ECOLOGICAL PERCEPTIONS IN MARXISM AND GANDHISM

ECOLOGICAL PERCEPTIONS IN MARXISM AND GANDHISM

Edited by
RAJDEVA NARAYAN
Advocate

and

JANARDAN KUMAR
Former Vice-Chancellor, L.N. Mithila University, Bihar

Foreword by
JUSTICE RAJINDER SACHAR
Chief Justice (Retd.)
High Court of Delhi, New Delhi

INSTITUTE FOR SOCIO-LEGAL STUDIES
Kalambagh Chowk, P.O. Ramna, Muzaffarpur, Bihar

In collaboration with

DEEP & DEEP PUBLICATIONS PVT. LTD.
F-159, Rajouri Garden, New Delhi-110027

ECOLOGICAL PERCEPTIONS IN MARXISM AND GANDHISM

ISBN 978-81-8450-302-9

Typeset by S.S. COMPOSERS,
3190, Mohindra Park, Shakur Basti, Delhi-110034.

Printed in India at MAYUR ENTERPRISES,
WZ Plot No. 3, Gujjar Market, Tihar Village, New Delhi-110018.

Published by DEEP & DEEP PUBLICATIONS PVT. LTD.
F-159, Rajouri Garden, New Delhi-110027.
Phones: 25435369, 25440916
E-mail: ddpbooks@yahoo.co.in • ddpubs@gmail.com
Showroom:
2/13, Ansari Road, Daryaganj, New Delhi-110002 • Telefax: 23245122

Contents

Part II
ECOLOGY AND GANDHISM

RAJINDER SACHAR
Chief Justice (Retd.)
High Court of Delhi, New Delhi
Chairperson Prime Minister's High Level Committee on Status of Muslims (Ex.)
UN Special Rapporteur on Housing
Member, UN Sub-Commission of Prevention of Discrimination and Protection of Minorities (Ex.)
President, Peoples Union for Civil Liberties (PUCL) India (Ex.)

A-19, New Friends Colony,
New Delhi-110065 (India)
Tel: 091-11-26847786, 26830194
E-mail: rsachar1@vsnl.net
rsachar23@bol.net.in
Fax: 091-011-26313393
Mobile: 9810006944

Foreword

The Institute for Social Legal Studies founded by Sri Rajdeva Narayan spreads knowledge not only for the State of Bihar but has also been a powerful medium to the spread of various current issues in the rest of India.

The present collection of articles expounded by well known writers, political commentators, economists on the importance given by Gandhi, Marx on the impact and importance of ecology is indeed a very important and urgently needed reminder of the proper utilization of natural resources if one wishes to prevent ecological disaster.

Of course in India ecology importance has been a constant feature and it was easy too because of late industrialization coupled with the reverence for nature and the source of knowledge, the abode of saints in the early history of India gave an intellectual and real understanding of place of environment in our daily life coupled with spreading the preachings of old wise men to try to keep one's needs within reasonable limit. But when Industrial Revolution took place and capitalist means of production took over on Europe, Marx though so brilliantly pointed out the disaster of capitalist mode of productions and a crusade for its destruction by a socialist mode of production still did emphasise the wanton destruction of soil inevitably damaging the ecological balance. Since ecology as a discipline was developed only in early 20th Century, Marx noticed it, though not with that depth as he dealt with danger of capitalist mode of production.

Of course for Gandhiji, in the twentieth century, and because of his faith in the welfare of the poorest and in a country where 2/3 population lived in villages, seeing the destructiveness of capitalism run wild on the whole environment, it was logical for him to proclaim his faith in balanced development, self-sufficiency of villages with smaller instruments of production. Socialist party believed as propounded by Dr. Lohia thus: "Villages and towns of our country have abundant raw material of various kinds. It is being wasted. Its processing and manufacture would be possible only when small machinery is available. I foresee the time when overall in our country, in towns and villages, will be spread millions of little power driven machines for producing wealth and easing the pressure on land."

But an economy must steadily aim to realize flexible techniques wherever possible. Only so can an economy hope to achieve real and under pressing expansion and an equal distribution of wealth and social understanding. Only so can an economy acquire balance, in which man's various demands are orchestrated in a harmony of all-round application of science.

That the mode of production has startling effects on ecology is clear now from the danger universally recognised of carbon emissions. But at the same time we in India and the developing countries must be alert enough not to allow our urgency in developing our productive capacities to be blocked by the vested institution of capitalist countries of North who by exploiting environment are the worst violators of ecology.

The danger to ecology by the present insistence on following the pattern of large scale machinery, colossal dams like Narmada and other similar ones which result in causing untold miseries to the poor tillers is obvious. It is in that connection that Gandhiji's emphasis and total commitment to the concept of self-sufficient villages is an acceptable revolutionary concept. To Dr. Lohia the thoughts and philosophy of developmental strategy propounded by Gandhiji was most suitable for our country as has been elaborated by Dr. Lohia in his "Fragments of World Mind."

This book contains very knowledgeable and well considered material on this important matter. I have no doubt that readers will benefit by this book, which is of greater urgency because of Doha round of negotiations which are said to be in the final phase of negotiations between all nations of the world. The editors of this book, Sh Rajdeva Narayan and Sri Janardan Kumar deserve due appreciation for their efforts in bringing out of this book.

New Delhi RAJINDAR SACHAR

Preface

This book is a research-study on the concept of ecology as may be found in the Marxism literature and the Gandhian literature. Marx and Gandhi should be jointly studied as the thinkings are the living forces of history today which are relevant for the present time also. Ecological concept in both the cases should be studied by comparing their views on the subject. A basic difference between them is that the Marxism movements in India was started as a part of the international movement whereas Gandhism originated in India and was practiced and developed by Gandhi himself.

What makes the earth unique and different from other planets is the presence of life on the earth. The relationship between the living organisms and their environment is the subject of relatively young of branch of science called ecology.

However, awareness about the environment is not recent or western in origin. The great political theorist and economist of ancient India, Chanakya, also known as Kautilya, said as far back as the 4th century BC, that the stability of an empire depends upon the stability of its environment. Please, refer to T.K. Omman's "State and Society in India: Studies in Nation Building." (New Delhi: Sage Publications, 1990):

Study of ecology appears to be an urgent task to be taken up with a view to stop destruction of nature and develop an urgent sense of awareness in the common people regarding the utility and use of nature for the existence of mankind on the earth.

Views of Marx and Gandhi on ecology have to be studied in this context.

I am grateful to the contributors for their articles included in this book. The authors are scholars of repute and deserve appreciation for presenting difficult topics in a simple language for the benefit of the common reader.

I hope, the readers will find the book worthy of their interest. I am confident that the book will advance the study of ecological sustainability and promote the open exchange of knowledge ingrained in the Marxian and the Gandhian literature. Our Institute will consider its efforts fruitful and rewarding if the book catches the attention of the reading public. The Institute invites suggestions from them for its improvement.

(Smt.) PRIYA RAJHANS
Joint Secretary
Institute for Socio-Legal Studies,
Kalambagh Chowk, Ramna,
Muzaffarpur-842002.
Bihar (India)

Acknowledgements

We express grateful thanks to the Gandhi Peace Foundation, New Delhi for allowing us to include in this book two articles already published in the *Gandhi Marg* in Volume 27, Nos. 3 and 4 and Volume 29, No. 4. We are further obliged to the Gandhi Peace Foundation for allowing us to publish the article "Gandhian Environmentalism" which is a chapter of the book "Modernisation and Ecology: A Gandhian Perspective" written by Shri Manoj Sinha. We are obliged to Cornerstone Publications, Kharagpur (W.B.) for giving us permission to include in this book the English version of the article named 'Marx and the Environment' by John Bellamy Foster. We are also grateful to the editor, the *Mainstream*, New Delhi for permitting us to include the article 'Socialism and Ecological Crisis' in the book.

We are indebted to Prof. Dr. Prabhakar Sinha, and Shri Surendra Kumar of the Gandhi Peace Foundation for helping us in various ways in publication of this book.

Thanks are due to Sri Sanjeev Kumar Anwar who has been consistently encouraging us to get the book ready for publication and also going through the type scripting of the articles in the book and also for his constant encouragement without which the book would not have seen the light of the day.

PRIYA RAJHANS

List of Contributors

Ashok S. Chousalkar, C/o Gandhi Marg, Gandhi Peace Foundation, 221-223, Deen Dayal Upadhyaya Marg, New Delhi-110002.

Bindeshwar Pathak, A-1-82, Panchsheel Park, New Delhi-110017.

C.K. Vershney, School of Environmental Science, Jawaharlal Nehru University, New Delhi-110067.

D.P. Sharma, C/o Prof. Janardan Kumar, Near Zenith Petrol Pump, Ramdayalu Nagar, Muzaffarpur-842002 (Bihar).

John Bellamy Foster, C/o Cornerstone Publications, P.O. Hijli Cooperative, Kharagpur-721306 (W.B.).

Krishna Kumar Khanna, B-705, Leela Sagar, Yari Road, Varsowa, Andhiri (W), Mumbai-400061. Phone: 26344068/09833422631

Manoj Sinha, C/o Gandhi Marg Gandhi, Peace Foundation, 221-223, Deen Dayal Upadhyaya Marg, New Delhi-110002.

Prof. Janardhan Kumar, Near Zenith Petrol Pump, Ramdayalu Nagar, Muzaffarpur-842002 (Bihar).

R.K. Prasad, Professor Colony, Near Aghoria Chowk, Muzaffarpur-842002 (Bihar).

Rajindra Sachar, Chief Justice (Retd.), High Court of Delhi, A-19, New Friends Colony, New Delhi-110065 (India).

Ramjee Singh, Bhikhanpur, Bhagalpur-812001 Phone-2420305

Randhir Singh, C/o Sumit Chakravartty, 145/1D, (First Floor), Shahpur Jat, (Near Asiad Village), New Delhi-110049 Phone-29497188.

Sachchidanand Singh, C/o Prof. Prabhakar Sinha, Nepali Kothi, Club Road, Muzaffarpur-842002 (Bihar).

Sarmistha Pattanaik, C/o Gandhi Marg, Gandhi Peace Foundation, 221-223, Deen Dayal Upadhyaya Marg, New Delhi- 110002.

Smt. Priya Rajhans, Kalambagh Chowk, P.O. Ramna, Muzaffarpur- 842002 (Bihar).

Sri Rajdeva Narayan, Kalambagh Chowk, P.O. Ramna, Muzaffarpur (Bihar).

Sunderlal Bahuguna, C/o Navjeewan Ashram, Post-Sigyara, Tehri Garhwal.

Introduction

Marx and Gandhi were the two legendary thinkers of the 19th and 20th century respectively whose thinkings are the living forces of history and their full effects are yet to be realized. Marx and his Marxism was the product of western renaissance, industrialism and the concept of resurrecting the dignity of labour. Western renaissance had greatly insisted upon the reign of reason instead of subscribing the dogmas and outdated thoughts. Industrial revolution had been not only upsetting the ancient mode of production and had been slowly but surely giving birth to the rise of few millionaires and millions miserable. The concept of the dignity of labour and the proper share of labour in the profits arising out of industrialization was being thrown to the winds. Drawing heavily upon the Hegelian concepts of thesis, antithesis and synthesis Marx vigorously assailed imperial exploitation and its mode of production and extolled the dignity of the working class and wanted to establish their supremacy not only on the means of production but also on its distribution. Discarding the tenets of Fabian Socialism, Guild Socialism and Syndicalism and terming them as mere utopian socialism he became the harbinger of scientific socialism. He effectively believed in the maximization of production and their equitable distribution as the only panacea which could bridge the gulf between the rich and the poor.

The very thought of maximization of production entailed in its trails unbriddled exploitation of natural and nature resources. In the entire writings of Marx there are no specific references as to how the uncontrolled exploitation of nature and natural resources would be taken care of so that the pyramidical balance in nature was not disturbed. It is true that the concept of ecology as its stands today was not in sight during Marx's times. It is, therefore, not surprising that there was virtually black out of the word ecology in his famous book, 'Das Capital' published in 1948. It was, however, in the writings of his disciple Engles and others that we come across with casual references on ecology. It is on the basis of these references that the neo-Marxists of Germany, France and also of elsewhere have traced and stretched Marxian perceptions of ecology. This idea would be expanded later on by scanning the writings of Marx's followers specially, the neo-Marxists thinkers.

It is worth-mentioning that while Marx from the very start of his thinking process strove hard to compress his ideas into a system which resulted in his theory of scientific socialism, Gandhi never tried to compress his ideas into straight jacket of a system. The very title of his book, My Experiments with Truth, is fully indicative of his trend of thinking. His was a journey of experiments with truth which unfolded his ideas step by step on various problems that confronted his mind. One believed in the material interpretation of history and the other in spiritualist interpretation. For one the labouring class was the God who had to be venerated, respected and given proper share in earnings. Gandhi on the other hand drawing heavily from Ruskin's *Unto This Last* and the ancient scriptures of *Ramayana* and *Gita* and having experienced the pangs of racial discrimination in South Africa he concentrated on his concepts of 'Satya and Ahimsa' as the only means which could salvage the common men from imperial exploitation and bondage. Gandhi's primary concern was freeing Indians from the tentacles of British imperialism. Marx and Gandhi stood on the same planks so far as imperialist exploitation and the consequent creation of acquisitive society was concerned. They however differed diametrically on the means of halting this exploitation. While Marx believed in class struggle and gave a clarion call to the workers to rise and unite for, according to him, they had nothing to lose but chains. Marx believed in the maxim of unity of the labouring class for in unity lay the strength. Gandhi, however, believed in the theory of changing the heart of the exploiters and creating a society free from the cankers of social, economic and political bondage. It is through the means of satya and ahimsa that the dessipated and desolate Indians could bring down to dust the mighty edifice of British imperialist power.

Earlier we have referred to that the concept of ecology had not developed as a discipline in science and matter of social and political concern. It became a buzz word in the latter half of the 20th century when environmental degradation threatened human health hazards, damaged monumental building and possible extinction of many species. Naturally, therefore, the term remained alien to Marx and Gandhi. However, with regard to nature, its exploitation of resources and human activity, the ideas of the two great thinkers are worth comparison.

Marx was a materialist and his ideas were rooted in developments in science and technology which, he believed, could lead to amelioration of the woes of the vast masses through large scale production. Marx's time saw the growth of large industries resulting from the developments in science which ultimatly led to the emergence of capitalism, a new system of exploitation with two sharply warring antagonistic classes, the capitalist and the labour. He made a deep study of the situation and offered a doctrine for the emancipation of the poor exploited labour class—the doctrine of scientific socialism—through sustained class struggle. Gandhi, on the other hand, was an idealist and a believer in the man's purity of soul. Though not against science he was certainly against high technology which he felt was a job-killer. He did not believe that emancipation lay in large scale production and consumption but in controlled austere living. He did not spell out his anguish against capitalism but he was unhappy at the exploitation. He laid great stress on individual's character building. He also recommended struggle without any violence against injustice. With Capitalist as trustee of industry and the capital and not the owner, the bitterness would end. This, of course, according to him required a change of heart on the part of both the capitalist and the labour. Machine is all right as long as it remains under man's control and does not impinge upon Gandhian concept of Gram Swaraj. Marx too believed that unplanned and chaotic ways of production for profits are responsible for job killing not the machine. Gandhi was also not against machine but against mechanization.

For Gandhi nature is sacrosanct, worth worship. It has enough to fulfil everyone's needs but not greed. And only greed is responsible for individual's woes. Limit your needs and do not be luxurious, live plain and think high should be one's motto. But Marx's approach to nature is dialectical. According to Marx man lives in nature and struggles with it too. For survival, he has to depend on it and to meet its vagaries he has to fight and gain control over it. He is not enimical to nature but since in nature everything is not found in the needed forms he makes tools which he continuously improves, there lies the growth of technology. According to Marx the history of man begins with production and technology. He believed in the maxim 'No Production History'. The march is undirectional and irreversible. At the present time ecology concerns with environmental pollution which has resulted in global warming, green house effect and disturbances in seasonal changes. During Marx's time the chief ecological concern was soil fertility and forests. Industries had started cropping up for the large scale production of artificial fertilizers for use in agriculture. The researches of the great agricultural chemist Von Liebig in Germany pointed out that the continued use of artificial fertilizers destroyed the capacity to gain nutrition from nature and so would do more harm than good to the agriculture in the long-run. Marx was associated with him and influenced by his researches. He had written several articles against the unrestricted use of fertilizers. The large scale deforestation in Europe unleashed by industrialists had taken away, through acts of parliament, the traditional rights of the poor peasants to use the dead woods of the forests for fuels and warming of homes. Marx fought against this through his writings in the journal which he edited on depletion of coal resources, Marx and Engels wrote and warned that over exploitation of nature would cause it to avenge in the long-run. (*Collected Works*, Vol. 5).

Marx was thinker and writer, Gandhi too was thinker but mainly a man of masses. For masses, especially downtrodden masses, he fought more than he wrote. During his days, and even now a large majority of masses were farmers, though industries were also taking roots. The indigo cultivation in Champaran forced by the British rulers robbed the farmers, damaged the soil fertility and the environment but benefitted the British imperialists. When it was brought to the notice of Gandhi he lost no time to come and lead the non-violent struggle of the farmers and won the battle. This constitutes a very important chapter of the history of independence movement of India. This story has been vividly described and immortalized by Dinbandhu Mitra in his famous works " Neel Darpan" Marx lay the blame of India poverty on the Asiatic Mode of Production, Gandhi believed that the root cause of the poverty of the Indians was the continued bluntings of indigenous industries in India by the British imperialists and the exhilarated dependence on agriculture. Gandhi was of the firm view that so long as imperial foreign ruler is not forced out of the country the fate of the Indian farmers can not be improved. Gandhi was a visionary but also an ardent activist. Marx was all in all a scientific thinker and believed that the emancipation of the labour class lay in their unity and sustained struggle against the capitalist class. To Marx the capitalist class has to be tolerated as necessary evil so long as the dictatorship of the proletariate is not firmly established. This he calls the period of gastation in which nature will be exploited freely by the capitalist class and it has to be at the mercy of this class for unbriddled profits. But Gandhi believe in the efficacy of non-violent means of Satya and Ahimsa for changing the heart of the capitalist class and making them conscious of their obligations towards society at large which in other words has been defined by Gandhites as ममता भरी समता, i.e. equality tinged with comparison. Marx was the proponent of an equalitarian society, Gandhi was a champion of egalitarian society. To secure nature against pollution Gandhi laid great stress on cleanliness of environ for him cleanliness was next to Godliness. He also strove hard in such food habits which were not only congenial to nature but enervating to health. Marx on the other hand was not concerned with these details owing to the varying situations in which they thought and worked.

While Marxian model of development centres around maximization of mundane goods with their equitable distribution among the masses so that the profits of economic activities are not pocketed by emerging capitalist class born out of rapid industrialization. He also emphasized that economic activities should be labour-intensive. Gandhi too believed in labour-intensive activities so that vast masses of indigent population of India is properly fed and freed from the problem of making both ends meet. Apart from this, Gandhian model of development centered around the crafting of an agrarian society of village republics making low level demands on the resources of the earth by living close to subsistence. Gandhi was given to simple inexpensive lifestyle and was deadly against materialistic, expensive and luxurious way of life. In other words, Gandhian wanted that the rich should live a contented life by exercising self-restrain in all their enjoyment and indulgences and let them remember the verse in Bhagwat Gita 'Whatever leaders of society do, the others will follow'. In his book *Swapna Ka Bharat* he said that Indian village will be so constructed as to live in perfect sanitation. It will be a cluster of cottages built of materials available and obtainable within a radius of five miles of it. In short, Gandhi dreamt of a society in which the tyranny of the richer class has no say. Gandhian model of development promised no surplus resources by tapping nature unnecessarily and channelizing it to the elite class who is entrenched on the power, purse, and people of the country. On the contrary his model called on the capital apparatus of the state to surrender its power in favour of the masses in the country. But this was not to be actualized by his followers and the natural resources are being continually depleted. An United Nations publication of 1995 by Madhaw Gargil and Ramchandra Guha has divided people affected by ecological disaster into two parts—the beneficiaries and non-beneficiaries. They have called the beneficiaries as omnivorous and designated the non-beneficiaries as displaced, damaged and deprived lot of people. The beneficiaries are in no mood to abjure the right of using nature indiscriminately. The developed nations of the world considered it their birth right to use nature as they like to.

They throw the guilt and guile of ecocide on the other side of the frontiers, that is, Asia and Africa. That has been the root cause of the failure of so many world conferences on ecological compability. The beneficiary class do not care for their efficient use of natural resources and pollution control. They freely import technology and do not care for environ-friendly technology and therefore, harsh action by the people has to be taken against this class.

According to the Marxists those who are displaced by ecological disaster have to be given far more control and access to natural resources as well as massive economic aids. The state should act swiftly in this regard. Marxist also distinguishes between human made capital and machine made capital. They do not lay their hands on human made capital but want better access to this capital for the displaced people.

For the vast number of people who feel greatly disturbed by ecological disorder the neo-Marxists are of the opinion that since it effects the largest segment of people personally as water and air pollution, the citizens have to force the government to take remedial action.

Gandhian approach to three segments of people by the eco crisis is grounded on moral imperatives. According to Gandhi the displaced persons by eco crisis should be a given access and control over natural resources based in their own locality. They should also be given large share in decentralised system of governance. They have to be content with their requirement of subsistence without access to material goods and aspiring for material goods. The building up of human made capital at the cost of considerable loss of natural capital was an anathema to Gandhi and should be halted for the sake of either rapid industrialization or intensive cultivation. The benefitters out of depletion of natural resources have to give up their greed and undue power to establish their Octopus grip over nature as well as human made capital. India according to Gandhi should half the drain of its national resources or capital to the outside world by doing away with the need for foreign exchange through acceptance of a way of life with very low material demand and a foreign policy based on non-violence and low military demands.

The perceptions of Marx and Gandhi differ from one another in respect to solving the problems of wounded nature. While Gandhian views are hermitic and visionary. Marx's perceptions are class strife torn and demonic.

It is left to the better judgement of the readers to weigh the difference between Marxist Perception of nature and the Gandhian Perception bearing in mind the observations made above.

RAJDEVA NARAYAN
JANARDAN KUMAR

PART I

ECOLOGY AND MARXISM

Marx and the Environment

John Bellamy Foster

It has become fashionable in recent years, in the words of one critic, to identify the growth of ecological consciousness with "the current post-modernist interrogation of the metnarrative of the Enlightenment." Green thinking, we are frequently told, is distinguished by its postmodern, postmodern, post-Enlightenment perspective. Nowhere is this fashion more evident than in certain criticisms directed at Marx and Engels. Historical materialism, beginning with the work of its two founders, is often said to be one of the main means by which the Baconian notion of the mastery of nature was transmitted to the modern world. The prevalence of this interpretation is indicated by its frequent appearance within the analysis of the left itself. "While Marx and Engels displayed an extraordinary understanding of and sensitivity toward the "ecological costs of capitalism." Socialist ecofeminist Carolyn Merchant writes," ... they nevertheless bought into the Enlightenment's myth of progress via the domination of nature."[1]

* John Bellamy Foster teaches sociology at the University of Oregon and is a member of the board of Monthly Review Foundation. His book 'The Vulnerable Planet' was recently published by Monthly Review Press.

It is of course undeniable that many of those who claimed to be following in Marx's footsteps treated nature as an object to be exploited and nothing more. It is common for today's critics, however, to argue that the worldview of Marx and Engels themselves was rooted before all else in the extreme technological subjugation of nature, and that despite the ecological sensitivity that they displayed in particular areas, this remains the primary context in which their theoretical contributions must be judged. Marxism and ecology are therefore never fully compatible. The chief complaint upon which this general criticism is based is that Marx adopted what the socialist environmentalist Ted Bention—himself a critic of Marx in this respect—has called a "Promethean 'Productivist' view of history." Reiner Grundmann concurs, writing in his Marxism and Ecology that "Marx's basic premises" was "the Promethean model" of the domination of nature a position that Grundmann attempts to defend. For liberal Victor Ferkiss, no defense is possible: "Marx's attitude toward the world always conquest of nature." Social ecologist (ecological anarchist) John Clark goes further:

Marx's Promethean ... "man" is a being who is not at home in nature, who does not see the Earth as the "household" of ecology. He is an indomitable spirit who must subject nature in his quest for self-realization... For such a being, the forces of nature, or the menacing powers of external nature, must be subdued.[2]

There are of course other common environment criticisms directed at Marx and Engels (not to mention Marxism as a whole) in addition to this one. Benton, for example, argues that Marx was unmistakably anthropocentric" and that he resisted any framework that would recognize the natural limits to economic advance. Marxian value theory, we are frequently told, designated labor (power) as the source of all value, thereby denying any intrinsic value to nature. Then there is the dismal ecological performance of the Soviet Union and other Eastern European regimes before the fall, which is seen as general reflections of Marx's failure to incorporate ecological concerns into his master narrative.

Yet it is the charge of Prometheanism that occupies central place in green criticisms of Marx. True environmentalism, we are led to believe, demands nothing less than a rejection of modernity itself. The charge of Prometheanism is thus a roundabout way of branding Marx's work and Marxism as a whole as an extreme version of modernism, more easily condemned in this respect perhaps than liberalism itself. Thus postmodern environmentalist Wade Sikorski writes that, "Marx . . . was one of our age's most devout worshippers of the machine. Capitalism was to be forgiven its sins because . . . it was in the process of perfecting the machine."[3]

This claim that Marx's work was based on a crude "Prometheanism," it is worth recalling, has a very long history. Bourgeois critics of Marxism have long sought to use Marx's frequent literary references to Aeschylus' Prometheus Bound to demonstrate that underneath his apparent commitment to scientific understanding lay "mythical-religious" foundation. Yet it is crucial to remember that Marx was not the only thinker attracted to the Greek myth of Prometheus, who was the predominant cultural hero of the entire Romantic period, and who stands in Western culture not only for technology but even more for creativity, revolution, and rebellion against the gods (against religion). Rubens, Titan, Dante, Milton, Blake, Goethe, Beethoven, Byron, Shelly, and numerous others incorporated Prometheus as a central motif in their work.[4]

In Marx's own work, Prometheus is invoked more often as a symbol of revolution than as symbol of technology. It is true that in Greek mythology the god (Titan) Prometheus brought fire to humanity. But more important to Marx was the fact that Zeus in retaliation bound Prometheus in chains for eternity, from which he sought to free himself. For the great tradedian Aeschylus, as Ellen Meiksins Wood observes in Peasant Citizen and Slave, Prometheus is "the personification of the Athenian opposition to servitude and arbitrary rule, as he resists the tyranny of Zeus and scorns the servility of the god's messenger, Hermes." Moreover, what is celebrated in Aeschylus' Prometheus Bound, a version of the Promethean myth reflection the values of

Athenian democracy, is not technology as it is now understood but the gift of labour, craftsmanship, and creativity- the practical arts underpinning democracy. So central was the myth of Prometheus to ancient Athens that the class opposition between laboring citizens in the democracy and the aristocratic opponents of democracy can be seen in the radically different treatments of this myth, as represented respectively by Aeschlus, Prometheus Bound and Plato's use of the same myth in his States man. Understanding the revolutionary class character of this conflict within antiquity, Marx clearly identified with the Prometheus of Aeschlyus rather than Plato.

All of this, though crucial for understanding Marx's own references to Prometheus, may seem irrelevant, since none of this rich cultural background, stretching back over a millennium and a half to the very beginnings of Western civilization, exists at all in the work of those among today's cultural and environmental critics who now commonly level the charge of Prometheanism at the entire Enlightenment tradition and at Marx and Engels in particular. Shorn of most of its historical and cultural meaning, the myth of Prometheus has been transformed, in the work of such critics, into a cultural symbol of modernity itself, standing for extreme Prometheus has been transformed, in the work of such critics, into a cultural symbol of modernity itself, standing for extreme productivism and the domination of nature (including human nature). Indeed, the fact that the very idea of human creativity, as symbolized by the Greek myth of Postmodern critics with crude productivism and the technological subjugation of nature provides assertling indication of the extent to which the dominant word-view of capitalism has penetrated such thinking.[5]

The classic reformulation of the Promethean myth along these lines is to be found in Herbert Marcuse's Eros and Civilization, which argued that Prometheus the predominant culture-hero [of European culture] is the trickster and (suffering) rebel against the gods, who creates culture at the price of perpetual pain. He symbolizes productiveness, the unceasing effort to master life.... Prometheus is the culture-hero of toill, productivity, and progress through repression.

In opposition to this one-sided emphasis of Western modernity, Marcuse insisted that,

> Another reality principle must be sought at the opposite pole. Orpheus and Narcissus... stand for a very different reality. They have not become the culture-heroes of the Western world: theirs is the image of joy and fulfilment... They recall the experience of a world that is not to be mastered and controlled but liberated.[6]

Marcuse was developing a critique of the instrumental rationality that characterized Western industrial cultural as a whole (encompassing both capitalism and what Roy Medvedev has called "barracks pseudosocialism"). His argument was however seen by some as a "trenchant criticism" of Marx in particular. Marccuse's text is interpreted in precisely this way in Marshall Berman's All That Is Solid Melts into Air, which nonetheless argues that it is wrong to see Marx as a proponent of crude Prometheanism. According to Berman,

If Marx is fetishistic about anything, it is not work and production but rather the far more complex and comprehensive ideal of development—"the free development of physical and spiritual energies" (1844 manuscripts)... Marx wants to embrace Prometheus and Orpheus; he considers communism worth fighting for, because for, because for the first time in history it could enable men to have both... He knew that the way beyond the contradictions would have to lead through modernity, not out of it.[7]

It is certainly possible to argue, as socialist environmentalist Kate Soper has in her essay, "Greening Prometheus," that there was a certain "ambiguity" in "Marx's Prometheanism" that one can exploit to develop a green interpretation of his thought. However, what seems to be mere "ambiguity" on the surface is more adequately understood as a dialectical tension resulting from Marx's attempt to transcend the usual ways in which human production and the mastery of nature were depicted in the Enlightenment tradition. As Marcuse's student Willaim Leiss has observed in his indispensable study the Domination of Nature, such phrases as "the mastery of nature," "the control of nature", and "the domination of nature" were almost universal within nineteenth-century thought, and as such took on varied and complex forms. The mere use of such terms on occasion by Marx and Engels does not therefore establish that they adopted an extreme productivist point of view. Indeed, taken together, the writings of Marx and Engels, Leiss contends, "represent the most profound insight into the complex issues surrounding the mastery over nature to be found anywhere in nineteenth the mastery over nature to be found anywhere in nineteenth-century social thought or a fortiori in the contributions of earlier periods."[8]

What was clear from Marx's analysis was that humanity and nature were interrelated, with the historically specific form of production relation constituting the core of that interrelationship in any given period. As he wrote in the Economic and Philosophic Manuscripts of 1844,

> Man lives from nature, i.e. nature is his body, and he must maintain a continuing dialogue with it if he is not to die. To say that man's physical and mental life is linked to nature simply means that nature is linked to itself, for man is a part of nature.[9]

Far from being mere worshippers of productivism, Marx and Engels were two of its foremost critics. As the young Engels were in 1844, "To make the earth an object of huckstering—the earth which is our one and all, the first condition of our existence—was the last step toward making oneself an object of huckstering." Under capitalism all nature and human relationships, Marx arguer, have dissolved into money relationships. Rather that in a society ruled by "callous 'cash-payment'" and by the necessity for continual increase in productivity, he looked forward to a social order that would promote the many-sided development of human capacities and the rational human relation to the nature of which we are a part. The further growth of human freedom, he wrote in the final part of the third volume of *Capital*, consists in "socialized man, the associated producers, rationally regulating their material inter-charge with nature and bringing it under common control, instead of allowing it to rule them as a blind force."

The human community, Marx believed, can no more free itself from the need to control its interaction with nature than it can free itself from the need to take into consideration the natural conditions of human existence. Yet rational control of the relation between nature and humanity is inherently opposed to the mechanistic domination of nature in the interest of the ever increasing expansion of production for its own sake. In a society of freely associated producers, Marx argued, the goal of social life would not be work and production, in the narrow forms in which they have been understood in possessive individualist, society but the all-around development of human creative potential as an end in itself, for which "the shortening of the working day is a basic prerequisite." This would set the stage for the achievement of a realm of freedom in which human beings would be united with each other and with nature.[10]

The realization of these conditions, Marx recognized, necessitated a radical transformation in the human relation to nature. With the elimination of private ownership of land and the development of a society of freely associated producers, global sustainability in the relationship to nature would become feasible for the first time. Pointing to the imperative of protecting the globe for further generations Marx stated:

> From the standpoint of a higher economic form of society, private ownership of the globe by single individuals will appear quite as absurd as private ownership of one man by another. Even a whole society, a nation, or even all simultaneously existing societies together, are not the owners of the globe. They are only its possessors, its usufructuaries, and like *boni patres families* [good fathers of families], they must hand it down to succeeding generations in an improved condition.[11]

It was the proper purpose of agriculture, Marx argued,

"to minister to the entire range of permanent necessities of life required by chain of successive generations"—in contradiction to "the whole spirit of capitalist production, which is directed toward the immediate gain of money." There was thus a direct conflict between capitalism's short-sighted expropriation of the earth's resources and the longer term character of truly sustainable production. Economic advance in a society of freely associated producers, Marx insisted again and again, would have to occur without jeopardizing the natural and global conditions upon which the welfare of future generations would depend. This is precisely the definition now given to the concept sustainable development, most famously in the Brundtland Commission report, Our Common Future, which defined it as "development that meets the needs of the present without compromising the ability of future generations to meet their own needs."[12]

Although Marx did not concentrate on the ecological critique of capitalism in his writings—no doubt because he thought that capitalism would be replaced by a society offreely associated producers long before such problems could become truly critical his allusions to sustainability indicate that he was acutely aware of the ecological depredations of the system. Central to his concerns in this respect was the effect of capitalist industrialization on the degradation of the soil.[13] The best known passage in this regard, from capital, Vol. 1., is to be found in the section on "Large-Scale Industry and Agriculture," which constitutes the final, culminating part of Marx's key chapter on "Machinery and Large-Scale Industry" (on the effects of the Industrial Revolution).[14] There Marx argues that,

> All progress in capitalist agriculture is a progress in the art, not only of robbing the worker, but of robbing the soil; all progress in increasing the fertility of the soil for a given time is progress towards ruining the long-lasting sources of that fertility. The more a country proceeds from large-scale industry as the background of its development, as in the case of the United States, the more rapid is this process of destruction. Capitalist

> production, therefore, only develops the techniques and the degree of combination of the social process of production by simultaneously undermining the original sources of all wealth the soil and the worker.[15]

These were not causal or isolated comments but reflected careful study of the work of the German agrarian chemist Justus von Liebig, often known as the founder of soil chemistry, Until the early 1860s, Marx thought that the progress of capitalist agriculture might be so rapid that it would outpace industry. But the time he wrote *Capital,* however, his studies of the work of Liebig and other agronomists had convinced him otherwise. "Large landed property," he explained in the conclusion to his most important chapter on capitalist agriculture ("The Genesis of Capitalist Ground Rent")

> reduces the agricultural population to a constantly falling minimum, and confronts it with a constantly growing industrial population crowded together in large cities, it thereby creates conditions which cause an irreparable break in the coherence of social interchange prescribed by the natural laws of life. As a result, the vitality of the soil is squandered, and this prodigality is carried by commerce far beyond the borders of a particulars state (Liebig).

Large-scale industry and large-scale agriculture under capitalism thus had the same results: both contributed to the ruining of the agricultural worker and the exhaustion of "the nature power of the soil." The "moral of history." Marx observed

> is that the capitalist system works against a rational agriculture, or that a rational agriculture is incompatible with the capitalist system (Always though the latter promotes technical improvements in agriculture) and needs either the hand of the small farmer living by his own labor or the control of the associated producers.

For Marx "the rational cultivation of the soil as eternal communal property" was "an inalienable condition of the existence and reproduction of a chain of successive generations of the human race."

Marx and Engels did not confine their discussions of ecological limits to the issue of the soil, but also explored numerous other issues of sustainability, in relation to forests, rivers, and streams, the disposal of waste, air quality, environmental toxins, etc. "The development of culture and industry in general", Marx wrote, "has ever evinced itself in such energetic destruction of forests that everything done by it conversely for their preservation and restoration appears infinitesimal." With regard to industrial waste, he argued for "economy through the prevention of waste, that is to say, the reduction of excretions of production to a minimum, and the immediate utilization of all raw and auxiliary materials required in production."

The chief source of ecological destruction under capitalism, Marx and Engels argued, was the extreme antagonism of town and country, a characteristic of capitalist organization as fundamental to the system as the division between capitalist and laborer. "When one observes," Engels wrote,

> how here in London alone a greater quantity of manure than is produced by the whole kingdom of Saxony is poured away every day into the sea with an expenditure of enormous sums, and what colossal structures are necessary to prevent this manure from poisoning the whole of London, then the utopia of abolishing the antithesis between town and country is given a remarkable practical basis.[16]

Such ecological insights, so unusual among nineteenth century thinkers, all derive from Marx and Engles' early recognition of the essential point that sustainability must lie at the core of the human relation to nature in any future society.

It is therefore wrong to argue, as Ted Benton has, that Marx and Engels "sustained and deepened those aspects of capitalist political economy which exemplified its hostility to the idea of nature limits to capital accumulation. "To be sure, they had little to say about the absolute natural limits of the golobe. In this sense, some, Benton included, have viewed Marx's analysis as ecologically inferior to that of Malthus, who emphasized the growth of population in relation to food supply (not primarily from and ecological or carrying capacity perspective but in order to justify subsistence wage levels and the dismantlement of the English Poor Laws). Yet Marx and Engels were unusual in the degree of emphasis they placed on the natural conditions of production, and in their recognition of the fact that a sustainable economy demanded a sustainable relation to nature on a global basis. In this sense, natural limits are very much a part of their argument.

As with other natural limits to population growth, to the extent that they existed, Marx and Engels believed, only reinforced the case for socialism. "Even if Malthus were completely right" (with respect to the relation between population and food supply), the young Engles had observed in his very first essay on political economy, this only provided a further argument for a "social transformation" for the creation of a society in which the "population and destruction" of human beings would no longer be a mere commodity relation dependent "on demand." Of course, neither Marx nor Engels believed that Malthus was "completely right." Malthus' expectation that population would outpace food supply because of the inexorable nature of the former and the limited supply of cultivable land had, as Marx and Engels understood, underestimated the dynamism of capitalist agriculture unleashed by the commercial, agricultural and industrial revolutions. Ironically, it is mainly because Malthus' expectations were defeated and the age-old cycle of famine (what Fernand Braudel has called "the biological ancient regime") was transcended for the first time in human history beginning in the late eighteenth century, that population has grown since Malthus' time to the point that overpopulation now poses a serious threat to the ecology of the planet as a whole. Moreover, if there is reason to believe that agriculture today is increasingly incapable of supplying the basic needs of a still growing would population, this is more related to Marx's analysis of the unsustainability of capitalist agriculture, which robs the soil itself, than to Malthus more abstract notion (following Ricardo) of the diminishing marginal productivity of agricultural as more and more marginal land is brought under cultivation.[17]

No less mistaken is the criticism of Marx for in the words of socialist ecologist Jean-Pual Deleage-attaching "no intrinsic value to nature resources" in his theory of value. For Marx, the law of value was a historically specific feature of capitalist society. Marx's comments on value relations no more indicate support for this set-up (and the denial of intrinsic value) than they indicate support for capitalism itself (and the denial of the prospect of a non-alienated society). In Marx's theory, it is explicitly stated that capitalist value relations treat nature as a "free gift", as something given to capital "gratis." This was not at all inconsistent, however, with Marx's other point that the land and soil were "robbed"—or, in other words, that conditions sustainability, which must take account of the reproduction of nature, were expressly violated by the system.[18]

For Marx, material wealth in its widest conception (understood in terms of use values) has to be distinguished from value creation under capitalism (the would of exchange value). "Labor," he wrote, "is not the only source of material wealth, of use-values produced by labor. As William Petty puts it, labor is its father and the earth is its mother." It is a contradiction of capitalism that it pursues exchange value (profit) while largely ignoring the qualitative conditions associated with use value and wealth in its larger context, which includes the nature environment and the productivity of nature. Marx seems to have clearly understood the basic ecological principal that "nothing comes from nothing," popularized in recent years by Barry Commoner and others. As Marx himself wrote,

What Lucretiussays is self-evident: "nil posse creari de nihilo," out of nothing, nothing can be created. Creation of value is transformation of labor-power into labor. Labor-power itself is energy transferred to a human organism by means of nourishing matter.[19]

We can more fully, understand the historical significance of Marx and Engels' ecological thought by comparing their ideas with those of the great Vermont environmentalist George Perkins Marsh, widely recognized as the greatest ecologist of the nineteenth century and (in the words of Lewis Mumford) "the fountainhead of the conservation movement." In one of the best-known passages of his classic work, Man and Nature (1864), Marsh wrote:

There are parts of Asia Minor, of Northern Africa, of Greece, and even of Alpine Europe where the operation of causes set in action by man has brought the face of the earth to a desolation almost as complete as that of the moon; and though, within that brief space of time which we call "the historical period," they are known to have been covered with luxuriant woods, verdant pastures, and fertile meadows, they are now too far deteriorated to be reclaimable by man ... The earth is fast becoming an unfit home for its noblest inhabitant, and another era of equal human crime and improvidence.... would reduce it to such a condition of impoverished productiveness, of shattered surface, of climatic excess, as to threaten the depravation, barbarism, and perhaps even extinction of the species.[20]

This statement by Marsh can be compared to a closely related interpretation of long-term ecological developments put forward by Engels in his essay, "The Part Played by Labor in the Transition from Ape to Man," written in 1876:

Let us not, however, flatter ourselves overmuch on account of our human conquest of nature. For each such conquest takes its revenge on us..... The people who, in Mesopotamia, Greece, Asia Minor, and elsewhere destroyed the forests to obtain cultivable land, never dreamed that they were laying the basis for the present devastated condition of these countries, by removing along with the forests the collection centers and reservoirs of moisture. When, on the southern slopes of the mountains, the Italians of the Alps used up the pine forests so carefully cherished on the northern slopes they had no inkling that by doing so they were cutting at the roots of the dairy industry in their region... Thus at every step we are reminded that we by no means rule over nature like a conqueror over a foreign people, like someone standing outside nature but that we, with flesh, blood, and brain, belong to nature, and exist in its midst, and that all our mastery of it consists in the fact that we have the advantage of all other beings of being able to know and correctly apply its laws.[21]

A close examination of these passages will reveal that there is a broad similarity in the way in which the issue of ecological destruction is approached by Engles and Marsh. Both refer in detail to great ecological disasters that have confronted civilizations. Both see this primarily as a question of sustainability. In Marsh's terms, such "improvidence" in the exploitation of nature must be ended, while Engels insists on the facts that we "belong to nature" and must "correctly apply its laws." Both adopt a broadly anthropocentric perspective, in the sense that they emphasize the consequences of such destruction for the fate of humanity.

The point here is not that Marx and Engels singly or together were the equal of Marsh in their understanding of ecological science; they were not. Yet their views were by no means incompatible with that of the greatest (and still widely respected) ecologist of their day. Moreover, it is no mere coincidence that Man and Nature, the leading work on planetary ecological devastation to be written prior to the twentieth century, was published only three years before the publication of the first volume of Marx's *Capital* (1867). Both were responses (though Marsh's less consciously so) to the effects of the Industrial Revolution. Marx's work helped inspire working class revolts, while Marsh's ideas gave impetus to a wide-ranging struggle on behalf of nature. Only by combining the analyses represented by these works do we have anything like a complete ecological critique of machine capitalism. The reason for this, of course, is that while Marsh was the premier ecologist of this, of course, is that while Marsh was the premier ecologist of his time, it was Marx and Engels who most acutely understood the historical conditions underlying such ecological destruction in the nineteenth century. Indeed, since the roots of the global environment crisis are to be found not in nature, but in society, Marx and Engels may have much more to teach us today about what is necessary in order to address the ecological problem than what can be learned from Marsh.

The key to Marx and Engels' understanding of modern society lay in their critique of capital accumulation. They were convinced that capitalism was economically and politically unsustainable. It would eventually give rise to the revolutionary forces that would overthrow it. The same critique of capital accumulation led them to conclude—beginning with their very earliest writings that the system lacked a sustainable relation to nature. In their analysis, however, this problem did not yet loom so large that it would affect the future of capitalism (which they thought would soon die a natural death as a result of its economic sustainability was frequently raised in their works, this has more to do with their understanding of the needs of the future society of freely associated producers than with the conditions of capitalism's demise. The stability of any future society. Marx clearly reorganized, would be dependent on the creation of a wholly new and more balanced relation to the natural world.

Today radical ecologists see differently only in the sense that it is now understood that global ecological destruction will play a central role in capitalism's end game. We are for the first time in human history confronting the problem of ecological survival on a planetary scale—a problem that nineteenth century thinkers, Marx and Engels included (though Marsh might be considered an exception to this), could scarcely have imagined. Nevertheless, we cannot even being to understand the complex of problems that presently face us unless we approach them as Marx and Engels did in relation to the critique of capital accumulation. It would be a mistake to see the answer to the ecological problem as one of rejecting "modernity" in the name of some abstract and amorphous "postmodernity," at the same time rejecting of capitalism. Rather, we must recognize that it is necessary to come to grips with modernity above all capitalist modernity and transform it. Since the destruction of the living would as we know it is otherwise certain, the great mass of humanity has nothing to lose but its chains. It has a planet to save.

Notes and References

1. Zaheer Baber, "The Vulnerable Planet" (Review), Contemporary Sociology (January 1955): 82; Merchant, Ecology (Atlanitc Highlands, New Jersey: Humanities Press, 1994), p. 2.
2. Benton, "Marxism and Natural Limits," *New Left Review* 178 (November-December 1989): 82; Reiner Grundmann, Marxism and Ecology (New York: Oxford University Press), p. 52 and "The Ecological Challenge to Marxism," *New Left Review* 187 (May-June 1991): 120; Frekiss, Nature, Technology and Society (New York: New York University Press, 1993), p. 180; Clark, "Marx's Inorganic Body," *Environmental Ethics* 11, No. 3 (Fall 1989): 258.
3. Sikorski, Modernity and Technology (Tuscaloosa: University of Alabama Press, 199), p. 138.
4. Leonard P. Wessell, Jr. Prometheus Bound: The Mythic Structure of Karl Marx's Scientific Thanking (Baton Rouge: Louisiana State University Press, 1984), p. 3; Linda M. Lewis, The Promethean Politics of Milton, Blake and Shelley (Columbia, Missouri: University of Missouri Press, 1992), p. 2.
5. Wood, Peasant Citizen and Slave (London: Verso, 1988), pp. 141-44.
6. Marcuse, Eros and Civilization (New York: Vintage, 1962), pp. 146-49.
7. Berman, All that is Solid Melts into Air (New York: Simon and Schuster, 1982), pp. 126-29; Medvedev, Let History Judge (New York: Columbia University Press, 1989), pp. 852-59.
8. Soper, "Greening Prometheus," in Peter Osborne, ed. Socialism and the limits of Liberalism (New York: Verso, 1991); Leiss, The Domination of Nature, Boston: Beacon Press, 1974), pp. 85, 198.
9. Marx, Early Writings (New York: Vintage, 1975), p. 328.
10. Frederick Engels, "Outlines of Critique of Political Economy," in Marx, The Economic and Philosophic Manuscripts of 1884 (New York: International Publishers, 1964), p. 210; Marx, Early Writings, pp. 377-79; Marx and Engels, The Communist Manifesto (New York: Monthly Review Press, 1964), pp. 5-6; Marx, *Capital*, Vol. III (New York: International Publishers, 1967), p. 820: Erich Fromm, Beyond the Chains of illusion (New York: Simon and Schuster, 1962), pp 36-37.
11. Marx, *Capital*, Vol. III, p. 776.
12. *Capital*, Vol. III, p. 617, World Commission of Environment and Development (the Brundtland Commission report), Our Common future (Oxford: Oxford University Press, 1987), p. 43.
13. Marx, *Capital*, Vol. I, pp. 637-38.
14. Marx, *Capital*, Vol. III, pp 121, 812-13; Ronald Meek, "Introduction," in Marx and Engels, Malthus (New York: International Publishers, 1954), pp. 13-14, 28-31. For a brilliant analysis of the contributions of Liebig and Marx to the critique of capitalist agriculture see Kozo Mavumi, "Temporary Emancipation from Land: From the Industrial Revolution to the Present time," *Ecological Economics*, 4, No. 1 (October 1991), pp. 35-56.

15. Marx, *Capital,* III, pp. 101-03; Marx, *Capital,* Vol. II (New York: International Publishers, 1967), p. 244.
16. Engels, The Housing Question (Moscow: Progress Publication, 1975), p. 92.
17. Benton, "Marxism and Natural Limits," *New Left Review,* 178 (November-December 1989):. 64; Engels, "Outlines of Critique of Political Econoy," p. 221; Marx, *Capital,* Vol. 1, p. 505; Fernand Braudel, The Structures of Everyday Life (New York: Harper and Raw, 1979), p. 70.
18. Jean-Paul Deleage, "Eco-Marxist Critique of Political Economy," in Martin O'Connor, ed., Is Capitalism Sustainable? (New York: Guiford, 1994). p. 48; Marx, *Capital,* Vol. III, p. 745, Vol I, p. 510, A similar interpretation to the one presented here has been developed in forthcoming work by Paul Burkett.
19. Marx, *Capital,* Vol. I (New York: International Publishers, 1967), pp. 43, 215n. While Commoner refers to the informal ecological law "there is no such thing as a free lunch," other ecologists have translated this as " nothing comes from nothing," See Foster, The Vulnerable Planet (New York: Monthly Review Press, 1994), pp. 118-20.
20. Marsh, Man and Nature (Cambridge, Massachusetts: Harvard University Press, 1965), pp. 42-43; Mumford, The Brown Decades (New York: Dover, 1971). p. 35.
21. Engels, Dialectics of Nature (New York. International Publishers, 1940), pp. 291-92.

2

Marxist Approach to Ecology

R.K Prasad

Non-Marxists have characterized Karl Marx as an anti-ecological thinker saying that:

(i) he failed to address the exploitation of nature,
(ii) his work have little to do with modern ecology,
(iii) he showed all interest in technology but not on its effects on environment, and
(iv) he showed no concern for species other than man.

Marxists, on the other hand, contend that even though ecology poses questions before the present day society answers to it can be sought in the purview of Marxist thought and, to a substantial extent, found in Marx's own writings, particularly his concept of nature. The challenges can be met by properly planned utilisation of resources and appropriate choice of technologies.

Within the contemporary Green thought there is a strong tendency to attribute the entire course of ecological degradation to human endeavour for scientific and technological revolution from the 18th through the 20th centuries. Marxists refute by saying that growth of human civilisation occurred so far would be well nigh impossible in the absence of science and technology. Not the science but the lust for capitalist profit and chaos in production that are responsible for the ecological degradation that occurred so far, Marxism is rooted in growth of scientific ideas as well as technology. It is more essential to comprehended the views about nature that arose with the development of science and technology in the said period which promoted Marx's thoughts rather than to project science and technology as enemies of nature. Marx, along with his friend and collaborator Engels closely followed the developments in science, especially the Darwin's theory of evolution Liebig's works on agricultural chemistry and several other and had frequent interactions with them which actually formed the basis of Marx's ecological perspective.

What is Marxism ?

Marxism, broadly speaking, is a doctrine for the emancipation of the exploited poor class of people. The doctrine is elaborated by its four components—dialectical materialism (the philosophy), political economy, surplus value theory of capitalism and scientific socialism. But basic to all Marxist thoughts is the theory of dialectical materialism.[1]

'Materialism' and 'idealism' refer in the ultimate sense, to the question regarding existence of spirit and spiritual power. While 'idealists' assert the primacy of spirit, the 'materialists' regard nature as primary, and natural phenomena as results of changes and transformations of matter and energy. For the latter, matter and energy are eternal as against the idealists' concept of their 'creation'.

Prior to the emergence of Marxism, the idealist philosophy of W.F. Hegel, based on "laws of dialectics", dominated the most part of Western Europe, particularly Germany. According to this law the social development goes through emerging ideas which in turn are the results of interaction of antagonistic forces and tendencies. At the same time, Europe in 18th and 19th centuries witnessed intellectual movements—Enlightenment, Rennaissance based mainly on science, logic and rationality.

While a student in Berlin, Karl Marx came under the spell of both—Hegel's dialectics and the Enlightenment. With respect to former, however, he was ambivalent Hegel was basically and idealist on social plane and his idealism was not in tune with the spirit of Enlightenment. Marx made a wide reading of literatures available—theological as well as scientific—and was deeply inspired by the ancient Greek philosopher Epicurus' works on materialism. The initial proposition of Epicurus, natural philosophy was that nothing could be created out of nothing nor could be reduced to nothing. This is what, in modern science, is known as law of conservation of matter and energy. For Marx and Engels, Epicurus was the "inventor of empirical natural science" and an avowed materialist. The work of Epicurus had been lost in the middle ages when theological views dominated and he was considered among the leading heretics opposed to Christianity. It was the Copernican revolution of the 16th century and researches of Bruno and Gailileo coupled with movement of Enlightenment and Rennaissance, challenging the authority of church, which resurrected the ancient materialism of Epicurus. A host of materialist philosophers emerged—Hollbach, Diderot in France, Feurbach in Germany to name of few. Hollbach in his "System of Nature" said that the idea of divine power ruling the world is associated with terror and hence and impediment for the progress. Feurbach held the view that God is the creation of human mind and urged people to forsake religion and embrace radical humanism.[2]

Marx affirmed Feurbach's view making improvement on it by stating that we invent God and religion to find solace from our miseries on earth. The cause of our misery has to be sought in the material would. Influenced by Epicurus, Hollbach, Feurbach and Enlightment, Marx provided his first critique of religion calling for the removal of all supe ıatural and teleological principles from nature amounting .o rejection of idealist (religious) view of nature. Applying Hegel's dialectical approach to the materialist concept of nature as well as society, he propounded his own theory of dialectical materialism. This theory says that events in nature and society occur owing to contradictions inherent in natural and social forces respectively and the character and trend of any development is governed by objective laws derived precisely from scientific investigations. In his 'Dialectics of Nature', F. Engels has mentioned three formal laws of dialectics, viz.,

(i) transformation of quantity into quality,
(ii) interpenetration of opposites, and
(iii) negation of negation.

The first law is illustrated by the concept of inseparability of matter and motion (energy). Continuous addition of energy (heat) to liquid water transforms the liquid to vapour. The dialectics of nature, or of thought, is refection of motion through opposites; this is second law. Attraction and repulsion, positive and negative charges, matter and anti-matter, north and south poles or magnet, etc. are opposites in inorganic nature; heredity and mutability, growth of new cells and atrophy of old ones, etc. are opposites in organic (living) nature. A corollary to this law is the law of inter-connectivity according to which the parts of the whole are connected and they interact with each other. Engels calls it the 'struggle of opposites'—a basic feature of nature. The interaction is seen in the process of evolution, emergence of living organisms, interaction of animals, plants and microorganisms as well as the material dependence of living organisms on environment. The third law of dialectics determines the relationship of the old to the new in the development of nature and social world. In the transition of an old object, or a phenomenon, to new Engels regards the latter tending to negate or be opposite to the former. The negation is however, not complete destruction of the old rather retaining some aspects of it. This progressive development of living organisms reveals continuity of relation of biological species. In Biology this is called Biogenetic law. In repeated transformations of things into

* The dictionary meaning of dialectics is the art of arriving at a truth and solving problems by discussions over opposite views and logical arguments

their opposites each successive step "negates" its preceding step and a single chain of development connects all the links in living nature. The history of vegetation and animal kingdom is evidence of the regularity in rise from lower to higher forms, the emergence of new and more developed form out of the demise of the old forms.[3]

Theory of Evolution

Marx's materialism received strong backing from the researches of Charles Darwin who, after years of continued observations on the habits of plants and living species, developed his theory of "Nature Selection" which is commonly known as 'Evolution'. The key point of the theory is adaptability of the environment which means standing up to the conditions of climate, temperature, sunlight soil nutrients, etc., ancient materialists also held the view that species survive by adapting the environment; those who could not, got eliminated. The essential features of Darwin's theory, contained in his "On the origin of Species by Nature Selection"[4] can be summarized as follows. All organisms have the tendency to produce many more off springs than can survive. These off springs vary among themselves and are not just replicas of the original. Since not all can survive, there is struggle for existence. Those who, by the process of innate variation, adapt to the local environment tend to survive. This is called "Natural Selection"*. Favourable variations over the long span of geological time resulted in the evolution of species.

What is Ecology?

Ernst Haeckel, a leading follower of Darwin coined the term 'Okologie' in German which was subsequently known as 'ecology' in English, a year before the publication of *'The Capital'* by Marx. Put simply, ecology means science of

* Darwin used the term natural selection and, very occasionally, survival of the fittest. In Biology the notion of the fittest means survival of an individual organism to the point that it can pass on its progeny. So it is frivolous to see that the concept has been (mis) utilized by some American social scientists in offering

relation of the plants, animals, insects, humans, etc. to both inorganic and organic environment including friendly and inimical relations. This science of ecology has thus far formed the principal component of what is usually referred to as Natural History.

Ecology as a discipline in science and as a matter of social and political concern came in the later half of the twentieth century, Marx and Engels were acquired with the works of Haeckel but preferred the term Natural History. The contemporary Green thoughts on ecology follow from Barry Commoner's third informal law of ecology: "Nature knows best" better put as "Evolution knows best." Species, including man, in the course of evolution, have adapted themselves to their environment through the process of natural selection operating over a time scale of million years. We can introduce into the environment materials synthesized by man, that are not the products of evolution, only at the perils of ecological destruction. This view acknowledges supreme authority of nature and stresses that only nature's laws can be the foundation stone of a society which will solve ecological problems.

Marxist Approach to Nature

Marxist approach to nature and ecology, on the other hand, is dialectical, Man's existential situation is characterised by the fact that he has to live simultaneously "in" as well as "against" nature. That is, he has to depend on nature for his survival but since naturally occurring materials are not necessarily available in the needed from, he transforms them by making suitable tools. Marx does not consider nature as all powerful. Unlike plants and animals who can survive only within a limited geographical and climatic zones man can inhabit any place on the planet. Even in insecure environment man can survive by building around himself a "second nature." He can change his relation with nature through the use of tools which other species cannot.

This does not, however, mean that man is inimical to nature. He receives matter and energy from nature as 'input' and gives something to nature and society as 'output', a process which Marx called 'metabolism' or 'interchange with nature'. (The term metabolism refers to material exchange within a body related to respiration. It is a key concept in biology and biochemistry used to explain the interaction of organisms with the environment. An organism draws materials and energy from its environment and converts them by way of various reactions into the building blocks of growth. Biologists employ the concept of metabolism to all biological levels—from a single cell to large ecosystems).

Marx's Theory of Labour and Production

According to Marx' the evolution of human beings from their primate ancestors arose out of labour and making of tools for production. As a result, early humans could alter their relation to local environment, radically improving their adaptability. Those who could make and use tools were likely to survive and progress.

This tool making ability distinguishes man from other species which cannot do so and hence cannot produce. This also provides a natural historical basis for Marx's theory of labour in the development of human society. Human history began the day man started production. It is the history of changing mode of production which comprises the productive force (labour+tools) and production relation. Based on this materialistic concept Marx interpreted history to have passed through stages of primitive communism, slavery, feudalism, capitalism and a future society under scientific socialism and, later communism a society that would be classless and hence stateless. Based on dialetics, Marx's "historical materialism" conceived this within an evolutionary perspective—new productive force and new production relation emerging out of prior formation, or to paraphrase Marx's own metaphor, "the old being pregnant with new."

---

* Justification for the law of the stronger and for the superiority of those on the top. Herbert Spencer in his "Introduction to Origin of Species" used the concept as basis for his theory of human progress based on the elimination of the unfit. John Bellamy Foster has quoted, in his 'Marx's Ecology', several other arguing like "millionaires are a product of natural selection"; "the growth of a large business is merely survival of the fittest" and things like that.

Relating historical materialism to Darwin's theory of evolution, Marx goes further to compare the development of organs in plants and animals of the specialized tools in the historical process of production; in both cases they are adapted to specialised functioning. He called the latter "human technology" and the former "natural technology." Technology is "mediator" in man's relation to nature. Man builds machines by transforming naturally occurring materials into organs of human will over nature.

Man's relation to land is through labour—the agriculture labour. Under capitalism he gets virtually reduced to the status of commodity governed by the laws of supply and demand. This "proletarianisation" of labour transforms the relation to land causing displacement of peasantry which Marx termed "alienation of labour", and this, according to Adam Smith led to "primitive accumulation." Those who monopolized the land and subsequently the power of the capital dominated the earth, and then all gifts of nature—land, mines, forest, animals, etc.—became private property. Marx called this a contempt for and degradation of nature and ecology.

Ecological Problems

Contempt for nature is reflected in ecological crisis. The capitalist mode of production has led to three broad categories of ecological problems:

(1) Pollution of environment including proliferation of hazardous wastes and introduction of toxic materials,
(2) Depletion of resources as also extinction of species, and
(3) Growth of population causing both pollution and depletion.

What led this situation? Idealsits and exponents Green thought attribute it to the growth of science and technology and unitended inevitable consequences of economic growth and human action. Fundamentalist ecologists have even demanded an end to industrial production, break with modernity and return to simple old ways of living. For Marxists this is just a romantic dream.

The level of production has gone very high and is likely to go unchecked far enough to make a return to the society of idealists' dream impossible. What is needed is planned economic growth and appropriate choice of technology rather that outright rejection of technology. R. Grundmann says, "Ecological problems are a feature of modern society which they have to live in and cope with. It is likely that the problems can be reduced, transformed and displaced, but will not be abolished completely." The ill-effects (anti-ecological) of technology must be attributed to the capitalists' greed for profit and not to man's efforts to build technology. In a planned economy it would be a means of conscious control over nature like taming a river for a wild animal.

Human relation to nature is not direct unlike other species. It is via society which is his immediate environment, the society having nature as its environment. In the chapter on "Equilibrium between society and nature" in "Historical Materialism"; N. Bukharin, a noted Marxist whom Lenin had called the golden boy of Bolshevik revolution, wrote: "the society applies human labour and obtains certain quantity of energy from nature. The balance of what it gives and what it receives determines the growth of the society. If what is obtained exceeds the loss important consequences follow for the society depending on the amount of excess.

The whole process of social reproduction is the process of adaption of human society to nature. Therefore, rejecting the teleological view that God created man with nature for his use, Marx argues, consistent with the theory of evolution, that human beings are in constant active struggle to adapt. Also, Levin in his 'Dialectical Biologist' has written, "Organisms not only adapt to their environment, they also change it..." This is dialectical approach in contract to the idealist view that ecosystems have inherent property of growing diversity, stability and complexity.

Marx's Concern for Ecology

During the days of Marx the chief environmental

concern was depletion of soil fertility, forest and coal reserves arising in the course of burgeoning industrialisation and capitalist agriculture. But Marx's concern arose in the context of the arbitrary and blatant exploitation unleashed by capitalist forces on poor peasants and workers. While an editor of the 'Rheinische Zeitung' in 1842 he went through a series of parliamentary debates leading to the dissolution of the rights of the poor peasants to collect "dead wood" (i.e. wood from dead or fallen trees) in the forest for cooking food and heating homes a right they enjoyed since time immemorial. Under growing capitalism the big forest owners managed to turn the dead wood with no market value into a 'value' and source of private property. Laws were made subsequently and the customary rights of peasants were made acts of theft and hence of penal offence. Marx took up the poor and wrote articles in his journal on "Debates on the Law of Theft of Wood" However, as a result of government repression and lack of support he was forced to reassign from editorship.

Meanwhile he went through the researches of Justus von Liebing, a renowned agricultural chemist, who worked on the circulation of soil nutrients and their relation to plant and animal metabolism, Prior to Liebig's works Europe, in the 18th and the 19th centuries witnessed two revolutions in agriculture that laid the found of industrial capitalism, Technical changes includes in demand for fertilizers and growth of fertilizer industries. This led to a phenomenal increase in demand for fertilizers to the extent that European farmers, in search of bones, even raided the battle fields of waterloo and Austerlitz to dig up catacomba. Deposits of guano which were rich in nitrogen were discovered in Peru and several South American islands, and later of sodium nitrate in Chile, which the British colonialists rushed to take possession of, Liebig, in his researches publication in his 'Agriculture Chemistry' pointed out that the use of external fertilizers tended to diminish the soil fertility by imparing the return of nutrients to the soil. Impressed by Liebig's works, Marx made a systematic critique of capitalist agriculture as well as exploitation of soil which was being robbed of its own capacity to maintain fertility. In his discussion on 'Large scale Industry and Agriculture, he wrote:

> "Capitalist production collects the population together in great centres and causes the urban population to achieve an ever growing preponderance. This has two results. On the one hand it concentrates the historical motive force of society; on the other hand it disturbs the metabolic interaction between man and the earth, i.e. it prevents the return to the soil of its constituent elements consumed by man in the form of food and clothing; hence it hinders the operation of the eternal natural condition for the lasting fertility of the soil.... All progress in capitalist agriculture is a progress in the art, not only of robbing the worked but also of the soil; progress in increasing the fertility........ Capitalist production, therefore, only develops the technique and the degree of combination of the social process of production by simultaneously undermining the original sources of all wealth the soil and the worker."

Marx's critique of capitalist agriculture and its contribution to the ecological thought have to be understood in the context of the decline in soil fertility, use of artificial fertilizers and the emerging awareness of the crisis in European and North Amercian agriculture. Marx future observed that the large scale agriculture and industry, long distance trade and growing centrality of the market was creating a rift between county and towns.

Marx's Theory of Metabolic Rift

These observations led Marx to develop the theory of metabolic rift in man's relation to nature. The key point in the Marxist concept of ecology, based on Darwin- Marx and Liebig-Marx relations lies in the metabolic interaction between human beings and nature or society and environment, through the process of labour. Regarding labour Marx writes:

> "Labour is first of all a process between man and nature, a process by which man, through his own action mediates, regulates and controls the metabolism

> between himself and nature. He confronts the materials of nature as a force of nature. He sets in motion the natural forces which belong to his own body, his arms, legs, hands heads in order to appropriate the materials of nature in a form adapted to his own needs. Through this movement he acts upon external nature, and changes it, and in this way he simultaneously changes his own nature..."

Under capitalism, therefore, the conditions of sustainable agriculture are violated due to the metabolic rift between human beings are soil. The leads also to the antagonism between towns and the country because the failure to return to soil its nutrients that had been removed in the form of food and fibre has its counterpart in the pollution of cities. Accordingly, Marx writes:

> "The conscious and rational treatment of land as permanent communal property is the inalienable condition of the reproduction of the chain of human generations." Thus Marx believed that the main problem in agriculture was not large scale production but metabolic interaction between human beings and the soil. Large scale capitalist agriculture was possible only if the condition of sustainability was maintained.

Addressing to other ecological problems like deforestation and depletion of coal reserves that characterised the growing industrial civilization, Marx and Engels warned against over exploitation of nature, "Let us not, however, flatter ourselves much on account of our human victories over nature. For each such victory nature takes its revenge on us. Each victory, it is true, in the first place brings about the results we expected, but in the second and third place it quite different unforeseen effects which can only too often cancel the first. On the depletion of coal reserves, Engels wrote to Marx that the "working individual is not only a stabiliser of the present but also a squanderer of the past; for example, solar heat stored in our coal reserves, forests, etc. Marx too referred to the exploitative relation of nature that had characterised all civilisation up to the present

Marxist Ecology after Marx

After the death of Kari Marx Europe saw generation of social thinkers drawn towards Marxism. In 1886 Eleanor Marx (the daughter of Marx) along with William Morris, a British social scientist who turned Marxist after going through *'The Capital'*, Founded a socialist league which became the centre of their activities. A case of lead poisoning was reported in which a factory worker was killed by being compelled to work in a lead factory. The owner did know the hazards of working in a lead factory but he did nothing to prevent his speedy death nor, in his quest for bigger profit, did he give him adequate compensation. This affected Morris much and he envisioned in his fantasy a socialism in which factories would be set among gardens which would befoul no water and poison no air.

Subsequent Marxist thinkers chief of whom were Bebel, Kautsky, Bukharin, Rosa Luxemberg and many others attempted to build ecological components of Marx's thoughts. Augustus Bebel wrote in his 'Woman under Socialism' (Later appearing as 'Woman in the past, present and future'), "The mad sacrifice of forests for the sake of profit is the cause of appreciable deterioration of climate and decline in the fertility of soil in Prussia, Syria, Italy, France and Spain........" He pointed to the "need of rational reorganisation of production under socialism." Kautsky presented his critique of the fertilizer treadmill resulting from the metabolic rift, "the growth to towns and expansion of industry increasingly exhausts the soil and imposes burden on agriculture in the form fertilizers needed to combat this exhaustion .... The increasing use of pesticides was attributed to the growth of pests, to the killing of insect-eating birds owing to extension of cultivation and to the replacement of natural selection with artificial selection in the growth of plants which tended to reduce resistance of disease and pests. Hence the cost of agriculture increased due to the fertilizer and pesticides." Bukharin who closely studied Natural Science remarked in his 'Historical Materialism' that the ultimate basis of materialism was to be found in ecology, in the theory of biosphere full of infinitely varied life from the smallest microorganisms in water, land and air to human beings.

In the 20th century, in England, a strong tradition of left wing scientist with deep commitment to dialectical materialism emerged in the period 1930-1980 which included stalwards like J.D. Bernal, J.B.S. Haldane, Joseph Needham—all fellows of Royal Society and many others. Bernal emphasized the "inexhaustible stability of the ever moving material world and man's power to change it." To the Cambridge biochemist Needham, Marx and Engels were bold enough to assert that the nature evolves itself dialectically. Haldane, a leading figure in the development of "New-Darwinian Synthesis within Biology" was a strong adherent of Engels' dialectical Materialism and wrote the preface to a later edition of the latter's 'Dialectics of Nature.'

In 1920's, N.I. Vavilov, a brilliant plant geneticist of Russia applied materialist principles to the question of the orgin of agriculture. He determined that there were a few centres of plant gene diversity—the richest banks of germ plasms that are the basis of all cultivation all located in under developed countries of tropical and sub-tropical mountainous regions. These centres of plant gene diversity are the products of human culture which arose in "seven principal centres" out of which all principal crops originated.

The tradition of dialectical materialistic researches gained impetus in 1980's, 90's by the works of some noted thinkers like Richard Lewontin Stephen J. Gould and Richard Levins, all professors of Harvard University (USA). Having derived their materialism from Darwin and Marx they have set in motion a long debate on materialism and teleology providing the basis for a thorough going materialist ecology. They point to the continuing importance of Marx, Engels, Darwin and dialectical materialism in the analysis of ecological phenomena.

Imperialist Threat to Ecology

Human history is the history of class struggle, says Karl Marx. In the era of imperialism it assumed global character in the form of national liberation movements, resistance to blackmail, intimidation, economic sanction and even belligerent occupation of territories by developed and powerful countries. From Marxist stand point, imperialism, the highest form of capitalism in the words of Lenin, poses the greatest danger to ecology. Imperialist powers do not spare any means to gain control over the natural resources of weak and developing countries despite latter's liberation from slavery.

After alluring the gene-rich developing countries to join the world trade organisation in the name of free and fare trade they have been pressed to change patent laws to suit imperialists interests. Giant multinational companies (MNC) of the west, taking advantage of the lack of capital and technology in the developing countries, have fund entry into latter's territories. A decade's experience of such "economic reforms" has revealed the emergence of a tiny consumer class with sky rocketing income, impoverishment and joblessness for the bulk of population and gradual decimation of small industries. On the other hand, problem of large scale waste disposal and depletion of resources and biodiversity have threatened the ecology. Industrial projects and big dams erected ostencibly catering to the aquatic needs of the people actually serve capitalists' interest and have certainly ruined the life of millions of tribals and even non-tribals on account of their eviction without rehabilitation. While suscepticism prevails about the proposed interlinking of rivers in India, some rivers are already under consideration for private bidding.

The atmosphere is already getting polluted with toxic emissions green house gases, heavy metals, pesticides and chlorofluorocarbons, eighty percent of which is due to rich countries of the West USA, the greatest emitter of green house gases in the world, is not prepared to slash any of its projects even though it means flouting the environment-related international agreement, "Kyoto protocol."

An obvious ecological impact of opening the market of developing countries to MNC's can be seen on the former's food and agriculture systems. High priced junk and tasty foods in attractive packs are being increasingly marketed. We have no clues to know their effects on health but reports of rise in diabetes, blood pressure, heart problems, etc. have been appearing in the press. To add, the introduction of genetically modified (GM) crops in agriculture has played havoc with farmers. By purchasing and ssowing Kargil 900 M Mazie seeds (GM) in Bihar and Bt cotton seeds (GM) at very high prices the farmers in both states found themselves shortchanged due to total failure of crops. The Mansanto Co. of USA who deals in GM seeds has been extolling the outstanding performance of GM seeds on the basis of the data obtained from a few trial plots owned by the company rather than conducting trials on farmers' fields. This amounts to data manipulation as the company's trial plots are experimental plots with optimum conditions for GM crops which are different from normal fields. When investigations are still going on with respect to the benefits of G.M. crops the hasty use in open to risk. Its use disregards not only human beings but all living organisms. Cattle fed on GM food could transmit its effect through dairy products. Reckless use of biotechnology has already produced wittingly or unwittingly hundreds of new viruses which we are at a loss to handle. We do not know their number or the mutants they may have spawned. To add more of these microorganisms into our atmosphere is to severely affect our ability to sustain life.

Ecology Destruction due to Imperialist Wars

Sources of energy (fossil fuels) and raw materials are the key to industrial development. Nature has endowed the countries of the third world with these sources which have been the targets of the imperialist powers of Europe and north America. Inter-imperialist rivalry coupled with quest for market have led to two world wars in the past century and frequent armed conflagrations in the post-war period. Imperialists armed as they are with the power of capital consider virtually their right to control the resources of the poor and weak countries and residence to this can lead to flash point. For this the former have quipped themselves with such high-tech weapons laser bombs, neutron bombs, chemical and biological bombs. Napalm bombs, killer satellites and a host of nuclear bombs, besides convention weapons which can not only destroy life but also cause environmental Foundation of America, USA has stockpiles of chemical weapons like mustard gas (Agent 4) which can cause cancer, Sarin gas (G.B.) which causes eye burn and respiratory problems leading to death, V.X. gas (trade name) which is 170 times more toxic than G.B. gas and V.X. gas which causes loss of memory and heart diseases. Such weapons can make endemic birds and plants become extinct. In 1991, Gulf War, violation of coastal biosystems affected precious animal and bird life. Thousands of migratory birds who survived the war could not escape the oil slicks and were trapped in them mistaking them for water. Jet fuel emissions contained nearly half a billion tons of ozone depleting gases. Toxic pollution of air and water, chemical and biological contamination of important natural habitats, loss of wild life and biodiversity and depletion of resources did irreversible damages to the environment. Much of the depleted uranium, a nuclear waste product, used in the war got converted into cancer-producing radioactive aerosol. The world has seen the clouds of black smoke over regions of constant US bombings in Iraq in Gulf War II—"the operation Iraq Freedom",—2003. What do they do to the lungs of Iraqi People ? The UN Environment Programme (UNEP) issued the warning: "This smoke contains dangerous chemicals immediately harmful to people, particularly children and those suffering from respiratory problems. The plumes of smoke rising in the sky from the oil fields threaten inhabited areas with smog. Smoke from oil fires contain a range of contaminants such as sulphur, mercury, dioxins and furnace. The black smoke from oil field trenches as well as bomb ignited fires coupled with increase in plankton productivity have led to fish death on a big scale." Many have raised concern about the ecological impact of depleted uranium munitions used by USA and Britain against Iraq.

Ironically, USA and its have been launching wars under the euphemisms of freedom, democracy, human rights, developing the undeveloped, etc. for imperialists no interest is bigger than their own economic interest. USA has been held responsible in 'earth summit' for pollution of air on global scale, nut it is not prepared to slash any of its war-related industrial projects. While ecology is destroyed, developed nations flourish at the cost of the developing, cities flourish at the cost of the villages, rich become richer at the cost of the poor—a dictum consistent with Marx's doctrine of the "ton country rift."

References

Ann Bramwell: Ecology in the 20th century, New Haven, Conn, Yale University Pross, 1989, p. 44.

Augustus Bebel: "Woman in the Past, Present and Future", London, Zwan, 1958, p. 204.

Baron d' Hollbach: System of Nature (1970).

Barry Commoner: The closing circle, London, 1971, pp 37-41, 178, 179.

Charles Darwin: "The Origin of Species", and Karl Marx: Grundrisse, pp. 489, 973.

F. Engels: Lectures on the Philosophy of Hegel.

F. Engels: Dialectics of Nature, Foreign Languages Publishing House, Moscow, 1954.

Herbert Spencer: Editors' Introduction, p. 53.

Johan Bellamy Foster: Marx's Ecology, Monthly Reviw Foundation, New York, 100001, Published in India by Corner Stone Publication, Kharagpur, p. 188.

Johan Bellany Foster: Marx's Ecology, Cornerstone Publication, Kharagpur, p. 73.

John Bellamy Foster: "The Vulnerable Planet," pp. 94-95.

John Bellamy Foster: Marx's Ecology, Cornerstone Publishers, Kharagpur, p. 66.

Justus Von Liebig: Published as a part of complete works on chemistry, Philadelphia, T.B. Peterson, 1852.

K. Marx and F. Engels: "*Collected Works*", Vol. 45, pp. 50-51.

K. Marx and F. Engels: "*Collected Works*", Vol. 5, pp. 480-81.

Karl Marx: *The Capital,* Vol 1, p. 352.

Karl Marx: *The Capital,* Vol. 1, pp. 637-38.

Karl Kautsky: "The Agrarian Question" (London) Zwan, 1998, Vol. 2, pp. 214-15.

Karl Marx: *The Capital,* Vol. 3, p. 748.

N.I. Vavilov: "The Problem of the Origin of Agriculture in the light of the Latest Investigations in Bukharin, *et al.,* in Science at the Cross-Roads, pp. 97-106.

Nikolai Bukharin: "Historical Materialism", pp. 180-12.

Reiner Grundman: New Left Review, 1995 (185), p. 106.

Reinner Grundman: New Left Review, 1995 (185), pp. 104-20.

William Morris: "Selected Writings", New York, Random House, 1934, p. 647.

3

Ecology and Related Themes in Classical Marxism

KRISHNA KUMAR KHANNA

From the standpoint of a higher economic form of society, private ownership of the globe by single individuals will appear quite as absurd as private ownership of one man by another. Even a whole society, a nation, or even all simultaneously existing societies taken together, are not the owners of the globe. They are only its possessors, its usufactuaries, and like bone patres familias, they must hand it down to succeeding generations in an improved condition.

—*Karl Marx*

STRADDLING the space between cultural ecology and ecofeminism, and taking in its stride the more proximate areas of ecological economics, ecopolitics and, somewhat ridiculously, ecotourism, ecology is today's buzzword. It is perhaps a sign of the times that in his recent volume on the history civilizations, Felipe Fernandez-Armesto should look upon civilization 'as a relationship between our species and the rest of nature' and organize his long narrative around five broad ecosystems.[1]

And yet, as Raymond Williams had noted, ecology is not a word that was common in English before mid-20th century, though its use goes back to the last quarter of the 19th century through translation from the German zoologist Haeckel. The word then stood for the study of the relation of plants and animals with each other and with their habitat. Such concerns were first expressed by environmentalist and its associated words and it was only from the late 1960's that these came to be replaced by ecology and its associated words.[2] However, ecology did not for long remain a mere study of relationships between animals and plants and their organic and inorganic surroundings but soon exfoliated into a body of thought that sought to reinterpret economics, politics and social theory in terms of man's relation to his natural surroundings. In this sense it has truly become, to adopt Edward Thompson's expressions devised for other occasions, a 'junction term' ('which lies at the point of junction between analytic disciplines')[3] or a 'junction point' (which 'leads us not into a single argument but into a concourse of arguments').[4] Ecology has in its substantive polyvalence, then, tended to offer itself as a complete Weltans chauung, an entire world-view, under girded by philosophical Naturalism.[5] Whence and why this broadening of the scope of ecology as a concept an ambitious expansion of its thematic claims to encompass and answer larger questions of life and reality? And why now?

Three sets of causal occurrences may have converged to make this eventuation possible. The first is the perceived threat to the very life of the human species due to grave and escalating environmental degradation. In his book, 'The Vulnerable Plant'. John Bellamy Forster has given a long list of factors threatening to cause ecological catastrophe:

> These include: overpopulation, destruction of the ozone layer, global warming, extinction of species, loss of genetic diversity, acid rain, nuclear contamination, tropical deforestation, the elimination of climax forests, wetland destruction, soil erosion, desertification, floods, famine, the despoliation of lakes, streams and rivers, the drawing down and contamination of ground water,

> the pollution of coastal over-fishing, expanding landfills toxic waters; the poisonous effects of pesticides and herbicides, exposure to hazards on the job, urban congestion, and the depletion of non-renewable resources.[6]

The frightening prospect of impending planetary disaster teams up with the advent of what Ernest Mandel calls the Third Machine Age or 'late capitalism', the era of multinational or consumer capitalism and globalisation.[7] After listing the economic features of globalised capitalism,[8] Fredric Jameson explains the 'cultural logic' of late 'capitalism':

> Implicit in all this is.....the effacement of Nature, and its pre-capitalist agricultures...the essential homogenization of a social space and experience now uniformly modernized and mechanized (where the generation gap passes between the models of the products rather than between the ecologies of their users).[9]

It results in the characteristic post-modernist angst of which Jameson has elsewhere given us a vivid glimpse:

> Thus we are faced with the peculiar impression that life becomes meaningless in direct proportion to people's control of their environment and that a humanisation of the world goes in hand with a spreading philosophic and existential despair. It is as though the meaningfulness of the world remains intact only so long as some portion of that world—an imperfectly dominated Nature, a blindly theocratic hierarchical social tradition hung beyond human reach....[10]

We shall do well to keep these representations of the historically conditioned post-modernist despair in mind assessing some of the views of mainstream ecologists which might strike us as somewhat regressive and even reactionary.

A third coordinate of the new situation lies in the political and ideological convulsions of our times, more specifically, the collapse of the states of the so-called 'existing socialism' and the general crisis of Marxism to which Marxists themselves have long been calling attention. Thus Perry Anderson had noted that Marxism, both as theory and practice, was facing challenges from different quarters and hazarded the guess that the more powerful challenge to historical materialism will come from Naturalism, raising issues of relations between humanity and nature 'which lie athwart rather than within the relations between classes that is the central concern of Marxism'.[11] Earlier still, Sebastiano Timpanaro had said that as result of the 'increasingly monstrous development of "capitalist rationality" on the one hand, and the crisis of world communist movement on the other, that tranquil faith in the historical progress as a certain bearer of communism has vanished'.[12]

These three coordinates in concert constitute some of the basic features of our time: a fear of planetary disaster, the triumphal sway of global capitalism, an emphatic set-back to the Left and consolidation of the political Right worldwide, and the perceived crisis of Marxism calling for radical revaluation of its theoretical categories. It is this historical conjuncture which may explain why ecology, aiming to fill the vacuum presumably left by retreating Marxism, today offers itself as an alternative ideology that seeks to give definitive answers to questions left unanswered by Marxism. On the other hand, the ecologist challenge may provide fruitful provocation to Marxists to foreground some of the themes in classical Marxism which had remained in the shadows.[13] This may also help them to compose the specifics of a Marxist ecology within the broad framework of historical materialism.

NOT THE QUESTION of ecology narrowly conceived, but that of society as a system of human relations of production and reproduction, where contradictions arise which then constitute historical evolution, is the central concern of classical Marxism, i.e. the writings of Marx and Engels. If one were to go by sheer numerical count of explicit references in their works to what are today called ecological problems, it will have to be admitted that their incidence is not very large. Why this is so is a matter that shall be touched on later in this paper. John Passmore has listed five characteristically ecological issue, viz. pollution, depletion of natural resources, extinction of species, destruction of wildness, and population growth.[14] Now, except for the criticism of Malthus on the question of population (about which even a sympathetic ecologist like Ted Benton is at best equivocal),[15] some stray observations on industrial waste, depletion of coal reserves and destruction of forests,[16] and Engels's description of living conditions in industrial Manchester,[17] the only sustained discussion of what may be called an ecological issue concerns Marx's critique, in volumes I and III of *Capital* of large sale capitalist agriculture as it inevitably tended to bring about a systematic degradation of the soil. In the concluding passage of the last section of the chapter on "Machinery and Modern Industry" in *Capital*, I, Marx registers of full-throated protest against wilful squandering of natural resources at the hands of capitalist landlords.

> Capitalist production, by collecting the population in great centres and causing an ever-increasing preponderance of town population on the one hand concentrates the historical motive power of society; on the other hand, it disturbs the circulation of matter between man and the soil, i.e. prevents the return to the soil of its elements consumed by man in the form of food and clothing; it therefore violates the conditions necessary for lasting fertility of the soil... But while upsetting the naturally grown conditions for the maintenance of that circulation of matter, it imperiously calls for its restoration as a system, as a regulatory law of social productions and under a form appropriate to the full development of the human race.[18]

The entire passage in illustrative of Marx's oxymoronic style of thought that tells us, in the words of Marshall Berman, 'how the bad things and the good things in the world spring from the same place.'[19] Its significance for the overall nature and direction of Marxist ecological thinking will emerge later in our discussion. In the meanwhile, it may be noted that, while referring to the violation of the 'conditions necessary to lasting fertility of the soil', Marx replicates the argument of the German agronomist Leibig (whose work he cites in the footnote to this passage) who had drawn attention to the polluting deposits of human and animal wastes in towns and had deplored their loss as nutrient to rural fields, thus causing depletion of natural fertility of the soil.[20] The passage is also remarkable for the way Marx graphically describes the metabolism taking place between man and nature, insists on the need to maintain a consistent ecological balance by returning to nature in full measure what is taken away from it by man, equates the pillaging to nature with the exploitation of laboures and cautions against tinkering with nature for short-term gains that might prove disastrous in the long-run. These are precisely the issue that ecologists, more than hundred years after Marx, find to be central to their concern.

However, Marx does not stop there. In the same passage he ties the matter up with the larger social issue of the separation of town and country that he had earlier called 'the foundation of every division of labour' and the primary 'antithesis' in the economic life of society.[21] But, as he elsewhere notes the process of this separation was itself set in motion by natural causes.[22] Still, what Marx presents here is not only a fact of social history but also of the ecological history of the soil. For his observation, following Leibig's on the loss of nutrient due to crowding of towns by dispossessed peasantry has indeed been validated by recent scientific research on soil ecology as a historical break in nutrient cycling traceable to the second agricultural revolution.[23]

The other extended discussion of the issue of the squandering of the natural fertility of the soil in capitalist agriculture occurs at the end of the chapter on "Genesis of Capitalist Ground Rent" in *Capital*, Vol. III. Here Marx draws attention to the ruinous collaboration of large-scale industry and large-scale agriculture, ruinous both of the life of the soil and of the life of the worker.[24] He, once again, relates the question of the soil exhaustion to that of the flight of dispossessed peasantry to towns where they become part of the vast reserve army of labour and to long-distance trade and colonisations, that is, to a whole set of attendant and causative circumstances marking this particular ecological problem.

Another aspect of the discussion relates to Marx's refusal to limit it to a strictly technical problem of mechanization of agriculture. Only a little earlier, he had commented upon the common complicity of small-scale as well as large-scale agriculture under private ownership in this plunder and waste of natural resources:

> In both forms, exploitation and squandering of the vitality of the soil..... takes the place of conscious rational cultivation of the soil as eternal communal property, an alienable condition of the existence and reproduction of a chain of successive generations of the human race.[25]

What is remarkable here is Marx's conscious attempt to relate the question of the soil (which he considered to be one of the forces of production) and of its depletion, in both large- and small-scale agriculture, to the question of the ownership and control of the land (the defining element in his concept of relations of production), thereby giving the ecological issue its proper place in a dialectical unfolding of his theory of historical materialism. The discourse moves on a terrain very different from one of debating, in abstract, the question of the desirability or otherwise of mechanization of agriculture and application of science to it, as in some ecological circles now. Marx, instead, raises the more pertinent question of the need for 'rational cultivation of the soil' in a rational order of society, free from the irrationalities of private ownership, reckless drive for profit and class domination. It is in such a society alone that ecological questions such as these can find their rational answers and the ecological 'evil' exorcised. It is this aspect of his historical materialist and communist concern which is uppermost in the memorable peroration on the patrimony of the earth in the lines that stand as the epigraph to this paper and in which Marx indeed appears at his 'ecologistic' best.[26]

It is a measure of his acute realism that although he has so sensitively described man's metabolism with nature in these and many other passages of *Capital,* Marx does not find untrammeled nature to be quite respectful to ecological niceties. Apropos the remarks of the German agriculturist Frass, he, in a letter to Engels, refers to depredations brought about by nature in ancient 'Persia' Mesopotamia and Greece'.[27] Bellamy Foster's narrative of ecological imbalances and even disasters in pre-industrial 'ecohistorical periods'[28] is clearly in line with Marx's thinking here.

Engel's and Marx's critique of Malthus on the question of population is, likewise, many-layered. That Malthus's idea geometrical and arithmetical progression of population and productivity respectively were refutable and refuted is not the most important aspect of the controversy. Engels's critique is important for a different reason. He in fact gives Malthus credit for having brought to the fore the question of precisely defining surplus population. From Malthus's contention that 'population is always pressing on the means of employment' Engels derives 'the most powerful arguments for social transformation'. To the question of social transformation Engels linked the question of measures to restrict population, 'for only this transformation, only the education of the masses which it provides, makes possible that moral restraint upon propagative instinct which Malthus himself presents as the most effective and easiest remedy for over population.'[29] It is one of the great merits of Engels's critique of Malthus that, so early in his career, he brought what was later to develop into a specifically ecological issue within the ambit of an evolving radical social theory.

For Marx, a notable feature of Malthus's doctrine was his proposal to create a class of buyers who were not simultaneously sellers of any kind so as to maintain an effective demand for goods. This rendered him, in the eyes of Marx, a spokesman of landed aristocracy and a target of his vitriolic attack in the pages of Theories of Surplus Value and elsewhere.[30] On a more theoretical level, Marx criticizes Malthus for generalizing a universal law of population on the basis of contemporary data forgetting that in 'different modes of social production there are different laws of the increase of population and of overpopulation;[31] a theme he develops at other places too.

Thus, in pre-industrial societies there was likely to prevail an inverse relationship between growth of population and productivity, which acted as a brake on population, the 'barrier' being put up by the mode of production itself.[32] Under the capitalist mode of production, however, the situation is different. Here two contradictory processes are simultaneously at work. From his observation that for both 'population growth' and 'latent wealth of nature' the capitalist pays nothing, it can be surmised that the system has an in-built tendency to exploit both labourer and nature inasmuch as this dual exploitation under the aegis of capital leads to constant growth of capital.[33] On the other hand, capitalism not only thrives on an increase of population but also tends to secrete pauperism, that is, 'over-population' or the reserve army of labour.[34]

And, finally, the question of the relation between population and machinery. Here, again, Marx relates the question of machinery not to the problem of population in abstract but to the concrete question of the availability of the mass of the unemployed, not necessarily due to the introduction of machinery but also due to antecedent conditions in the countryside, the forcible uprooting of peasantry from land as described by him in harrowing detail in the chapter on primitive accumulation in *Capital*. He then makes the startling discovery that machinery 'inserts itself to replace labour only where there is overflow of labour powers'.[36]

What the discussion of the problem of population in Engels and Marx, especially in the latter, shows is the complex ways in which it meshes with so many aspects of social production and natural reproduction of different social groups in varied historical circumstances. In these discussions, the question of population takes its place beside the other ecological issue of fertility of the soil within the large framework of historical materialism to a consideration of which we now turn in order to get our bearings on the governing principles of a Marxist ecology.

IN THE EXPRESSION, 'historical materialism', the

noun affirms the material unity of man and nature man himself being a natural physical species who continues to live, produce and reproduce under 'everlasting Nature-imposed conditions of human existence';[37] and the adjective denotes the historically evolving differentiation within this unity which is marked by changing forms of nature as well as by purely natural determinations being increasingly replaced by social determinations. The latter process results in the 'retreat of the natural boundary', though never in its disappearance. This dual determination—an insuperable natural basis of human existence and social transformations of these natural conditions—is the defining principle of historical materialism.[38] The principle of dual determination is the leading thread in the reflections of Marx and Engels on the man-nature relationship.

Very early, Marx had acknowledged that 'the writing of history must always set out from these natural bases' 'the natural conditions in which man finds himself geological, orohydrophical, climatic and so on', and that through all the productive activities of man 'the priority of external nature remains unassailed'.[39] In his theory of history, therefore, 'the evolution of the economic formation of society is viewed as a process of natural history,[40] in that elements of pre-human history continue to exist in human society, e.g. the fettering of the productiveness of labour by physical conditions, both the condition of man himself and the surrounding nature.[41] Marx had also drawn attention to the similarity between his materialist conception of the role of productive forces in social production and reproduction and Darwin's theory of the formation of the organs of plants and animals, that is, his theory of 'Nature's technology'.[42] In another footnote earlier, while referring to Darwin's principle of natural selection as the process of adaptation of plant and animals as instruments of production, Marx spoke about their similarity with human instruments of production in respect of specialization of function.[43] He also attention to a striking analogy between natural law and social law:

> Castes and guilds arise from the action of the same natural law that regulates the differentiation of plants and animals into species and varieties..... [44]

A similar analogy is drawn between Darwin's theory of the storage of inherited traits and accumulation and transmission of labour skills.[45]

Engels's Dialectics of Nature gives a broad perspective on materialist ontology, at once scientific, philosophic and visionary. While defining materialist outlook as 'nothing more than the simple conception of nature just as it is, without alien addition',[46] he explains the cardinal principle of materialism as the principle of the 'universal connection' of natural phenomenon, the general interconnection of things'.[47] The whole nature accessible to us forms a system, an interconnected totality of bodies', that is, all material existences extending from stars to atoms, indeed right up to ether particles.'[48] In nature, therefore, 'nothing takes place in isolation. Everything affects and is affected by every other thing.'[49] The history of mankind is unimaginable without its prehistory: 'the evolutionary series of organisms from a few simple forms to increasingly multifarious and complicated ones as it confronts us today, and extending right up to man'.[50] Without the 'prehistory of the human mind', the 'existence of the thinking human brain remains a miracle.'[51]

However, while calling attention to the continuities between natural and social determinations, Marx and Engels sometimes in the same passage—also remarked upon the discontinuities and distinctions between 'the history we do not make' and 'the history that we make'.[52] The passage in *Capital*, I, where Marx speaks of the fettering of the productivity of labour by natural conditions like fertility of the soil is followed by an assertion that 'it by no means follows from this that the most fruitful soil is the most fitted for the growth of the capitalist mode of production'. There is also a hint of Nature working at cross-purposes, as it were, with men, for 'where nature is too lavish, she keeps him in hand like a child in leading-strings. She does not impose upon him any necessity to develop himself'. From this arises the necessity of bringing the 'natural force under the control of society, of economizing, of appropriating or subduing it on a large scale by the work of man's hand.'[53] Similarly, his remarks on the analogy between natural law and social law is followed by the observation that 'when a certain degree of development has been reached, the heredity of castes and exclusiveness of guilds are ordained as a law of society.'[54] In the passage in Theories of Surplus Value, Part III, where he draws an analogy between Darwin's notion of inherited traits and his own views on accumulation of labour skills, he goes on to note that man 'faces an already modified natural (and in particular natural factors which have been transformed into means of his own activity) and definite relations existing between the producers'[55] As for the discussion in The German Ideology, the 'natural bases' from which history begins are themselves 'modified in the course of history through the action of man.'[56] And while Marx speaks of the 'unity of man with nature' and of the compresence of an 'historical nature and a natural history', he also says though 'the celebrated "unity of man with nature" has always existed in industry', so has the struggle of man with nature right up to the development of his productive powers on a corresponding bases.'[57] In his eyes, the differentiation of man from nature has gone so far that 'nature, the nature that preceded human history, is not by any means the nature in which Feurbach lives, nor the nature which today no longer exists anywhere (except perhaps on a few Australian coral islands of recent origin').[58] Elsewhere he asserted that 'nature . . . taken abstractly, for itself—nature fixed in isolation from man is nothing for man.'[59] He brings out the new determinations which are wholly social and absent in nature:

> Nature does not produce on the one side owners of money or commodity, and on the other men possessing nothing but their own labour power. This relation has no natural basis, neither is its social basis one that is common to all historical periods.[60]

Like Marx, Engels had also stressed, equally, the element of unity as well as of struggle in man's relation with nature and had criticized any one sided emphasis on either term of this dialectical relationship.[61] He brought out the cardinal difference between animal and man: 'animals at most collect while men produce'.[62] The story of man's differentiation from animal is outlined in 'Part Played by labour in Transition from Ape to Man.'[63] The story of the differentiation taking place through the agency of labour and tools and also involving man's growing freedom from unilateral dependence on natural is the story of what Darwin calls the 'law of correlation of growth' and Bellamy Foster 'co-evolution.'[64] It is a psychosomatic growth of mankind, a simultaneous development in body, mind and sociability.[65] Growth in consciousness leads to a deepening of the knowledge of natural laws and to man's more many-sided engagement with natural, one aspect of which is the variation of strategy from adaptation to 'mastery of nature.'[66] However, whether mastering nature or adapting to it, man becomes increasingly aware of the inexhaustible richness of nature's properties.[67]

Engels, too, notes that in the course of human development purely human processes and categories emerge which are not to be found in animal or in natural. One of these is the capacity for intentional action. The further removed men are from animals, 'the more their effect on nature assumes the character of premeditated planned action, directed towards definite preconceived ends',[68] Another novelty lies in the way the very notion of struggle for existence or subsistence is transcended by the new-found concepts of development and pleasures.[69] And then, as history progresses, there emerge, in contrast to the 'eternal laws of nature,' 'economic laws' which are historical and which 'appear and disappear,'[70]

Engels knows that subjective human action take place within an objective order, natural and social. The international projects of men are, therefore, beset with three kinds of asymmetry and contradiction: between the 'more immediate and more remote consequences of interference with the traditional course of nature',[71] between the 'most immediate and directly useful effect of labour and the further consequences which appear only later;[72] and the asymmetry 'resulting from the interplay of unintended effects from uncontrolled forces',[73] It is precisely because these asymmetries are always present and active that Engels decries any triumphalist account of man's action upon nature much as any latter-day ecologist would do, sometimes without the rational underpinning of the kind offered by Engels.

> Thus at every step we are reminded that we by no means rule our nature like a conqueror over a foreign people like someone standing outside nature—than we, with flesh, blood brain, belong to nature and exist in its midst, and that all our mastery of it consist in the fact that we have the advantage over all our all creatures of being able to learn its laws and apply them correctly.

With this, the pejorative meaning with which terms like 'mastery' and 'control' of nature found in Marx and Engels are saddled in some ecological circles disappears, and these terms undergo a radical revision of meaning, suggesting by 'mastery' and 'control' nothing more than a 'deft handling' of nature. Engels had much less faith than some of his epigones in man's triumphal march into an unproblematic future.[75] This is evident from his 'judgment on the evolution' of species ('each advance in organic evolution is at the same time a regression')[76] and from the deeply tragic sense and tone of stoic acceptance that resonate through the memorable passage in which he draws the picture of the future end of the world.[77]

In Dialectics of Nature, Engels had given a panoramic view of the prehistoric man's differentiation from the animal under conditions still largely set by nature. The subsequent story, with elaborate structure of its plot and fine texture of its themes, when, in the words of G.A. Cohen, history came to substitute nature,[78] is told in the writings of Marx.

The plot is composed of several themes, a crucial one dealing with labour process as a metabolism between man and nature.[79] Of this metabolism, Marx gives us two versions. One, especially outlined in chapter VII of *Capital*, I, treats the labour process 'in the abstract, apart from its historical form, as a process between man and Nature.'[80] Here, labour begins by separating things from 'immediate connection with their environment'. Some of the subjects of labour are spontaneously provided by nature, others are those products of nature which are filtered though previous labour. The instruments of labour which man interposes between himself and the subject of his labour are the conductors of his activity and are themselves composed of mechanical, physical and chemical properties of some substance or matter. Nature, thus, 'becomes one of the organs of his activity'. 'As the earth is his original larder, so too it is his original tool house.'[81]

In this metabolism, then, there is an active dialectic of identity and non-identity between man and nature.[82] Man 'opposes himself to Nature as one of his forces, setting in motion arms and legs, head and hands, the natural forces of his body,'[83] or, as Marx had also noted: 'Man himself, viewed as the impersonation of labour power is a natural object .... and labour is the manifestation of this power residing in him.'[84] It is in this sense that while in Economic and Philosophic Manuscripts, 'Nature is the inorganic body of man', in Grundrisse, the individual is the 'organic body of nature.'[85]

However, the character of this metabolism is such that at the end of the process the relative autonomy of each, nature and man, is preserved. The materials of nature remain part of nature even after they have undergone the labour process: 'The forces of wood is .....'[86] On the other hand, man's actions 'effect an alteration' in the materials of nature, adapting them by a change of form with a view to producing use-values. 'The labour process... is human action with a view to the producing or use values.'[87] And yet, this process, the 'necessary condition for effecting exchange of matter between man and nature' is the 'everlasting Nature-imposed condition of human existence, and therefore independent of every social phase of that existence, or rather, is common to every such phase.'[88] Moreover, this metabolism is subject to laws of nature existing anterior to man. ['Man] can work only as Nature does, that is, by changing the form of matter.'[89]

A very significant aspect of this metabolism is that man's relationship to nature is at the same time man's relationship to other men. This in the sense that man collaborates with his fellow men for the purposes of production which is nothing other than a function of man's action and effect on nature. Marx had said: 'In production, men not only act on nature but also on one another.'[90] In

Economic and Philosophic Manuscripts, deeper ontological implications of this sociality is given in the philosophical idiom of the young Marx. Thus, 'immediate sensuous nature for man is, immediately, human sensuousness (the expressions are identical)—presented immediately in the form of the other man sensuously present for him.'[91] And '[a] being which does not have its natural outside itself is not a natural being, and plays no part in the system of nature..... A being which is not itself an object for some third being has no being for its object.'[92] Such an outlook, which brings together the concept of man as a 'generic being' in the Manuscripts and the notice of 'social relations of production' in *Capital*,[93] abjures a dualistic notice of man and nature, basic to all forms of Naturalism underlying contemporary ecological thinking and implicit in the controversy over ecocentrism *versus* anthropomorphism, the favourite hobby horse of some ecologists.[94]

The other version of the metabolism, complementary to the first we have discussed, deals with the process of labour, not in general and universal terms but under specific modes of production. The premise of such a study is that as 'the taste of the porridge does not tell you who grew the oats, no more does this simple process tell you of itself what are the social conditions under which it is taking place.'[95] This is so because labour process is always part of a larger social process of production which is 'always appropriation of nature by an individual within and with the help of a definite social organization.'[96]

One aspect of the historical evolution of nature forms is the transformation of nature by man. In The German Ideology, Marx and Engels, contra Feurbach, insisted that the sensuous world is 'not a thing given direct from all eternity, ever the same, but the product of history and of the state of society.'[97] Another is man's separation from nature through history, the 'separation of these inorganic conditions of human existence from the active existence', that is, from 'the unity of living and active human beings with the natural inorganic conditions of their metabolism with nature,' 'a separation which is completely posited only in the relation wage labour and capital.'[98] The story of this separation of man from nature, consummated under capitalism, is an important theme of Marx's historical materialism and is articulated in the crucial Marxist categories of alienation, reification of fetishism.

In the pages of Grundrisse, in which he deals with the question of the pre-capitalist historical formations, Marx defines man's relations with nature and with his community in pre-class societies as if these two relations mirrored each other: 'The earth is the great workshop, the arsenal which furnishes both means and material of labour, as well as the seat, the base of the community.'[99] And the "chief objective condition of labour does not itself appear as product of labour, is already there as nature; on one side the living individual, on the other the earth as the objection condition of his reproduction.'[100] Man has still not severed his umbilical cord with nature, such is the close symbiotic relation between them. A full separation has not taken place even in the class societies of slavery and serfdom: What happens is that 'one part of society is treated by another as itself merely an inorganic and natural condition of its own reproduction.'[101] The full separation occurs only under conditions of generalized commodity production, that is, under capitalism, which presupposes a historical process causing, first, a '[d] isolation of the relation to the earth—land and soil—as a nature condition of production—to which he relates as to his own inorganic being' and, second, a '[d] isolation of the relations in which he appears as proprietor of the instrument.'[102] This dual process, the expropriation of the agricultural population from land and the birth of modern proletariat sans any means of production of his own, has been described in great historical detail in Part VII—The So-called Primitive Accumulation—of the first volume of *Capital.*

Human labour in Marx, we have seen, is a materialization of nature. So what happens to labour under the capitalist mode of production is the key to understanding man's changed relation to nature under its aegis.[103] Unlike in classless primitive societies, under capitalism the labour of the individual producer is a private labour and not part of associated or social labour. It becomes so only through the mediation of exchange or market. But for this to happen producers must equalize their products so that exchange could at all take place. This involves abstracting from the natural, physical or use-value-qualities in which products differ from one another. That is, it involves abstracting from the concrete living labour of which products are the repositories. Thus, abstraction and equalization imply that individual labour-power is treated as abstract and separate from the real living individuals who are henceforth mere vectors or vessels of their labour-power. Abstract labour, estranged from concrete individuals, is alienated labour. The empirical individual, whose natural individuality and particularized labour-power is abolished in the generalized uniform abstract labour-power which is social only in the sense that it belongs to no particular individual, then, becomes subservient to his own labour-power which is no longer his labour-power. The living, natural labour of the individual is thus dominated by bead, abstract labour of a faceless collective.[104]

Mar's concepts of labour, production, and forces of production are likely to be misunderstood and have indeed been misconstrued in some ecological literature- unless they are seen as forming part of his ontology of social being. For in Marx, labour and production, tools and technology are expressive of man's species character, a mode of self-realization of man. As early as in 1844 Manuscripts, he had said that 'the history of industry and the established objective existence of industry are the open book of man's essential powers, the perceptibly existing human psychology.'[105] And: 'It is just in his work upon the objective world, therefore, that man really proves himself in his productive activities, opening out to the world around him, both natural and social.[106]

An animal forms only in accordance with the standard and the need of the species to which it belongs, whilst man knows how to produce in accordance with the standard of every species, and knows how to apply everywhere the inherent standard to the object. Man therefore also forms objects in accordance with the laws of beauty.[107]

The concept of productive forces in Marx implies a view of human nature, of human capacities and needs, and their rootedness in man's species character.[108] The special capacity of man which distinguishes him from animals is what Jhon McMurtry calls his 'projective consciousness' wherein 'man's activities express a mentally selected structured purposed or plan that is raised by his own imagination and then realized in project-commanded activity.'[109] This is McMurty's gloss on that famous passage in *Capital*, I, where Marx underlined the superiority of the 'worst architect' over 'the best of bees'.[110] This capacity is exercised in fulfilment of an essential need for 'self-realization' and 'objectification'[111] of man's creative potentialities. McMurtry has culled from various places in Marx a list of such needs—from the very mundane (and eco-friendly) ones as food, clothing, habitation, fresh air and sunlight, adequate living and working spaces, cleanliness of person and surrounding, rest from exertion and variation of activity to the more sublime ones such as creation of beauty and aesthetic enjoyment.[112] He concludes that the major ethical premises of Marx's theory of needs, capacity and production is: 'Men ought to materially realize themselves'.[113]

Productive forces are the primary historical expression of these needs and capacities of man. They both shape and fulfil them. Their close correspondence is noted by Marx when he says that 'the number and extent of his so-called necessary wants as also the mode of satisfying them, are themselves the product of historical development.'[114] In a later passage he was still more explicit on the question of a homology between development of productive forces and technology and realization of man's creative potential:

> Modern industry indeed compels society, under penalty of death, to replace the detail worker of today, crippled by life-long repetition of one and the same trivial operation, and thus reduced to a mere fragment of a man, by the full developed individual, fit for a variety of labour, ready to face any change of production and to whom the different social functions he performs are but so many modes of giving free scope to his own natural and acquired powers.[115]

The same parallel is suggested by the counterfactual examples he gives of earlier societies whose less developed or stunted forces of production and correspondingly constricting social relations were reflected in restricted social interconnections or what McMurtry calls the limited 'functionable range of human consciousness' or the 'range of man's ontic engagement' these conditions permitted.[116] 'Wealth' or plentitude of natural use-values available to society betoken the richness of human personality.

> .... when the limited bourgeois form is stripped away what is wealth other than the universality of human needs, capacities, pleasures, productive forces, etc. created through universal exchange? The full development of human mastery over the forces of nature, those of so called nature as well as humanity's own nature? The absolute working out of his creative potentialities......the development of all human powers... where he does not reproduce himself in one specificity but produces his totality? Strives not to remain something he has become but is in absolute movement of becoming?[117]

But time and again in history this coordination of rhythm between material technology and human personhood has broken down due to contradictions arising between forces of production and relations of production, between a society's productive and technological capacities and its social arrangement of class rule, never more acutely so than under capitalism. In the capitalist mode of production, there has been a general tendency for the economy, governed by laws of motion of capital accumulation, to introduce grave distortions into productive forces resulting, among other things, in deliberate over employment and/or underemployment of natural and other resources. G.A. Cohen, who has aligned use value with natural quality of products and exchange-value with their ghostly surrogate in the shape of commodities, finds in capitalism the final subjugation of use-value by exchange-value,[118] of nature by its antithesis. The antithesis is so great that, according to Marx, man's vaunted 'mastery over nature, results in man's enslavement to 'other man or to his own infamy'[119] What should indeed have been and achieved all-rounded development of human personality (a 'complete working out of the human content') turns out to be 'a complete emptying-out, this universal objectification as total alienation.'[120]

Communism of Marx's vision was to single the end of alienation and mark the reintegration of man and nature. After the capitalist mode of production and class rule are ended, firm foundation will be laid for 'socialized men, the associated producers' to rationally regulat[e] their interchange with nature, brin[g] it under their control... and achiev[e] this with the least expenditure of energy and under conditions most favourable to, and worthy of, their human nature'.[121] 'Nature' and 'human nature', separated under capitalism, will be brought into harmony with each other. In more practical, programmatic terms, it will involve combining 'agriculture with manufacturing industries, gradual abolition of the distinction between town and country, by a more equitable distribution of the population over the country'[122] and abolition of the 'enslaving subordination of the individual to the division of labour and therewith also the antithesis between mental and physical labour.'[123] These are precisely the objectives that figure on the agenda of environmentalists and social activists of out day.

The Ecology critics of Marx have, on the basis of his stipulation regarding productive abundance as a precondition for transition to communism, accused him of adopting 'Promethean', that is, protechnological, view. He has also been arraigned for being theoretically complicit in capitalism's blatant disregard for ecological harmony in its productionist drive. What these critics, however, fail to realize is that Marx's central concern was neither production nor growth but 'development' in a more complex and comprehensive sense than that posited by developmental economics to whose basic productionist, *albeit* petty-production, paradigm these ecologists themselves subscribe.[125] As Marshall Berman has observed, the development ideal in Marx stands for 'good life' and is synonymous with happiness of man is a happy society. Man's human development, according to Marx, gets a fillip in capitalist conditions but is also severely hindered and repressed by the self-same conditions.[126] Thus defined, the development ideal could hardly stand opposed to the idea of man's harmonious relation with nature. However, the basic requisite for a full realization of the ideal is heightened productivity leading to the 'shortening of the working day', thus expanding the space for civilized and meaningful existence for all. It is for this reason that Marx had said that 'if we did not find concealed in society as it is the material conditions production and the corresponding relations of exchange prerequisite to a classless society, then all attempts to explode it would be quixotic.'[127]

To call Marx a 'productivist' or a 'worshipper' of machines will be, ironically, to read him in the same 'economistic' and reductionist manner that partly accounts for the dogged indifference to ecological planning in the former Soviet Union and for its disastrous environmental record. For in the context of the wider human existential dimension of Marx's notion of labor process, production, and technology as aspects of man's metabolism with nature, it can be said, in the words of Jon Elster (a fairly critical reader of Marx's), that 'creation and not production was at the centre of Marx's anthropology.'[128] That Marx was not content to see human beings as mere producers has been persuasively argued by the well-know economist Amartya Sen.[129] As for being a 'worshipper' of machine, Marx well knew, none better, that under capitalism, machine technology and science were subsumed under capital, were part of (constant) capital, were 'pressed into service of capital' and 'gave capital a power of expansion.'[130] He also knew, none better, that the structural contradictions of capitalism were bound to make machine mutilate men and women, as he so vividly described in the chapters on 'The Working Day' and Machinery and Modern Industry' in *Capital*, I, and succinctly stated in The Poverty of Philosophy:

> ....by the introduction of machinery, the division of labour inside society has grown up, the task of the worker inside the worshop has been simplified capital has been concentrated, human beings have been further dismembered.[131]

Technology, including machinery, was for Marx analogous to 'Nature's technology' that 'discloses man's mode of dealing with nature'[132] and, according to Marx's discussion of man's metabolism with nature's resources crucially dependent on continual preservation and renewal of nature's resources as the prerequisite of its maintenance and development. So, going strictly by Marx's definition of productive forces, it would be a contradiction in terms to say that technology by its very nature brings in its train ecological degradation or nature's ruin. The latter, on the contrary, would involve irreparable loss of essential resources of technology and therefore cause a permanent setback to it. This would indeed be a prime instance of the capitalist contradiction whereby the ruling class would seem to be losing control over the productive forces of society, causing disequilibrium between the forces and relations of production, the central contradiction of capitalism which is always pregnant with immense revolutionary possibilities in terms of Marx's theory of social change.[133]

A major premise, stated or unstated, of the mainstream ecologist thinking is that it is technology as such, irrespective of its social form, which is responsible for the growth mania of the industrial society of today and that has led to large-scale despoliation of natural resources. On the contrary, it is a Marxist axiom, and an irrefutable truth of history, that social relations and forms of society provide the basis and use of the forces of production including natural resources. Howsoever autonomous role a productive force, say technology, may appear to play, there exists a necessary correlation between certain productive forces and certain kind of society defined by its dominant relations of production; otherwise terms like feudalism, capitalism and socialism will lose all their meaning.[134] The ever present social form of material productive activity is an imperative not only the economy of advanced capitalism but equally of the natural economies of primitive tribal societies, as any number of anthropological studies have shown.[135] Thus, productive forces are not technical, external to the social structure but internal to it. This is the meaning of Marx's statement that 'political economy is not technology'.[136] In developed capitalism, advanced technology can favour both output for the owner and leisure for the producer. But the fact that it is always increased output, and not free time, that is chosen as the objective to which the technology is geared can be explained only by the extra-technological fact that this technology functions within a capitalist economic form.[137] It is in the extra technological fact of the drive for incessant accumulation of capital, surplus-value and profit, without which the structure of capitalist mode of production cannot survive, that the secret of the manner and magnitude of the use of technology in modern industry is to be sought. The same drive ('the need of constantly expanding market for its products') which in the times of Marx 'chase[d] the bourgeois over the whole surface of the globe' has in out times induced it to mount an assault on the biosphere and made him, with his hydraheaded latest technologies, into a 'sorcerer, who is no longer able to control the powers of the nether would whom he has called up by his spells.'[138] It is today's free-floating globalised capitalism that, unlike the more restricted nation-centred capitalism of yesteryears, has, correspondingly, raised the ecological threat to planetary heights.[139]

Apart from theory, there are any number of incontrovertible facts of life. Every single industrial project that ends up degrading the ecology is visible seen to pile up profits for a capitalist undertaking, whether single or a conglomerate, national or multinational, operating directly through its own agencies or through the state working on its behalf or sometimes in joint operation with it, whether in agribus or automobile complex, petrochemical or military-industrial complex. The so-called Green Revolution in agriculture, with new types of chemical fertilizer and renetic experiments with hybrid plants, did result in loss of bioadversity and in increaded salinity of land. But equally indisputable is the fact of the commodification of seed production through the use of hybrid method that is motivated primarily by consideration of profitability.[140] The ecological degradation is an unintended consequence of the economies of large-scale penetration of capitalism in agriculture. These two (and more) sets of variables have to be correlated if an alternative mode of ecologically sustainable agriculture is ever to be found.[141]

We had earlier raised the question as to why explicit ecological issues did not find a prominent place in Marx and Engels. Ted Benton and Bellamy Foster have, in pertinent asides, suggested one reason each. Benton suggests that Marx, like his contemporaries, was profoundly impressed by the transformative power of modern industrial production because this sector was in the nineteenth century still tied to ecoregulatory labours as the necessary productive resources.[142] Foster suggests another reason. Speaking of the idea of 'ecological sustainability', he hazards the guess that Marx thought the idea to be 'of very limited practical relevance to capitalist society, which was incapable of applying rational scientific methods in this area, but essential to a society of associated producers.'[143] If we consider, as we must, how when Marx talks of ecological degradation in large-scale agriculture he invariably points out the social arrangement under which it is carried out ('capitalist') and also how every time he talks of amelioration in this regard he speaks not of rectification of reforms within the system, which is as if law-bound to produce and reproduce the mess, but of a post-capitalist society of associated producers,[144] we can understand why for him the question of ecology was neither primary nor secondary but conterminous with the problem of structural social change.

We shall touch on two other issues pertinent to any discussion of ecological themes in classical Marxism. Marx would have found the proposal, seriously canvassed by a good number of environmentalists, to dismantle, in the interest of sustainable ecology, the entire structure of modern technology in industry and agriculture to be quixotic in the extreme.[145] And this for the simple reason that '[m]en never relinquish what they have won' and that 'it is a matter of primary concern not to be deprived of the fruits of civilization, of the acquired productive forces.'[146] In other words, where a society is ready for change, the change will only be such that will preserve or develop but in no case forfeit the achieved stage of productive forces.[147] The irreversible and unidirectional movement of history was underlined by Marx when, speaking of the short-lived phase of petty production by independent producers in early stages of capitalism, he said: 'It is just as pious as it is stupid to wish that exchange-value into wages labour.'[148] So, those who would like the idealized lost tribal economies or those of petty production to reappear as dominant mode of production will, ever if such a miracle happened, only rue to see, in Marx's words, the 'filthy business' begin all over again. This yearning to escape from the bourgeois world to a simpler pre-industrial past is, as Marx had percipiently noted, itself spawned by a limited and limiting bourgeois consciousness.[149]

Two sympathetic readers of Marx—Cohen and McMurtry—have raised questions regarding the dilemma that the future communist society of Marx's imagining might encounter as it tries to come to grips with the contradictory realities besting that society: on the one hand, increased productivity dictating sparing use of depleting natural resources and, on the other hand, more intensive labour now needed to maintain the optimal level of productivity dictating sparing use of depleting natural resources, and, on the other hand, more intensive labour now needed to maintain the optimal level of productivity and a consequent fall in leisure time; abundance-induced need- expansion but which can only enlarge the 'realm of necessity' at the expenses of 'realm of freedom'.[150] With that extremely dense passage in *Capital*, III, as their text where Marx speculates about the 'socialised men, the associated producers, rationally regulating their interchange with Nature,' Cohen and McMurtry reach the same conclusion but different evaluations. Cohen think that since leisure means freedom from 'unwanted activity' and not from 'productive activity', it is 'possible to envisage creative labour processes which are less appetitive of scarce resources'. He, however, believes that Marx did not consider creative fulfilment to be compatible with labour and therefore, pessimistically looked for true freedom 'beyond the economic zone'. McMurtry, on the other hand, thinks that Marx's idea of men 'regulating their interchange with Nature'—of this ecological principle he gives an analytic description in a footnote[151]—will take care of harmonizing the imperatives of resources, labour and leisure in such a way that a happy and, in modern terms, an 'eco-friendly' society will emerge. McMurtry's outline of a Marxist ethics, pivoted on the notion of man's species character of 'projective consciousness', also hints at, with positive overtones, the possibility of need satisfaction in the Communist society as being realizable in non-economic terms, the nearest analogue of which be the kind of inner satisfaction an artiste or a scientist derives from his labours.[152]

IT IS, NEVERTHELESS, true that a Marxist ecology remains to be developed. What we have in classical Marxism are some of the socio-philosophical presuppositions of such an undertaking, not a concrete working out of the full terms of this discourse. Moreover, not all these propositions are free from ambiguities, while some are somewhat speculative. A case in point is Marx's notion of the 'realm of freedom' succeeding the 'realm of necessity' in the misty future of communism.[153] Another is Engels's theory of dialectics of nature wherein he sought to develop a unified science of nature, society and human thought. Some of the contemporary Marxist ecologists, e.g. John Bellamy Foster and Paul Burkett, see in the Engelsian dialectics of nature a basic constituent of a Marxist ecology. [154] There are, however, others, also writing from within the Marxist tradition, such as even the later Lukacs, Colletti (even in his Marxist phase), Schmidt, Timpanaro and many others, who have either denied that dialectics is an objective property of nature while upholding it as an attribute of the dialectics is an objective property of nature while upholding it as an attribute of the process of knowledge (Schmidt) or have accepted dialectics as an objective property of nature but have denied the possibility of applying dialectical method to nature (Lukacs) or have rejected the very notion of dialectics in Engels as an idealist Hegelian baggage (Colletti and Timpanaro).[155] So, even on such a fundamental issue, considered by many to be of central importance to a Marxist ecology, there is a good deal of dispute and not a little of obfuscation.

What however, is indisputable is that Marx and Engels whatever one might think of the nature of the causal laws determining the three realms of the inorganic, organic and social propounded by them, (that is, whether these laws are uniform or differentiated), firmly believed that the three realms are the diverse manifestations of a reality that is unitary and constitutes a totality. A denial of any absolute dualism between nature and man and an affirmation of the principle of dual determination in man and nature relationship will always remain the first principles of any future socio-ecology. Here natural forms do not appear as distant gods but as 'mans' worldly goods' to be valued, preserved and, if necessary, fought for in the social arena. This is the meaning of Marx's rebuke to Feurbach, that the letter referred too much to nature and too little to politics.[156] For, howsoever class-indifferent ecological issues may appear to be in the eyes of some environmentalists, in a class-divided society they are always nuanced, if not determined, in class ways.[157] Marx's words, therefore, also carry an implied admonition to Marxist theorists and activists who have for too long neglected the task of making a necessary politics of the ecological questions and of projecting them as a subset of strategic slogans in the economic, political and cultural struggles of the disadvantaged and the dispossessed. While the so-called existing socialist states now lie in ruins as travesty of genuine socialism and the 'mist enveloped' realm of communist freedom is not easily conceivable, nothing visible has yet emerged to refurbish the idea of socialism as a feasible and desirable ideal. On the other hand, as Perry Anderson says, a 'socialism that remains incognito' can hardly lay claim on people's aspirations.[158] By joining and leading new social movements around issues of sustainable economic struggles on class issues,[159] Marxists may help reconstruct and render visible in the very present the contours of a credible society of the future and thus revivify, in these distressing times, a redeeming socialist ideal.

Notes and References

1. Felipe Fernandez-Armesto, Civilizations (London: 2001), p. xii and passim.
2. Raymod Williams, Keywords (London: 1983), pp. 110-11.
3. E.P. Thompson, The Poverty of Theory and Other Essays (London: 1978), p. 110.
4. E.P. Thompson, Customs in Common (Harmondsworth: 1993), p. 259.

5. Ted Benton, 'Marxism and Natural Limits: An Ecological Critique and Reconstruction', *New Left Review*, No. 177. Sept.-Oct. 1989, 53 and Machthild Oechle, quoted in Reiner Grundmann, 'The Ecological Challenge to Marxism,' *New Left Review*, No. 185, Jan.-Feb. 1991, 13.
6. John Bellamy Foster, The Vulnerable Planet (Kharagpur: 1999), p. 13.
7. Ernest Mandel, Late Capitalism (London: 1978), p. 118 and passim.
8. Fredric Jameson, Postmodernism. Or, The Cultural Logic of Late Capitalism (London: 1999), p. xix.
9. *Ibid.*, p. 366.
10. Fredric Jameson, The Ideologies of Theory, Vol. 2 (Minneapolis: 1988), p. 10.
11. Perry Anderson, In the Tracks of Historical Materialism (London: 1983), pp. 86-88, 104.
12. Sebastiano Timpanaro, On Materialism (London: 1975), p. 11.
13. Cf. 'It is to gain, through Leopardi, in awareness of certain aspects of the man-nature relationship which remain somewhat in the shadows in Marxism....', *Ibid.*, p. 21.
14. Reiner Grundmann, 'The Ecological Challenge to Marxism', *op. cit.*, 105.
15. Ted Benton, 'Marxism and the Nature Limits,' *op. cit.*, 58-60.
16. John Bellamy Foster, Marx's Ecology (Kharagpur: 2001), pp. 166, 169.
17. Frederick Engels, cited in The Vulnerable Planet, *op. cit.*, pp. 57-59.
18. Karl Marx, *Capital*, Vol. I (Moscow: 1954), p. 474.
19. Marshall Berman, Adventures in Marxism (London: 1999) p. 97.
20. Marx's Ecology, *op. cit.*, pp. 149-54.
21. *Capital*, I, p. 333.
22. *Ibid.*, pp. 481, 332.
23. Marx's Ecology, *op. cit.*, p. 253.
24. Karl Marx, *Capital*, Vol. III (Moscow: 1959), p. 813.
25. *Ibid.*, pp. 812-13.
26. *Ibid.*, p. 776. Cf. 'Man is but a tenant of the soil and he is guilty of a crime when he reduces its value for other tenants who are to come after him', George E. Warring Jr. [1850] quoted in Marx's Ecology, *op. cit.*, p. 153.
27. Marx-Engels, Selected Correspondence (Moscow: 1975), p. 190.
28. Foster, The Vulnerable Planet, *op. cit.*, Ch. 2.
29. Frederick Engels, Outlines of a Critique of Political Economy in Karl Marx, Economic and Philosophic Manuscripts of 1844 (Moscow: 1974), pp. 137, 174.
30. Karl Marx, Theories of Surplus-Value, Part II (Moscow 1975), pp. 115-117.
31. Karl Marx, Grundrisse (Harmondswoth: 1977), pp. 604,605.
32. *Ibid.*

33. Karl Marx, Zur Kritik der politschen Okonomie (Manuscript 1861-63), quoted in Jon Elster, Making Sense of Marx (Cambridge: 1985), p. 249 and Karl Marx, Theories of Surplus-Value, Part III (Moscow: 1975), p. 246.
34. Grundrisse, p. 605.
35. *Capital*, I, Ch. XXVI.
36. Grundrisse, p. 702.
37. *Capital*, I, p. 179.
38. For principle of what I call dual determination, see Georg Lukacs, The Ontology of Social Being, I, Hegel (London 1978), p. 9 and The Ontology of Social Being, II, Marx (London: 1978), pp. 8-9 and passim. Also Theo Pinkus, ed., Conversations with Lukacs (London: 1974), pp. 29-30 and passim.
39. Karl Marx and Frederick Engels, The German Idelogy (Calcutta: 1945), pp. 7, 35.
40. *Capital*, I, p. 21.
41. *Ibid.*, p. 480.
42. *Ibid.*, p. 352 n.
43. *Ibid.*, p. 323 n.
44. *Ibid.*, p. 321 n.
45. Theories of Surplus-Value, Part III, pp. 294-95
46. Frederick Engels, Dialectics of Nature (Moscow: 1972), p. 198.
47. *Ibid.*, p. 44.
48. *Ibid.*, p. 70.
49. *Ibid.*, p. 178.
50. *Ibid.*, p. 181.
51. *Ibid.*, p. 197.
52. *Capital*, I, p. 352n, and Lawrence Krader, 'Theory of Evolution, Revolution and the State: The Critical Relation of Marx to his Contemporaries Darwin, Carlyle, Morgan, Maine and Kovalevsky' in Eric J. Hobsbawm, ed., The History of Marxism, Vol. I (New Delhi: 1982), pp. 198-200.
53. *Capital*, I, p. 480
54. *Ibid.*, p. 321.
55. Theories of Surplus-Value, Part III, p. 295.
56. The German Ideology, p. 7.
57. *Ibid.*, p. 34.
58. *Ibid.*, p. 35.
59. Economic and Philosophic Manuscript, p. 145.
60. *Capital*, I, p. 166.
61. Dialectics of Nature, p. 308.
62. Selected Correspondence, p. 284 and Dialectics of Nature, p. 308.
63. Dialectics of Nature, pp. 170-83.

64. *Ibid.*, p. 172 and Marx's Ecology, *op. cit.*, p. 203.
65. Dialectics of Nature, p. 173.
66. *Ibid.*, p. 179.
67. *Ibid.*, p. 173.
68. *Ibid.*, p. 178.
69. Selected Correspondence, p. 284.
70. *Ibid.*, p. 161.
71. Dialectics of Nature, p. 180.
72. *Ibid.*, p. 182.
73. *Ibid.*, p. 35.
74. *Ibid.*, p. 180.
75. See Raymond Williams, The Country and the City (London: 1973), p. 303, Politics and Letters (London: 1979), p. 312, 'Problems of Materialism of Culture', *New Left Review*, No. 109, May-June 1978, 8.
76. Dialectics of Nature, p. 307.
77. *Ibid.*, pp. 35-36.
78. Cf. 'Men break with one another in consequence of a process which began when they break with nature,' G.A. Cohen, Karl Marx's Theory of History: A Defence (London: 1991), p. 24.
79. For concept of metabolism in Marx's see Alfred Schmidt, The Concept of Nature in Marx (London: 1965), Ch. 2 and passim.
80. *Capital*, I, p. 476.
81. *Ibid.*, p. 175.
82. Schmidt, *op. cit.*, p. 84.
83. *Capital*, I, p. 76.
84. *Ibid.*, p. 196.
85. Economic and Philosophic Manuscripts, p. 67, Grundrisse, p. 388.
86. *Capital*, I, p. 76.
87. *Ibid.*, pp. 176, 179.
88. *Ibid.*, p. 179.
89. *Ibid.*, p. 50.
90. K. Marx, Wage, Labour and *Capital* in Karl Marx and Frederick Engels, Selected Works (Moscow: 1970), p. 80.
91. Economic and Philosophic Manuscripts, p. 98, emphases in original.
92. *Ibid.*, p. 135, emphasis in original.
93. See Lucio Colletti, Marx and Hegel (London: 1973), Ch. XI.
94. Reiner Grundmann has quoted Machthild as affirming that Naturalism is the prevent viewpoint of contemporary ecological thought. She says: 'Naturalism means to attempt to explain Society from the viewpoint of the laws of nature, to derive organizing principles of society and norms and social life from ecological principles' (Grundmann, *op. cit.*, 114). Ted Benton, too, finds Naturalism to be the philosophical basis of ecologies thinking

(Benton, *op. cit.*, 53-54). Even though, as Arthur C. Danto has noted, there is room within the naturalist movement for any variety of otherwise rival ontologies' (Arthur C. Danto, 'Naturalism', in Paul Edwards, ed., The Encyclopaedia of Philosophy, Vol. 5 (London: 1967), p. 448), broadly two main streams of thought within Naturalism may be discerned. In the first, exemplified in the critical philosophy of Kant, nature is the totality of systems of laws governing events in the natural world, that is, nature as seen by scientists like Kepler and Galileo (See Georg Lukacs, History and Class Consciousness (London: 1971), pp. 136ff). But man, who in Kant Exists as a natural being, is yet conceived by the latter as a single individual contemplating the world, and not active in a productive and transforming relationship in a society of men where he could objectify himself in relation to other men. In the naturalistic materialism of Kant, therefore man remained an apriori proposition in a pre-given setting from which history is absent (Coletti, Marx and Hegel, *op. cit.*, pp. 221, 223). From this arises the well-known Kantian bifurcation between phenomenon and noumenon as also the ethics of receptivity characteristic of the Romantic cult of nature of much of Naturphilosophe in which a pure and unchanging nature is seen bestowing its bounties on man who gratefully and passively receives them. In the other version of naturalism, the supernatural becomes the mode of appearance of the natural. Nature is here invested with the attributes of an objective spirituality conceived in the form of a diety as in the naturalist theism of Samuel Alexander whose god is 'present in the thunderstorm' (Samuel Alexander, Space, Time and Deity (London: 1927), II, p. 375). Both versions of Naturalism involve a dualistic metaphysic which denies man's active mediation with nature. While in its agnostic Kantian form Naturalism posits an unbridgeable chasm between nature and man, in its theistic version it considers nature as the 'Other' of man into which man should ideally seek his own dissolution. Once these features of Naturalism are noted and their implications properly grasped one may grow wise to the great theoretical discordance between the Naturalism of the mainstream ecological thought and Marx's historical materialism. Benton is, therefore, wide of the mark when he identifies Marx's philosophical thought with Naturalism tout court (Benton, *op. cit.*, 53-54). For a critique of ecologists' valorization of ecocentrism as the 'other' of anthropomorphism, see Grundmann, *op. cit.*, 111 ff. For a perceptive discussion of the problem, see Conversations with Lukacs. *Op. cit.*, First Conversation.

95. *Capital*, I, p. 179.
96. Karl Marx, A Contribution to the Contribution of the Critique of Political Economy (Moscow: 1977), p. 192.
97. The German Ideology, pp. 33-34.
98. Grundrisse, p. 489.

99. *Ibid.*, p. 472, emphasis in the original.
100. *Ibid.*, p. 485, emphasis in the original.
101. *Ibid.*, p. 489, emphasis in the original.
102. *Ibid.*, p. 497, emphasis in the original.
103. For a brief but lucid exposition of the theme of alienation in labour process under capitalism, see 'Bernstein and the Marxism of the Second International' in Lucio Colletti, From Rousseau to Lenin (London: 1974), pp. 76ff.
104. See *Capital*, I, 'The Fetishism of Commodities and the Secret Thereof', pp. 76ff.
105. Economic and Philosophic Manuscripts, p. 96.
106. *Ibid.*, p. 69.
107. *Ibid.*
108. For this part of the argument I draw heavily on John McMurtry, The Structure of Marx's World-View (Princeton: 1978), Ch. I and passim.
109. *Ibid.*, p. 23.
110. *Capital*, I, p. 174.
111. Grundrisse, p. 611.
112. John McMurtry, *op. cit.*, p. 33.
113. *Ibid.*, p. 53.
114. *Capital*, I, p. 168.
115. *Ibid.*, p. 458.
116. John McMurty, *op. cit.*, pp. 45, 49n.
117. Grundrisse, p. 488.
118. G.A. Cohen, *op. cit.*, Ch. IV and p. 298.
119. Karl Marx in People's Paper cited in Jon Elster, *op. cit.*, p. 264.
120. Grundrisse, p. 488.
121. *Capital*, III, p. 820.
122. Karl Marx and Frederick Engels, Manifesto of the Communist Party in Selected Works, *op. cit.*, p. 264.
123. Karl Marx, Critique of the Gotha Programme in Selected Works, *op. cit.*, p. 320.
124. Anthony Giddens, John Clark and Ted Benton *et al.* in Foster, Marx's Ecology, *op. cit.*, pp. 9-10, 136-137, Kostas Papaiannon in Jon Elster, *op. cit.*, p. 267 and ecologists alluded to in Grundamnn, *op. cit.*, passim and in Benton, *op. cit.*, 52 fn I.
125. Jurgen Habermas, 'A Philosophico-Political Profile', *New Left Review*, No. 151, May June 1985, 96. Also see Pranab Bardhan, 'The State Against Society: The Great Divide in Indian Social Science Discourse' in Sugata Bose and Ayesha Jalal, eds, Nationalism, Democracy, Development (Delhi: 1998), 99, 184-95.
126. 'Marx imagines communism as a way to make people happy. The first aspect of this happiness is "development"—that is, an

experience that doesn't simply repeat itself, but that goes through some sort of change and growth.... But bourgeois society, although it enables people to develop, forces them to develop in accord with market demands: what can self gets developed; what can't self gets repressed, or never comes to life at all. Against the market model of forced and twisted development, Marx fights for "free development", development that the self can control'. Marshall Berman, Adventures in Marxism, *op. cit.*, p. 265.

127. Grundrisse, p. 159.

128. Jon Elster, *op. cit.*, p. 267. cf. 'even production for the sake of production means nothing more than the development of the productive energies of man and hence the development of the wealth of human nature as an end in itself'. Marx quoted in Preface to the New Edition (1967) of Lukacs, History and Class Consciousness, *op. cit.*, p. xvii.

129. Amartya Sen, Inequality Reexamined (Delhi: 1991), pp. 119-21.

130. See Grundrisse, p. 690ff.

131. Karl Marx, The Poverty of Philosophy (Calcutta: 1936), p. 116, emphases added.

132. *Capital*, I, p. 352n.

133. McMurtry, *op. cit.*, p. 320.

134. For the centrality of social form as a determinant of technology, see Cohen, *op. cit.*, Ch. IV, William Shaw, Marx's Theory of history (London: 1978), p. 74 and Etienne Balibar, 'The Basic Concepts of Historical Materialism in Louis Althusser and Etienne Balibar, eds. Reading *Capital* (London: 1983), pp. 199ff. Cf. 'Whether a natural force, a natural element, promotes or inhibits the economic development is decided by the economy,' Georg Lukacs, Conversations with Lukacs, *op. cit.*, p. 124.

135. Cf. '.....anthropologists find it difficult to consider economic relations as a separate field, independent of social organization,' Maurice Godelier, Perspectives in Marxist Anthropology (Cambridge: 1977), p. 25.

136. Grundrisse, p. 86.

137. Cohen, *op. cit.*, pp. 302 ff.

138. Communist Manifesto, *op. cit.*, pp. 38, 40.

139. Cf. 'The pressure to sustain and expand output makes for a more rapid exploitation of existing resources than could otherwise be expected to occur, and the finite time horzon of the capitalist firm discourages investigation of alternative paths of development. What is more, the consequent conditioning of society to forms of consumption which draws upon prodigious quantities of irreplaceable material makes new paths harder to embark upon. The longer Capitalism and its bias prevail, the more difficult will be the transformation which appears to be necessary.' Cohen, *op. cit.*, pp. 322-23.

140. Foster, The Vulnerable Planet, *op. cit.*, p. 117.

141. In the Indian context, especially, the Green Revolution is more than an episode in India's ecological history. It is part of a larger socio-political scenario whose other elements are: the growth of commercialization of agriculture and spread of capitalist relations in agriculture with their investment-driven strategies giving tremendous boost to agro business and related technologies mergence of well-off middle and rich farmers, especially of the intermediate castes, rise of regional parties decisively affecting the form and structure of Indian polity and also the opening up of a new terrain of conflict between the new kulaks, the children of the Indian Green Revolution, and the largely dalit wage labour in the countryside. To look at the Indian Green Revolution, with all the attending circumstances as remarked above, and more, as part of the grand desing of the late capitalism in the era of globalization to transform the relationship of the metropolitan centres to the peripheral regions of the third would from the old fashioned imperialist control to one of deep market penetration is of course to see the picture in its necessary totality. To miss on all these while assessing ecological impact of the new agricultural/industrial technologies in India is to trivialize the ecological issue itself and, instead of approaching it as a practical problem whose solution is the south within a certain set of extremely complex given conditions, to turn it into a sovereign subject, entirely existing in its own right, on which contending environmentalist scientists scholars pontificate at length (see Shiv Visvanathan, Chandrika Parmar, 'A Biotechnology Story: Notes from India,' *Economic and Political Weekly*, Vol. xxxvii, No. 27, July 6-12, 2002, 2714-27). It is this attitude that permits Vandana Shiva, notwithstanding much that is sound sense in her discourse, to weave a fanciful mytho-cosmological story of the Green Revolution [Vandana Shiva, 'The Seed and the Earth: Biotechnology and the Colonisation of Regeneration' in Shiva, ed. Minding Our Lives: Women from the South and the North Reconnect Ecology and Health (Delhi: 1999)]. It is no wonder that in these circles certain postures of stridently anti-Enlightenment and anti-science nature render the debate somewhat esoteric. For all the violence done to nature, it is not the capitalist order, not even the application of science and technology to specific economies, that are blamed, but scientific knowledge itself, that is, science as knowledge. This is how environmental theorists like Vandna Shiva, Claude Alvares and Ashis Nandy declare war on "scientific knowledge' in defense of some mythic 'traditional knowledge', 'alternative knowledge' or 'indigenous knowledge' which however they scrupulously refrain from defining except by throwing oblique and dark hints of the occult and worse as Alvares sings the praise of 'vibhuti' or as Nandy, in the name of 'tradition', winks at the sati incident at Deorala (For Vandana Shiva and Claude Alvares, see

Ashis Nandy, ed., Science, Hegemony and Violence (Delhi: 1996), pp. 233, 70 and their papers in the volume. For Nandy, his 'Sociology of Sati', *Indian Express*, (October 5, 1987). For trenchant critique of these positions, see, in particular, Meera Nanda, 'Reclaiming Modern Science for Third World Social Movements', *Political and Economic Weekly*, Vol. xxxiii, No. 16, April 18-24, 1998, 915-922 and *Ibid.*, 'Breaking the speel of Dharma: case for Indian Enlightenment', *Political and Economic Weekly*, Vol. xxxv, No. 27, July 7-13, 2001, 2551-66 and Radhika Desai,, 'Culturalism and Contemporary Right: Indian Bourgeoisie and Political Hindutva', *Political and Economic Weekly*, Vol. xxxiv, No. 12, March 20-26, 1999, 695-712. Also cf. 'It is too often assumed that the achievement of western science, pure and applied, lies mainly in the apparatus and machinery that have been developed from it... 'The real achievement lies in the accumulation of precise knowledge and this knowledge can be applied in a great variety of ways of which the current application in modern industry is only one', K. Schumacher, quoted in Cohen, *op. cit.*, p. 323, fn. 2.

142. Ted Benton, *op. cit.*, 70. Also Marx's Ecology, *op. cit.*, p. 140

143. Marx's Ecology, *op. cit.*, p. 164.

144. *Capital* I, pp. 473-75, *Capital* III, pp. 776, 812-13 Grundrisse, pp. 159, 590, second section of the Communist manifesto and the whole of Critique of Gotha Programme, among many others.

145. As against Claude Alvares's eager advocacy of a 'Luddite response of the third world' to science and technology, which he terms as 'two major oppressions of out time', one could quote Marx's remarks on the original Luddites: 'It took both time and experience before the workpeople learnt to distinguish between machinery and its employment by capital, and to direct their attacks, not against the material instruments of production but against the mode in which they are used'. But note also Lukacs's observations made more than three decades back: 'We should analyse how this transformation of capitalism into a form dominated by relative surplus value has created a new situation in which the workers' movement, the revolutionary movement, is condemned to a new beginning and in which such apparently long superseded ideologies as the machine-wrecking at the end of the eighteenth century are experiencing a renaissance'. (For Alvares, see his paper 'Science, Colonialism and Violence: A Luddite view' in Science, Hegemony and Violence, *op. cit.*, pp. 68-112; for Marx, *Capital*, I, p. 404, and for Lukacs, Conversations with Lukacs, *op. cit.*, p. 61.)

146. Selected Correspondence, p. 31 and Poverty of Philosophy, p. 101.

147. See McMurtry, *op. cit.*, Ch. 8.

148. Grundrisse, p. 249. On the basis of two types of cases, one hypothetical and another historical, Cohen has shown how the mode of petty production cannot but logically lead to a full-grown

capitalist mode of production as indeed it has done so in history. (Cohen, *op. cit.*, pp. 184-86, 314).

149. 'In earlier stages of development the single individual seems to be developed more fully, because he has not yet worked out his relationships in their fullness, or erected them as independent social powers and relations opposite himself. It is as ridiculous to yearn for a return to original fullness, as it is to believe that with this complete emptiness history has come to a standstill. The bourgeois viewpoint has never advanced beyond this antithesis between itself and the romantic viewpoint, and therefore the latter will accompany it is legitimate antithesis up to its blessed end.' (Grundrisse, p. 162).

150. Cohen, *op. cit.*, pp. 322-25 and McMurtry, *op. cit.*, pp. 227-28.

151. 'The regulating principle required here can be simply formulated as follows: A new product, x, is to produced if and only if x's production does not add to society's total necessary labour-time. Thus x qualifies for production if: (a) it replaces another product that requires the same or more necessary labour time for its production; or (b) it does not exceed in the necessary labour time it requires the amount of labour-time liberated elsewhere by some labour-saving device.' McMurtry, *op. cit.*, p. 228, fn. 26.

152. However, an interpretation of Marx on one aspect of this larger question, less pessimistic than Cohen's and less optimistic than McMurtry's is offered by Lukacs. See Conversations with Lukacs, *op. cit.*, pp. 135-36.

153. Even a sympathetic reader of Marx like Nilou Mobasser observes that Marx was 'notoriously vague about future society' and that while 'it would be very misleading indeed to suggest that Marx left us no clues as to his thought on the future', 'no blueprint for this vision actually exists'. Nilou Mobasser, 'Marx and Self-Realization', *New Left Review*, No. 161, Jan.-Feb. 1987, 119.

154. Foster, Marx's Ecology, *op. cit.*, p. 245, Paul Burkett, Lukacs on Science', *Economic and Political Weekly*, Vol. xxxvi, No. 48, Dec. 1-7, 2001, 4485-89.

155. For quotations from Lukacs, see Paul Burkett, *op. cit.*, Also see Schmidt, The Concept of Nature in Marx, *op. cit.*, p. 195, Colletti, From Rousseau to Lenin, *op. cit.*, pp. 121-27, Timpanaro, On Materialism, *op. cit.*, p. 71.

156. Quoted in Marx's Ecology, *op. cit.*, p. 71.

157. The Narbada Bachao Andolan, led by someone who is not a Marxist, vididly exemplifies this truism. See Arundhati Roy, 'The Greater Common Good', *Frontline*, Vol. 16, No. 11, May 22-June 4, 1999, 4-29. There is now a growing body of work on ecological dimensions of tribal revolts and peasant protests in colonial and post-colonial India, a short list of which is given in David Arnold, "Disease, Resistance and India's Ecological Frontier, 1770-1970" in Biswamoy Pati, ed. Issues in Modern Indian History (Mumbai: 2000), pp. 1-59.

158. Perry Anderson, In the Tracks of Historical Materialism, *op. cit.*, p. 99.

159. Most of the Green parties in Europe have now on their agenda the proposal for a universal grant, i.e., to give every permanent inhabitant, whether waged, self-employed or jobless, a completely unconditional universal grant or basic income sufficient to cover at least fundamental needs. See Philippe Van Parijs, 'A Revolution in Class Theory' in Erik Olin Wright, et Always, end, The Debate on Classes (London: 1998), pp. 239-41. Shouldn't our ecologists, when they demand shutting down of urban factories, big and small, for reasons of environmental pollution, pause to think also of the wider issue of unemployment and, more particularly, of the condition of workers in the unorganized sector? To put it rather strongly, must ecocentrism be allowed to turn into something akin to misanthropy?

4

Ecologism and the New Left

D.P. SHARMA

> Capitalist growth is in crisis not only because it is capitalist but also because it is encountering physical limits.....the crisis also possesses a number of new dimensions which Marxists have not seen and socialism does not contain adequate answers. It is a crisis in a relation between the individual and the economic sphere as such, a crisis in the character of work, a crisis in out relations with nature, with out bodies with society, with future generation, with history, a crisis of urban life, of habitat, of medical practice, of education, of science.
>
> —*Andre Gorz*

[I]

During the second half of the twentieth century two sets of 'endist' theories ('The End of Ideology' by Bell in 1960 and 'The End of History' by Fukuyama in 1992) came to suggest that the age of ideologies is coming to an end. The horrors of fascism, totalitarianism and communism were so terrifying that all 'grandiose visions' became suspect 'ideologies' and lost this appeal to intellectuals. The collapse of communism after 1989 shattered the hopes eclipse during the intervening decades and helped Francis Fukuyama to formulate his thesis predicting the 'end of history'. He tried to show that all competing ideologies professing to forge perfect society are bankrupt and false. For example, communism's commitment to give real peoples' democracy became citadel of dictatorial elitism; similarly its promise to produce economic abundance landed Soviet land in the labyrinth of unending shortage and poverty. Same thing happened with other ideologies with which liberalism was in conflict and as a final outcome came 'an unabashed victory of economic and political liberalism'. Critics vehemently opposed that 'endist' theory and argued that the 'end of ideology' thesis is itself ideological containing an element of Western triumphalism seeking to prove that in a fight against other contending ideologies capitalist liberalism finally won the battle and world, today, has only one choice before it to follow its path.

During postwar era from 1945 to the second half of the 1960s Bells thesis seemed to succeed. There existed a broad ideological consensus on many issues, that there be a mixed economy, state welfare provision and the enhancement of individual liberty within this framework. But this consensus soon proved to be fragile. The end of ideology thesis, during the late 1960s and full 1970s, started crumbing. In much of the world, communism seemed to be growing. More extensively in the Third world there were signs of growing radicalism and Islamic fundamentalism. During the same period the west witnessed the rise of a New Left and a New Right. Such varied developments seemed to damn the end of ideology to the intellectual dustbin. It is a fact the protest movements such as the counter-culture and violent student movement did not last long but they left the impression that everything is not well within the capitalist industrial society.

Although ideology *per se* is unlikely to end, it can be profoundly changed. And that is precisely happening as the twentieth century nears it end. Some ideologies, such as the Marxist-Leninist version of socialism, appear to be dying, whereas others—such as the newer ecological or 'green' ideology are emerging and gaining influence and importance.

All ideologies are born of crisis of one kind or another. If there is one crisis that looms large on the near horizon of history, that is nearly the ecological crisis. Far from being a single crisis this is in fact a series of interconnected problems requiring immediate attention. These range from the technical to the philosophical one such as how shall we dispose of toxic materials, what is our place in and relation to nature; what duties or obligations, if any, do human beings have towards animals or towards rivers, mountains, and forests and what are obligations towards future generations ? But the older ideologies including liberalism cannot answer these questions in any satisfactory way and in order to fill up the void, 'ecologism' as an alternative ideology has emerged.

[2]

In the late 1960s and 1970s ecolism as a systematic and self-contained ideology began to emerge out of the radical, libertarian politics of the era. The New Left movements which appeared in the United States and Western Europe were particularly important in this context. They combined their concern for the effects of modern industrial practices upon human living conditions, with a denunciation of the artificiality of capitalist culture and the inability of the system to satisfy basic human needs. The New Left highlighted environmental degradation and supported the notion of a counter culture, a space away from capitalist values where a new life based on cooperative ethics may be developed. The Green movement that followed a decade later was inspired by the nation of escaping from the imperatives of modern industrial life and developing a more self-sufficient, rural and harmonious context for living with other humans and nature.

In the post-war era the first generation of young people to protest against their society were the Beatniks (beaten by the system) who sought beatitude in another world. Although they did not relate the emphasis on individual freedom to collective freedom, there was a link between their beliefs and the way they lived in practice.

They exemplified the various trends: rootlessness, rejection of the affluent society and all social values, a predilection for Jazz, resort to ill assimilated oriental religions (eg. Zen) and to drugs, pseudo relaxation and free sexuality. Politically the Beatniks found expressions in pacifist and anti-nuclear bomb movements. Moreover, they provoked discussion over norms, values and ways of life because of their rejection of the ethics of achievement and consumption. The Beal culture later exercised powerful influence on the American and West European student movements.

Both in the United States and in the Netherlands there emerged, in the early 1960s, groups which sought to put these ideas into practice. The 'Provos' in the Netherlands demanded free public transport, the disarmament of the police, a ban on advertising for alcohol and tobacco and the introduction of measures to curb pollution of the atmosphere. It was an urban movement of Dutch radical youth of an anti-industrialist, individualist, anti-establishment kind. They used cycle to prevent pollution. Similar attempt was made to offer constructive ideas by the Hippies in the United States. They owed to Beatniks numerous cultural and behavioural debts but in contrast to the earlier generation of Beatniks they tried to offer a positive count-image to the negative world. There is misleading conception in some minds that the Hippies were the escapist who simply wanted to drop out but in fact most of them were not fleeing from society but they were leaving it in order to build a new order of values. Their missionary zeal and moral self-righteousness inspired them not to accept any material support from their parents, even though they were mostly from a wealthy background. Their world view was intuitive and their search for truth was centred around themselves. Their philosophy included a philosophy of Peace and Love together with a rejection of things material, a devotion to drugs as instruments of enlightenment and pleasure, a propensity for communal lifestyles and libertarian sexual behaviour, and a style of dress included beads, bells, and long hairs.

This movement could not last for various reasons including the threat of hunger, sickness and chaos, in the Hippie communities. Most of them returned to their homes after staging a 'Death of Hippie' parade in Sanfrancisco in 1968 and many joined the Youth International Party. The Hippie movement consciously buried itself because of its own contradictions and the wave of commercialism that had began to make profits out of the Hippie culture. The idea of building shops, hospitals, restaurants and clubs for the Hippie community came from the so-called Diggers. The Diggers established contact with existing land communes along with setting up of clinics and self-help schemes as well as the opening of free shops in various American cities and Western Europe. The action by the Diggers was an important historical step in the formation of the 'counter-societal' or alternative movements.[1]

The solipsism of the Hippies gave way to a desire to confront the political and economic power of the system.[2] Thus a Youth International Party (YIP/Yippies) was formed. It was not a traditional party, rather, it stood for action-street politics, agitation and guerrilla theatre.[3] The Yippies tried to carry the values of the movement into society. Politics was understood existentially, growing out of the life of the actors and indivisible from this life. Instead of giving due attention to the necessity of forming a viable organisation, the Yippies engaged themselves to much in spontaneous and permanent revolution.

West European protest movements in the sixties were strongly influenced by the Hippies and Yippies. This reflected, moreover the continuing influence of the Beatniks. In the Federal Republic of Germany many young people felt alienated from the political culture and this was most clearly expressed by an introspective movement which turned its back on society. Communes were seen as places in which an individual could raise his or her 'consciousness' and also as base from which change could be carried into society. In the same manner as the Provos in the Netherlands and the Yippies in the United States, the Communards in West Germany relied on their ability to ridicule authority. When this met with only limited success greater emphasis was laid on the 'revolution of the self' and on experiments in communal living. Most communes sought to change the consciousness of the members. But the practical experience of the well-known Kommune-1 and Kommune-2 showed how difficult it was to achieve this.

The communal movement was characterized by two aims directed towards a change to the individual and his or her consciousness and also towards social change. Thus the dialectical relationship between the two aims which the communes encouraged could not be realised. As with the Hippie movement many turned towards the use of drugs and psychedelic techniques and meditation as a means of self-liberation, others, following the dissolution of the anti-authoritarian movement formed different groups which tried to constitute, a counter-power to one that prevailed in the society.

[3]

Public awareness of environmental problems grew enormously during the post-war era and this caused the emergence of ecological ideas on the political agenda in the 1970s. The publication of Rachel 'Carson's Silent Spring' (1969) focused on the dangers of pesticides and chemical defoliants for the human food chain, marked the arrival of environmental concern at a popular level. The publication of 'Limits of Growth' (1972) heightened concern with respect to human survival resulting from the relentless resource extraction, population growth and usage of non-renewable resources such as gas, coal and oil. This study caught the imagination of many and the idea of defending nature against excess of modernity became theme of post-war protest movements in America and elsewhere. 'Limits of Growth' marks the birth of ecologism as a distinctive and separate ideological perspective. This changed the political scenario in the West with the winning of Green political parties throughout Western Europe and Australia and the 'greening' of a number of political parties in response to the increased concern about the environment manifested by the people.

The ecology or 'green' movement is a relatively recent arrival on the political scene. And, like other political movements, it has its own ideology ecologism. This ideology is critical of other mainstream ideologies, right and left alike.

Liberalism, Marxism and Modern Conservatism are alike, the Green say, in picturing human beings as 'master' or 'conquerors' of the nature, which in turn is viewed as being without intrinsic value or worth. But ecologism treats mankind as part of a intricate and complex web of life called nature or ecology which means that every species, including our own, lives in interdependent relations with every other species, and with the environment that sustains us.

Ecologism is wedded to two ideals: one is to develop mutulistic relationship between man and nature in order to overcome the alienation of human beings from nature and from each other; second is to effect fundamental overhaul in social and political life of men.

Modern industrial society is dedicated to unrestricted economic growth which depends upon the relentless exploitation of natural resources in utter disregard of the basic fact that an infinite growth in a finite system is not possible. Besides it has destroyed the social fabric and man's relation with nature and one-another. Green's view the principles of economic growth, centralization, bureaucratization and materialism as central to the modern industrial society. They argue that time has come to change our values if the present civilization is to survive for long, and these include sustainability, small-scale/local organization, the limiting of population level individual responsibility and a spiritual reawakening. The present model of economic development involves the relentless extraction of natural minerals and resources to feed an increasingly greedy manufacturing system. This, in turn is, pouring pollutants to make air unbreathable, the soil infertile and the oceans and rivers sterile. If it goes on as such "we shall all be dead" since ozone depletion cannot forgive us. This system is sustained by the creation of artificial desires which are satisfied through wasteful and unnecessary levels of human consumption. As a remedy to it, ecologism propose the principle of sustainability: humans have to be educated to consume less and to produce more and to achieve self-sufficiently in satisfying their basic needs. The thesis of "Zero growth" will not do since even at zero growth the continued consumption of scarce resources will inevitably result in exhausting them completely. The point is not to refrain from consuming more and more but to consume less and less—and there is no other way of conserving the available reserves for future generations.

At the same time, the industrial system needs to be dismantled and replaced by a smaller-system of manufacture sustained by a number of self-governing local communities. Greens challenge the belief that economic growth is an essential goal, and assumption common to all other ideological perspectives. Greens propose to organize 'a steady state' economy around essential human needs and to keep them subordinated to the collective interest of the community. It will use the lowest possible levels of materials end energy in the production phase and emit the least possible amount of pollution in the consumption phase. Conventional economic growth cannot alleviate present economic ills and inequalities. The sustainability principle places just distribution of resources firmly on the political agenda since without it self-reliant communities cannot be made viable in which men live according to their basic needs.

The commitment of sustainability in concrete terms varies widely across the Green movement. For same fundamentalist ecologists, it involves a frugal pattern of living as a part of a return to pre-industrial society. For other Greens the sustainability means reordering the priorities of the contemporary society so that genuine human needs will take precedence over frivolous wants. The latter cannot be abolished entirely is an important countervailing principle to be taken note of.

Many Greens have adopted their ideals in their personal lifestyle as part of their rejection of conventional materialist values in order to present models for collective adoption of sustainable living patterns by the masses. The expansion of organic farming; the adoption of non-monetary exchange economies in certain localities and the growth in greener lifestyle are similar to the notion of the counter culture which appeared in the 1950s and became central to contemporary Green politics.

But all individual efforts to bring about a radical

change in the society will not be much effective unless efforts are made at different levels including at the national and international levels of governance. Greens are of the view that it is important to devise tough international laws at the international level particularly on issues related to toxic emissions into biosphere since such issues cannot be resolved within the boundaries of one nation state.

The ideas of Gandhi exerted largest influence on the minds and thoughts of the Greens. Following his ideals, the Greens not only adopted simple and frugal lifestyles, they also encouraged spiritualism within the movement. Any fundamental reordering of modern society can only be achieved by a radical transformation in 'consciousness' of man and in our relationship with nature. Various spiritual movements have found favour with the Green movement that led to the celebration of a number of spiritual values, from the Chinese philosophy of Taoism to Hindu mysticism. Another significant impact made by spiritual thinking upon Green ideas came from Gaia philosophy among ecological activists. Gaia (the Greek word for earth) theory was developed by a British Scientist, James Lovelock. He proposed that the earth's biosphere is a self-regulating system in which various living and inorganic elements function as a part of a larger being or life force which hold them together in a complex equilibrium. The life system consistently works to perpetuate the conditions necessary for its own survival. The principles of holism sustain Gaia which means that every element is connected with the elements as a part of larger whole maintaining the integrity of the system. These principles from the core ideas of the Green ideology. For some Greens there is now a new God to worship nature itself. Many others remain unconvinced by Gaia philosophy, yet welcome Gaia as a metaphor to encourage a more holistic attitude to life.

[4]

The environmental movements and Green parties have come to prominence in the past decades but they lack coherence of ideas. They have give bewildering range of interpretations of the depth and nature of the ecological crisis and how to find suitable remedies of them. Diversities in their ideas are so great that these ideas have been divided into a number of mutually exclusive camps. Fundamental opposition has been proposed between: environmentalists and conservationists, 'dark' and 'light' greens, 'deep' and 'shallow' ecologists, ecologists and environmentalists and 'fundis' (for political fundamentalists) and 'relos' (for realists).[3]

Preservanists belong to Johan Muir's school of thought who argue for the preservation of wilderness for own sake while Gifford Pinchot and others take a more practical line in arguing for the conservation of natural resources because of their utility value. So, they are called conservationists. Environmentalists and ecologists are united by their concern for the environment but they differ in two different ways. First, environmentalists are concerned, with the extent of environmental damage while ecologists go beyond it to find its economic and political causes; and second, the former believe that such damage can be corrected by tinkering with 'industrialism' while the latter think it needs to be dismantled and replaced. Both have common target to raise awareness of the visible symptoms of environmental degradation but the environmentalists stop there and they donot proceed beyond that point while the ecologists produce critique of present practices in the light of their transformative ideology. Ecologism argues that care for the environment needs in our relationship with it alongwith in our mode of social and political life, whereas environmentalism argues for 'managerial approach' to environment without any change in the present patterns of production and consumption.[4]

Almost all major political parties in the West have grafted green agenda on their already existing manifestos without affecting their agenda on their already existing manifestos without affecting their fundamentals in any way with apparent belief that environmental degradation can be successfully confronted within existing practices. In other words, it is possible to be a socialist, a conservative or a liberal and an environmentalist. But it is not so simple to be a socialist, conservative or liberal and a political ecologist because ecologism itself is a distinct political ideology which calls into questions too many assumptions on which socialism, conservation and liberalism are based. It is true that ecologism contains elements of these three ideologies but it remains distinct from them. It proposes radical changes in our living habits and political system.

Recent commentary has opted for two different kinds of definition of ecologism. Its philosophical school was founded by the Norwegian philosopher Arone Naess in the early seventies known as 'deep ecology' different from 'shallow ecology' the second variant of ecologism. Shallow ecology is anthropocentric, or human centered. It views humans as above or outside of nature, as the source of all values, and ascribes only instrumental, or 'use' value to nature. Deep ecology does not separate humans—or anything else—from the natural environment. It does not see the world as a collection of isolated objects but as a network of phenomena that are fundamentally interconnected and interdependent. Deep ecology recognizes the intrinsic value of all living brings and views human as just one particular strand in the web of life.

Deep ecological awareness in spiritual or religious awareness since it means the mode of consciousness in which the individual feels a sense of belonging, of connectedness, to the cosmos as a whole in which nature and the self become one.

The expansion of the self all the way to the identification with nature is the grounding of deep ecology, as Arone Naess observes:

> "Care flows naturally if the 'self is widened and deepened so that protection of free Nature is felt and conceived as protection of ourselves.... Just as we need no morals to make us breathe.... [so] if your self in the wide sense embraces another being you need no moral exhortation to show care........"

One's self becomes ecological self and in this way a psychological connection gets established between the individual self and the ecology. Hence, deep ecological awareness of being part of the web of life will be inclined to care for all living nature. The link between ecology and psychology included in the concept of the ecological self has been explored by several authors. Deep ecologist Joanna calls it "greening of the self", while warwick Fox coined 'transpersonal ecology' and Theodore Roszak calls it 'ecopsychology' to express deep connection between 'self and the ecology'.

Deep ecology questions the very foundations of modern scientific industrial growth-oriented, materialistic world view and way of life. In the words of Gorver Folley—"Deep ecology goes beyond the transformation of technology and politics to a transformation of humanity. Taking a holistic, total field view it denies any boundaries between man and nature" (The Ecologist, 1988) This does not mean to deify nature or to worship nature as god but to take account of a simple fact that human activity cannot go beyond certain limits in the natural world. During past hundred and fifty years 'industrial society developed through the accelerated looting of reserves whose creation required tens of millions of years' if it continues to go on as before the oceans and rivers will be sterile, and soil infertile and the air unbreathable. This blind orthodoxy cannot help mankind that science would find new paths; and technology would discover new processes undreamt of. But science and technology cannot undo the basic fact that the resources of the earth are extremely finite and limited.

It is not possible to derive any ethic from the economic reasoning since the economists are not concerned with what individuals thinks, feel and desire or what is good for man; they are only concerned with the material process which is economically thriving. Hence, deep ecology has its own rationality different from economic rationality that promotes production which destroys more than it cerates and beyond a certain threshold value, it has potentiality to create absolute and insurmountable scarcities. Disregarding the human concern has already set off a backlash affecting every aspect of human life, ultimately decreasing quality of life despite increasing levels of material consumption.

To overcome this situation, the ecologists advocate reduction in material production in order to conserve natural resources and to sustain natural cycles than interfere them. To achieve this end it is also necessary to impose limits on technology and to favour the development and autonomy of communities and individuals. Capitalism develops only those technologies which correspond to its logic and which are compatible with its continued domination. So, capitalist relations of productions and exchange are inscribed in the technologies capitalism develops and this made the inversion of tools a fundamental condition for the transformation of society. The size and structure of state is to a large extent determined by the level of technology. For example, nuclear energy—whether capitalist or socialist—requires highly centralized and police dominated state.

Decentralisation is the central theme of ecologism which intends to reduce the human impact on nature, and encourage communities to meet their needs as far as possible from local resources. Bringing the points of production and consumption closer would reduce waste and encourage self-reliance. This would also eliminate the necessity of centralised networks of transport and trade which causes waste of energy and pollution. In addition to decentralization of production, political decentralization would improve the quality of decision made and effectively implemented by those who are closest to the effects. Ecologists believe that most of the environmental damage caused by the present day large and centralized production techniques will have not place in a decentralized society.

The extent of decentralization is a matter of dispute among ecologists, but they are agreed on the basic features of the new sustainable society they want to create and they are: decentralization and local autonomy, labour-intensive modes of production, a de-emphasis on material things, individual self-sufficiency and cultural diversity.[8]

In addition to deep ecology, there are two other important philosophical schools of ecology; social ecology and feminist ecology. Anarchist Murray Bookchin is the prominent ideologue of 'social ecology'. Deep ecological awareness provides the ideal philosophical and spiritual basis for 'deep ecology' in forming its ideology but it does not tell much about the patterns of origination that have brought about the current ecological crisis. This is the main focus of social ecology. It is based on the recognition of the fact that the anti-ecological nature of many of our social and economic structures and their technologies is rooted in the 'dominator system' of social organization. Patriarchy, imperialism, capitalism and racism are examples of social domination that are exploitative and anti-ecological.

Social ecology strongly emphasize that 'hierarchy' in society is an institutional phenomenon, not a biological. It is a product of organized, carefully crafted power relationships. Unity in diversity does not only provided most needed stability to ecosystem, but it gives impetus to its evolutionary potential to create newer, still more complex life-forms and biotic interrelationships. By comparing ecosystems to societies, social ecology challenges the very 'function of hierarchy as a way ordering reality'. Social ecology ruptures the association of order with hierarchy and strongly advocates to experience the 'other' ecologically that enriches wholeness.

'The social ecologists are very critical of the fact that the hierarchy exists today as an even more fundamental problem than social classes; that domination exists today as an even more fundamental problem than economic exploitation,.... the abolition of classes, exploitation and even of state is no guarantee whatever that people will cease to be ranked heirarchically, dominated according to age, gender, race, physical qualities and often quite frivolous and irrational categories, unless liberation focuses as much on hierarchy and domination as on classes and exploitation. This is the point where socialism..... must extend itself into broader liberation tradition that reaches back into tribal or band type communities.' (Bookchin—"What is Social Ecology")

Politically, social ecologists are committed to the abolition of all human inequalities, of class, gender and race: But according to Bookchin Deep ecology overlooks and probably reinforces existing inequalities within society with its tendency to retreat into mystical 'ecolala' and occasional eco-fascism. Boockhin is very conspicuous in his political preferences for a system of dencentralised, quasianarchist communities. The notion of dominating nature literally defines all our social disciplines, including socialism and psychoanalysis. Until this faulty vision is removed from our sensibilities; and replaced by ecological sensibility that sees 'otherness' in terms of complimentarily rather than rivalry, we will never achieve human emancipation. However, Bookchin favoured technology of appropriate scale.

Concern for nature has given rise to 'ecofeminism' which can be viewed as special school of social ecology. Ecofeminists believe that women and nature have a common cause as both have been subjected to perennial subjugation. They see the patriarchial domination of women by men as the prototype of all domination and exploitation in the various hierarchical, militaristic, capitalist, and industrialists forms. They point out that the exploitation of nature, in particular, has gone had in hand with that of women who have been identified with nature throughout the ages. Most ecofeminists want to disengage women from association of nature in order to claim a place for women in the more valued realms of culture. Some ecofeminists think it to be wrong, primarily because denying association with nature amount to denying them their own true nature.

The philosophical dimensions of ecologism lack unity and cohesion due to which it failed to develop an acceptable political theory. Like any other radical political ideology, ecologism faces the problem of putting its ideas into practice. The gap between the realities in which the world is living today and where ecologists like us to go is so wide that ecologism's practical credibility is in question. Green political parties, no doubt have succeeded to a great extent in making impact on the minds of the people to change their lifestyles either in home or in sustainable communities but industrialism remains in practice all over the world and the more radical demands for the dismantling of industrialism and creation of a decentralized, low impact society, are as far as ever from being realised. Despite their critique of the existing system, sections of the ecologists still have faith in technology to solve problems and do not want to give up technology which would save work. Thus, ecologism remains a fragmented ideology, beset by a number of competing paradigms.

[5]

A 'new' left orientation quite distinct from Old Left and Marxist formations on the one hand and liberalism on the other, evolved during the years 1956, reached its climax in 1967-69 and then declined. The mood that led to the creation of the 'New Left-orientation largely came out of the writings of W.C. Wright and the literature of the Beats'. It is amongst the dissident communists of the West that the intellectual origins of the New Left are first discerned. Politically isolated and alone, the ex-communists were in search for a 'third way' beyond the 'empty cant' of current liberalism and the Marxist-Stalinist orthodoxies. They were deeply shocked to find that Marxism have become 'the mirror image of bourgoise, an image reversed, and yet unmistakably identical' because Marxism unabashedly shared most of the 'liberal-technocratic assumptions; its positivism, its materialism, its belief in progress'. In sum, the New Left emerged as an alternative to both liberal and Marxist orthodoxies. Its chief theorists are Leszek Kalkowski, S. Stojanovic, Herbet Marcuse, Jean Paul Stare, Frantz Fanon, J. Garandy, Theodre Adorno, Earnest Block, Jurgen Habermas, Charles Roszak and Che Guevra. They take inspiration from Marx and yet denounce much of what comes within the fold of classical Marxism. They denounce the affluent capitalists society as well. To them both capitalism and socialism have debased and dehumanized the life man.

A scepticism of purely political action and an ambivalence about 'politics attended the birth of New Left. The New Left thinkers, felt that we are living in a post-industrial society in which neither the laws of an Adam Smith nor that of a Karl Marx would work' since 'now the struggle is neither a purely economic nor a political affair', rather it is concerned with the very preservation of man's life as a man in face of the invisible, omnipresent dictatorship of which tend to integrate and assimilate all elements (including the human ones) into the system. For them objective of man's struggle is 'the reconquest of his individual autonomy' which is more important than all social and economic structures.[9]

Throughout the 1960s the ideological core of the New Left remained ambiguous. 'Marxist or non-Marxist, socialist or non-socialist, violent or non-violent, centralist or anarchist-no one was very clear on these points.[10] The Port Huron document, the initial manifesto of the New Left, stated that not even the socialist and liberal preachments of the past seem adequate to the forms of the present. Angry Youngman's anguished outburst of 1958 that there was an end to 'good brave cause' expressed similar disillusionment with all ideologies. As Bottomore put it.

> "The great 19th century ideologies which divided societies, have developed cracks and appear to be crumbling.... (this) no longer exercise anything like their former sway over the minds of social critics. Critics." And "no intellectual current emerged as clear alternative."

At this stage the New Left lacked any commitment to a comprehensive ideological position despite the existing vacuum of organized belief. But a general argument emerged among the new Left activists that such lack of ideology might eventually lead to crisis and that the anti-intellectual currents might be subsequent cause of weakness. Search for a new revolutionary strategy had inevitably involved dialogue with Marx but it would be quite erroneous to think that the New Left was ever a Marxist movement even after 1968.

The fact is that the new Left went through wide-ranging eclecticism: the early movement drew at least from as much as other traditions—the Anarchist, the Gandhian, and from classical sociology, Weber and Michels—as from Marx. Nevertheless, the movement shifted far enough towards Marxism. Thoughout the 1960s and early 1970s, many commentators used the term Anarchist to describe part or all of the New Left. In Zinn's view:

> "it (New Left) is anarchistic .... not just in wanting the

ultimate abolition of the state, but in its immediate requirement that authority and coercion be banished in every sphere of existence."

At the outset, Camu's emphasis on rebellion in thought and action had been widely influential on the early New Left. Subsequently, the ideas and events of May 1968 were described as libertarian Marxism with the spread of Marcusian ideas of the 1968. The terms libertarian Marxist with the spread of were used frequently for many of the New Left ideas and actions.

The Marxism of the New Left is based upon the 'young' Marx. The Marx these thinkers follow is not so much the economist, the 'Old' Marx the author of Das Kapital but rather the young Marx the sociologist, the author of the early philosophical manuscripts. Their Marx is, like themselves, a 'Hegelian', a metaphysician, neither a positivist nor a scientific determinist. Their Marx is the philosopher of alienation. New Left theoreticians took the Marxian idea of alienation and made it the fundamental tenet of the New Left.

In the Manuscripts Marx writes that 'human nature is man's true communal nature' but under capitalist order man 'gets separated from his work, separated from his products, separated from the material work, and also separated from his fellow men.... capitalism alienates man essentially from his own activity, from the product of his labour, thus tuning labour's product into an alien object, the more he works the more he finds himself dominated by the world of objects his own labour has created. The worker puts his life into the objects and his life then belongs no longer to himself but to the object. What is embodied in the product of his labour is no longer his own. The greater this product...... the more he is diminished." (D. Mclellan-Marx: Early Writings, pp. 123-24). What is left with the individual after all these changes have occurred is a mere rump." .... so long as man has not recognized himself as man has not organized his world in a human way, the communal nature appears in the form of alienation because its subject man is a self-alienated being.... alienated man is an abstraction because he has lost touch with all human specificity." (*Ibid.* p. 193) Man becomes stranger to himself, 'unattached', 'marginal', 'obsessive', 'normless', isolated individual due to breaking of the seamless mould in which values, behaviour and expectations were once cast into interlocking forms.

Alienation has acquired connotation such as a cultural fragmentation, social isolation, economic exploitation, philosophical abstraction and political non-existence. It causes profound dislocation in the primary associative areas of human life whether in its private or public manifestations and marks man unattached, marginal obsessive, normless isolated individual.

Marx was in search of a system (communism) in which man's self-alienation could be transcended, a possibility may be devised for "the complete return of man to himself a social (human) being with positive transcendence of all estrangements." The New Left thinkers draw inspiration from 'young' Marx but they agree with Marx that alienation will go with the abolition of capitalist order. They believe that the course of alienation can be eliminated in the present industrial society as well with the creation of feeman (Marcuse) or with the creation of a free community with a changed hearts (Fanon) which is not possible in any regimentated system be it communist or Fascist. Stare suggests that the state of disalienation can be achieved with 'the withering away not only of the state but of politics all together through full exercise of self government at every level'.

Eric Fromm believes that modernization is the sole cause of the political and social maladies of the contemporary world. Human nature craves for society and would like to be related to it in love and not in submission or dominance. In absence of such relations man develops a sense of 'alienation'. The state of near complete alienation has already been reached in the modern age and man has been rendered so helpless that he hardly has any control over the development of his character and his social character is so moulded by the mode of production that man begins to think of himself as a 'thing' which can be bought or sold in the market place. Fromm wants to establish "communatrain socialist" society in which there is perfect blending of centralization and decentralization at the economic level and on the political and social levels there should be division of society into small units bringing into existence a real primitive village accompanied with the decentralization of the government.

Rubert Nisbet is also against industrialization and modernization which have destroyed the primary groups in society. He believes in social pluralism and administrative decentralization. In his view the modern state is the cause of alienation.

Camus's humanism and non-violence were enormously influential on the first generation of movement activists. In the early 1960s, non-violence remained unchallenged in the movement since human optimism was predominant Fromm's taboo on tenderness could not capture the imagination of the New Left in 1965 and "the philosophy, or religious ideal of non-violence" remained the fundamental creed of the New Left.

A sense of urgency and impatience justified extra-institutional methods and all who held these views turned to militant illegal action. They openly opposed civil disobedience and ridiculed it as a "confession of impotence." Gradually, glorification of violence became the central theme of the New Left. Marx himself believed that revolutionary violence might be inevitable but he regretted it. Communist practice, assuredly involved violence—war, sabotage, torture, assimilation and terror—in pursuits of its aims. But as much as possible communist violence remained veiled. But the New Left thinkers gave several reasons for thinking that violence is good. Fanon believed that at the level of individuals, violence is a cleansing force since violence "frees a man from despair and inaction, it makes him fearless and restores his self-respect."

Satre was a champion of violence in politics long before he read Fanon: "one cannot do good in politics unless one is willing to soil one's hand with violent deeds such as assassination and "terrorism." Marcuse has even greater loathing than State for the world of present day reality. In what Marcuse calls the "hell of the affluent society", he thinks the working class are as much deceived and corrupted by material prosperity as everyone. Marcuse agrees with State that the institutions of existing societies rest on violence and that violence is required to overthrow them.

Summarising the above, the components of the New Left ideology can be sum up as below:

- Anit intellectualism, irrationalism and anti-theory.
- A stress on 'community' and the decentralization of society.
- Loose decentralized organization, the rejection of society.
- A stress on the means/ends continuum.
- The organization of the poor and the declasses the marginal elements.
- Direct Action, extra-institutional, extra parliamentary and extra-legal activity.
- The romanticization of spontaneous violence.

These dimensions which represent the significant ingredients in the New Left's ideological make up, found prominent place in ecologism also but its great emphasis is on the emancipation of man from all sorts of domination and repressions. Its focus on environment, on culture, on lifestyle and on free speech, free school, free radio and other alternative media is aimed to broaden the areas of freedom and disalienation of man is existing in existing society but its focus on ecology is marginal and the liberation of nature is secondary to the main goal of human freedom. For this reason Marxism and other left traditions are criticized by the ecologists since they treat the planet as an exploitable resource with the positive assumption that nature is subordinate to man. The New Leftism is primarily a political doctrine and its subsequent drift towards the adoration of violence made it quite alien to the mainstream ecological movements. Sudden decline in the New Left movement after 1970s, made it a social and cultural doctrine having extensive borrowings from Gandhi who remains to be the main guiding spirit behind ecological movements.[11]

Notes and References

1. T. Roszak, The Making of a Counter Culture, p. 100, Faber, 1970.
2. *Ibid.*, p. 110.
3. Porrit and D. Winner, The Coming of the Greens, p. 9, Fontana, London, 1984.
4. See J. Dryzek, Rational Ecology, Environment and Political Ecology, Blackwell, 1987.
5. Dolosn-Green Political Thought, p. 13, Unwin Hyman, London, 1990.
6. For details see Mike Robinson, The Greening of British Party Politics, Manchester University Press, 1992.
7. A. Naess, Ecology, Community and Lifestyle: Outline of an Ecosophy, Cambridge University Press, 1989.
8. D. Pirages (ed)., The Sustainable Society: Implications for Limited Growth, p. 164, Praeger, New York, 1977.
9. Massino Teodori, The New Left. Documentary History, p. 18.
10. E. Benello and D. Roussopoley, Participatory Democracy, p. 300.
11. For detail study see T.B. Bottomore, Critics of Society.

5

Socialism and the Ecological Crisis

RANDHIR SINGH

The following are two concluding sections of one chapter "Future of Socialism—As Bleak or Bright as Humankind's" of the author's book, Crisis of Socialism—Notes in Defence of a Commitment, published by Ajanta Books International, Delhi. These are being reproduced here with the consent of the author, a distinguished Professor of Political Theory (retired), University of Delhi.

—*Editor*

The environment has been damaged by all social systems, more or less, at least 15,000 years ago, since the agricultural revolution which brought in class-society, and the civilisation the way we have know it. But four odd centuries of capitalism have transformed the world far more drastically than all the millennia of previous human history combined. With capitalism, especially since the Second World War, the damage to environment has acquired an altogether new frightening dimension which is posing the threat of an imminent ecological disaster. Not a natural process nor the result of economic growth or industrialisation as such, this damage and the accompanying threat have grown directly out of the specific structural logic of capitalism. The productive forces which capitalism has unleashed have been caught up with and overtaken by the destructive powers it released simultaneously, and these are now about to break down the highly strained ecological equilibrium, putting a question mark on the very survival of humankind on this earth. As Foster recently put it,

> human society has reached a critical threshold in its relation to the environment. The destruction of the planet, in the sense of making it unusable for human purposes, has grown to such an extent that is now threatens the continuation of much of nature, as well as the survival and development of society itself.

The threat has been growing over the years and so have been the warnings, even if its linkages with capitalism have not been always clearly seen. Way back in 1864, George Perkins Marsh—the famous environmentalist and 'the fountain-head to the conservative movement' in the words of Lewis Mumford—taking note of the damage already done to environment by 'the operations of causes set in action by man' had warned:

> The earth is fast becoming an unfit home for its noblest inhabitant, and another era of equal human crime and improvidence..... would reduce it to such a condition of impoverished productiveness, of shattered surface, of climatic excess, as to threaten the depravation, barbarism, and perhaps even extinction of the species.

A century later, Rachel Carson saw this threat as 'the central problem of our age' argued:

> Along with the possibility of the extinction of mankind by nuclear war, the central problem of our age has... become the contamination of man's total environment with such substances of incredible potential for harm-

> substances that accumulate in the tissues of plants and animals and even penetrate the germ cells to shatter or alter the very material of heredity upon which the shape of the future depends.

The epigraph for Carson's book the environmental classic Silent Spring, was a quote from Albert Schweitzer: 'Man has lost the capability to forces and forestall. He will end by destroying the earth.' About a decade later, noting the disastrously negative consequences of capitalism and viewing resistance to capitalism as the necessary human defence, in the City and the Country, Raymond Williams wrote:

> Capitalism, as a mode of production....its abstracted economic drives, its fundamental priorities in social relations, its criteria of growth and of profit and loss, (have) over several centuries altered our country and created our kinds of city. In its final form of imperialism it has altered the world...Resistance to capitalism is the decisive form of the necessary human defence.

More recently, referring to five past mass extinctions (in which 65 per cent or more of species died out in a brief geological instant, and the last one saw the decimation of dinosaurs), scientists have been warning that we are on the verge of 'the sixth extinction'—this time at the hands of humanity. According to the 'World Scientists Warning to Humanity,' initiated by the Union of Concerned Scientists and signed in 1992 by 1575 of the world's most distinguished scientists, including more than half of all living scientists awarded the Nobel Prize,

Human beings and the natural world are on a collision course. Human activities inflict harsh and often irreversible damage on the environment and on critical resources. If not checked, many of our current practices put at risk the future we wish for human society and the plant and animal kingdom, and may so alter the living world that it will be unable to sustain life in the manner that we know. Fundamental changes are urgent if we are to avoid the collision our present course will bring.

The World, Scientists go on to emphasise 'the critical stress' in such areas as the atmosphere, the oceans, water resources, soil, forests, and living species—'the irreversible loss of species, which by 2100 may reach one-third of all species now living, is especially serious.' Their conclusion is unmistakably clear:

> We the undersigned, senior members of the world's scientific community, hereby warn all humanity of what lies ahead. A great change in our stewardship of the Earth and the life on it is required if vast human misery is to be avoided and our global home on this planet is not to be irretrievably mutilated.

Commenting on a government-funded study on the decline of species—butterflies, birds and plants—in the UK, recently reported in the magazine Science, Jeremy Thomas of the National Environment Research Council has said, the date 'adds enormous strength to the hypothesis that the world is approaching its sixth major extinction event.' And finally, stressing the need to fight capitalism before it destroys us and our planet, Paul Buhle has written:

> Today, human society, and the biosphere itself, cannot survive the organised greed and environmental ruination that the system demands for it continued vampire-like existence.

As we have argued, it is impossible for capitalism to counter the emerging threat to environment within its own parameters as an economic system. For a capitalism in crisis as it is today (recession, stagnation in economy, unemployment, etc.) it is doubly impossible. Retreating even from their earlier, mostly verbal, concern for the environment, the governmental and political leaders of global capitalism have made it clear (at international conferences and elsewhere) that they will not allow environmental controls to interfere with no 'hurt' the economy, that their only efficient concern is to keep capitalism going, and the environment be damned. They would rather defend and uphold the global capitalist interests, carry on with their consumerist, privileged way of life and shift the immediate pollution and environmental degradation from wealthy areas to poor areas within their own countries and form the advanced capitalist world to its peripheries in the Third World. Notwithstanding their cynical use of ecological concern to hinder economic development in countries of the Third World in the name of 'global interdependence', or otherwise gain advantage over them in the world market, they fail to see that environmental crisis recognizes no barriers within or without, that for it, it is no longer First, Second, Third of Fourth Worlds but only one world. This short sightedness has been compounded by capitalism's recharged domination of the world, following the collapse of the Soviet Union, which has given rise to an era of privatization and the market-knows-best-solution to all socio-economic problems. Rather than increase regulation and enforcement to reduce pollution or check ecological degradation, the strategy of the dominant capitalist powers is to set-up a worldwide 'free market', their dominion in which multinationals can freely buy and sell the right to pollute and further degrade the environment. Such dominance of the market in a period of economic crisis can ultimately lead only to an ecological disaster.

There are those who believe 'ultimately' means so far in the future, like the cooling of the sun, as to be for all practical purpose irrelevant. But those who know, reputable ecologists, environmentalists and scientists, have warned us that we are already on the brink of this disaster. Some ten years back an article in the reputed magazine Nature History, writing of a 'throw away society' which is 'strangling itself', had reported:

> if the world is not to fatally overtax its natural systems, we will need to achieve sustainability within the next forty years. If we have not succeeded by then, environmental deterioration and economic decline are likely to be feeding on each other, pulling us into a downward spiral of social disintegration. Our vision of the future therefore looks to the year 2030.

About the same time, pointing out that the global environment is what sustains us and in some ways we are the villains and victims of the changing environment, and that what lay ahead was drought all over the planet, conflict over water resources, massive flooding of coastal cities, disappearance of entire Bangladesh and so on, the eminent scientist, late Carl Sagan, had warned that human society faced disaster by the year 2050, if it did not change to a more life sustaining technology or development. A recent secret Pentagon report warns of much the same, of climate change over the next 20 odd years causing a global catastrophe—mega droughts, famines, nuclear threat and wars to defend and secure dwindling food, water and energy supplies, major European cities sun beneath rising seas and parts plunged into a 'Siberian' climate. Lester Brown, currently President of the Earth Policy Institute, even as he continues to look for solutions within the system (and collect awards) fears that time is running out for us, that 'we are losing the war to save the planet.' Oliver S. Laud, Professor or Physical Sciences at Antioch University, has written:

> On this, our planet, there have been about 1000 human generations since our species survived alone among several hominid species, to become the culture-creating species. And only the last 200 generations have been born into hierarchical, class-structural social systems. Five generations, three of them already here, will either win or lose forever the human future.

Forty to fifty years or a couple more generations may be too short a period and we need not be alarmist. Such warnings may only indicate the need for an all-sided struggle against the destructive tendencies or our existing social order which today are in full operation. Even so environmental destruction can no longer be viewed as a long-run problem. In these opening years of the twenty-first century, we can no longer afford the luxury of continuing to think in terms of traditional historical time. Form an ecological point of view the human species is indeed in deep trouble today. If things continue to develop as they have over the last fifty years for another century or two—a very short time by historical standards—it is virtually certain that civilized life as we know it today will no longer be possible. Unless we succeed in getting rid of capitalism within a hundred years, the end of human history may be actually not a bad dream, or the poor concoction of a Fukuyama, but a reality.

We indeed do not have much time. As Sara Parkin, spokesperson of the UK Green Party, has observe,

> Our numbers, our silence, our lack of outrage, could mean we end up the only species to have minutely monitored our own extinction. What a measly epitaph that would make-they saw it coming but hadn't the wit to stop it happening.

There is no guarantee of human tenure on earth, according to Carl Sagan. About 65 million years ago dinosaurs ruled the earth. They are extinct. This is a reminder to us to be careful. Alfred North Whitehead, one of the greatest thinkers of this past century, had written:

> I have never ceased to entertain the idea that the human race might rise to a certain point and then decline and never retrieve itself. Plenty of other forms of life have done that. Evolution may go down as well as up.

It is an unsettling but by no means far-fetched thought that the form and active agency of this decline may be taking shape before our very eyes in these opening years of the twenty-first century AD.

This is no 'environmental apocalypticism' or 'millenarianism', of 'doomsday' prophecy, as some critics have alleged. The terms used by critics, 'apocalyptic', 'millenarian' or 'doomsday', because of the sense of religious fatalism associated with them, imply something irrational in character—the wrath of God, the second coming Day of Judgment—which it should be obvious, has nothing to do with our argument. Our argument carries no suggestion of any kind of uncontrollable destruction of earth's natural conditions. What is suggested is that if humanity constructs a kind of society that systematically destroys the natural grounds of its own existence then it is heading for a disaster. Or, to put it more specifically, if our society continues to be dominated by capitalism, then it is only a matter of time be it a few decades or a few centuries, neither of which amounts to much in the long stretch of history before it expires from lack for essential life supports. It is not apocalyptic to warn about the disastrous dimensions that capitalism's threat to environment has now acquired.

This, however, is not the only threat looming on the horizon—the possible parting gift of capitalism to humankind. In yet another way the great capitalist powers, the overlords of contemporary bourgeois civilisation, with their accumulation of high-tech arms and arsenals of nuclear and chemical weapons, are proving incapable of a responsible stewardship of the world's affairs. David Edgerton has spoken of a 'liberal militarism' of the West, long exemplified by the US and British military policy, that today aims at the imposition of a global 'Pax Technologica', based on deployment of high-tech strike forces. This 'liberal militarism' achieves a distinctive fusion of economics and warfare, technology and globalism, with the 'new imperialism' that a Blair has even decreed necessary, recycling the synoptic warfare delusions of the 'old colonialism'. At the head of this 'new imperialism' stands the United States, with its long record of military interventions, regional wars, counter-revolutionary subversions, low-intensity conflicts and proxy wars the world over—since the second half of the 1970s alone, in China, Korea, Greece, Vietnam, Iran, Guatemala, Middle East, Cuba, Dominican Republic, China, Granada, Nicaragua, Afghanistan, Angola, El Salvador, Iraq and so on, invariably in order to either maintain or restore the status quo, or to pursue its imperialist interests. The 1991 Iraq war, on Afghanistan and another war on Iraq—was significant in more ways than one. It secured the US domination in the strategically important Middle East with its oil reserves which fuel the consumerist extravagance of the West—just as its recent war in Afghanistan has secured for it an assured military presence and political domination in yet another strategically important and oil-rich region of the world, something it has been wanting for a long time. IT also exposed the fragile ecology of the Gulf to the pyrotechnics of modern warfare as has again happened with America's recent wars in the region and beyond. Particularly significant, however, was the belief or the false presumption it generated about the demise of 'the Vietnam syndrome'—America had won a war in the Third World along with an assurance for the Americans that they can henceforth kill others but need no longer themselves die in the imperialist invasions abroad. Thus emboldened, and as the world's sole superpower, America has gone altogether adventurist in pursuit of its imperialist aims. It has claimed the right to pre-emptive strike, to unilateral, at will armed intervention wherever it wants. As an imperial power it has the world's largest stock of weapons of mass destruction and proposes to have more of them—including those which are about blowing people up on the other side of the planet even if no country on earth will allow us to use their territory, and its politics is not immune to Bushite marke—no mistake—'greatest nationalism' and the itch to bomb recalcitrant nations 'into the parking lot' to its being a rogue, even 'terrorist state', in Chomsky's words, which it indeed is today in its so-called 'war against terrorism'. However messy, politically and militarily, they may have turned out to be, through its wars on Iraq and Afghanistan, the United States has virtually served notice to people in the Third World that imperialist domination is a fate that must be accepted on pain of violent destruction. The people of the Third World may, and are likely to, defy and reject this notice. But this does not rule out the possibility that, with its short-run vision and arrogance as well as impotence of power, and long record of imperialist interventions, the US may yet, in the words of Paul Sweezy, come 'to play Samson in the temple of humanity'.

This is not to suggest that either irreversible evolutionary decline or military destruction of human species is inevitable. In human affairs nothing is today has a deadly potential for both.

Let me conclude by putting the argument in a historical perspective. Marx assessed the significance of capitalism in the development of mankind as creating the conditions for socialism. He visualized the construction of socialism on the basis provided by the productive and other achievements of capitalism. He saw socialism as necessary and possible but not as a smooth and unproblematic transition. There was no assumption that different countries involved in socialist transition would all actually exhibit a determinate degree of approximation the socialist goal on a liner scale. Nor was this transition seen as in any sense inevitable. Decisive here was political intervention that immediately Marx defined as 'proletarian revolution'—which, again, Marx certainly regarded as a necessary but not an automatic and inevitable, or necessarily violent, consequence of capitalist development. Proletarian revolution has remained delayed in the advanced capitalist countries, and where it occurred, as in Germany in 1981, it did not survive. And where it survived, as Russia in 1971, there were hardly any achievements of capitalism to build upon. The effort to build socialism there has now finally collapsed. Again this was possible but not inevitable. The post-revolutionary theoretical and political intervention was simply inadequate to cope with the unanticipated task. They could have built better and socialism could have survived, even if not as ideally conceived by Marx, but certainly with long-term possibilities of significant approximation to the ideal. Not inevitable, this first experiment in socialism has yet failed, which leaves capitalism every much 'over-developed', surviving much beyond the period of its historical legitimacy, with consequences now all to visible in the materially, morally mentally and culturally sick societies of the capitalist world. The entire world, the developed capitalist countries no less, are paying the price for the revolution that never happened in the West and the 'socialism' that has now failed in the East. None of this, however, in any way falsifies the theory of Karl Marx. He always maintained that there are alternatives in history, and the alternative facing the world today, the advanced capitalist societies no less than others, was long ago expressed by Rosa Luxemburg in the formula: 'either socialism or a descent into barbarism'. The emerging ecological catastrophe has only added to the meaning and the urgency, and the scope, of this statement. The real problem here is not the fact of pollution, the scarcity or resources or over-population, but the extent to which a world dominated by capitalist imperatives is able to tackle them. On this account, there is room here only for pessimism. Marx foresaw capitalism as carrying within itself the possibility of 'the total destruction of humanity', and also noted: 'Apre moile deluge' is the watchword for every capitalist and every capitalist nation. That is how capitalism is ruining the human habital and will continue to do so as long as it exists. It is an open question how far the destruction which it has wrought and continues to weak is still reversible. But give the tenacity with which the capitalist mode of production still asserts itself, it seems certain that in another hundred years or so, may be less, we will be beyond

RANDHIR SINGH: Socialism and the Ecological Crisis

The point of no return. The fight against capitalism has become a race with time which mankind is in danger of losing.

But the fight is not yet lost. Capitalism certainly holds no possibility of realizing Mar's project for the reconciliation of man and nature. But we can still fight and win against capitalism to realise it, to ensure that our sun continues to radiate stably into our cherished biosphere for the posterilty, which could well comprise 200 million more human generations. Concern for the future is indeed what has always provided perspective for and inspired the commitment of revolutionaries. So it has to in our struggle to save the environment.

Winning against capitalism means winning socialism, that is, winning conscious rational control of humanity's metabolism with nature. It is to win our freedom in the realm of necessity, as Marx called it, which capitalism by its very nature denies us, and which, to repeat Marx again,

> Can only consist in this, that socialized man, the associated producers, govern the human metabolism with nature in a rational way, bring it under their

> collective control instead of being dominated by it as a blind power, accomplishing it with the least expenditure of energy and in conditions most, favourable to and worthy of, their human nature.

It is not claimed that socialism offers an instant solution to the problems which confront our planet. But its rejection of capitalist imperatives and drives offers a chance that the problems would be tackled with the determination that is required. Socialism is no guarantee of salvation, ecological or any other, but there is no other possibility of salvation today. At the beginning of the twenty-first century, the choice still remains as, following Marx, Rosa Luxemburg formulated it: 'either socialism or a descent into barbarism.'

Years ago the French students in their May-June uprising of 1968 expressed this sharp contrast of alternatives magnificently in their slogan: 'Be practical! Do the impossible' Marcuse had suggested that the new generation that faces the next (that is, twenty-first) century needs to add to this demand the more solemn injunction: If we don't do the impossible, we shall be faced with the unthinkable!' The 'unthinkable' today is more than mere descent into barbarism. What is at stake is the actual existence of the world, and with it of the human species. And the task, as eco-feminist Francoise d'Eaubonne, paraphrasing Marx has said, is 'to change the world...so that there can still be a world.' Socialism is precisely the changed world we need. Once promise of liberation, socialism has now become a question of survival too. Human species needs socialism not only to realize its potentials but even to survive. That is how the chances of survival and realization of the potentials of both human species and socialism have come to be interlinked today. Which also means that the future of socialism is as bleak or bright as that of humankind.

PART II

ECOLOGY AND GANDHISM

6

Relevance of Gandhian Approach to Environmental Problems

C.K. Varshney

Gandhiji's message to the problem redden modern society is that every human being should lead simple austere life and reduce his needs to the minimum. This simple philosophy, if honestly practice, will reduce over consumption, avoid wanton destruction of finite resource, minimize waste, prevent pollution, lead to sustainability and promote a better quality of life. In the absence of frugal approach, whatever is done at higher intellectual and political levels is not going to provide a lasting solution to our present day environmental predicament.

Evidence of planetary crisis confronts us in the despoliation of the environment and the loss of meaning in the lives of individuals. In spite of material abundance which had been made possible today through technological advancement, there is widespread social and psychological tension and moral bankruptcy. Environmental degradation, global warming, depletion of natural resources, decimation of biodiversity, increasing economic instability, unemployment, and widening inequality are among the complex array of problems that threaten all human societies.

It is now widely realised that the current pattern of economic development, which has promoted industrialisation and encouraged consumerism, is the major cause under lining the contemporary environmental problems. Increasing number of people are seeking to resolve the challenges facing humanity. A paradigm shift is essential for charging the current scenario. An alternate development strategy is required not to manage nature but to manage human society. Gandhian philosophy, which lays down ground rules and norms for individuals and society, appears to be highly appropriate for solving many of the present day environmental problems which defy easy solution.

It is well known that throughout the history of eastern civilisations, nature has been held in great esteem. Non-violence and respect for all forms of life have been the major guiding principle of eastern cultures. Life and natural assets were considered sacred and worthy of preservation. The respect for nature was so deep-seated that various trees, animals and natural forces like sun, wind, water, etc. were considered as "manifestations of God." These values were passed on from one generation to another, were accepted by masses as an article of faith, and helped man to live in harmony with nature. There was a deep sense of continuum from man to nature.

Gandhiji, one of the greatest exponents of eastern civilisation, provided a very critical and realistic analysis of the impact of industrialism when it was still in its infancy and people all over the world were dazzled by its ill-conceived virtues. Gandhiji was able to clearly foresee the implications of industrialisation. He was convinced about the negative impact of industrial growth and throughout his life he preached that the path of industrialisation is not conducive to the fuller development of man. Gandhian philosophy has great value in solving the ills of our industrial civilisation.

Against Exploitive Industrialisation

Gandhiji was against over-exploitation of natural resources by any society for its own material affluence or by outsiders by neglecting human labour. He believed that such a policy is lopsided and can never establish human equality. He emphasised the importance and dignity of human labour and regarded it as the greatest potential capital which should be harnessed on a priority basis by providing job to all people. His opposition to machinery was due to unemployment caused by it. Security against unemployment is the first criterion of every healthy society. If this essential objective is sacrificed, then all other measures of economic development cannot bear fruit. Man and machines, according to Gandhiji, are substitute for raising national productivity, but the employment of the former. While doing so, environmental and social costs involved in indiscriminate adoption and import of technology need to be given serious consideration and the current environmental awareness has effectively demonstrated that indiscriminate industrialism is mainly responsible for most of the environmental problems. Gandhiji was opposed to it and his words in this connection are prophetic. "Industrialism is, I am afraid, going to be a curse for mankind. Industrialism depends entirely on your capacity to exploit on foreign markets being open to you and on the absence of competitors. . . . The future of industrialism is dark. . . . And my fundamental objection to machinery rests on the fact that it is machinery that has enabled these nations to exploit others. . . . Today, machinery merely helps a few to ride on the back of millions. The impetus behind it all is not the philanthropy to save labour, but greed." Gandhiji was opposed to exploitive industrialisation but was not against the judicious application of science and technology. Explaining the practical side of the question, he says "Machinery has its place." The implications of his teachings are wide and still relevant to the current situation. Restraints on rampant industrialisation are already being suggested by environmentalists to avoid over exploitation of finite resources resulting in environmental degradation.

---

* [Preference for cottage over large industries will not only generate local employment but may also help in reducing consumption of fossil fuels used to power industrial production]

Widespread Moral Bankruptcy

The control of ever-growing industrialization cannot be achieved in isolation. Our attitude and values towards life have to be carefully redefined and examined. We cannot afford to control industrial-consumerism or "growth mania" without reducing our wants and limiting luxuries. There has been no example to show that multiplication of wants and desires or increasing leisure has brought true happiness to any individual or society. Mere acquisition of artifacts does not bring happiness. Clearly, then, the philosophy of continued economic growth and consumption does not promise happiness. There is ample evidence to show that many early civilizations declined because of these precise causes. In spite of material abundance which has been possible today through technological advancement there is widespread social and psychological tension and moral bankruptcy. Gandhiji believed in "Plain Living and High Thinking" and emphasized that man's real happiness lies in contentment. He who is discontented, whoever much he possess, becomes a save to his desires." In today's world, self-restraint is not only sound morally but is the only practical way to avoid impending disaster by luxury consumption of finite from natural resources.

Alternative to Linear Growth

In a finite world unchecked linear growth cannot be sustained. Gandhiji's advise to curtail wants shows that he clear about it. He advocated that curtailment of demand and self-restraint do not mean the arresting of growth. It is difficult to think that human society can survive long under a no-growth atmosphere. But growth should not be interpreted to mean economic or material abundance only. Gandhiji emphasised that increase in wealth was necessary only as far as it helped moral advancement of the nation. Spiritual growth is the ideal for every individual as well as for every society, and material wealth is justified only in as far as it helps the unfolding of spirituality. We have to think of growth in broader terms, so that it can provide happiness, contentment and spiritual satisfaction. It is the growth of the soul that should be the prime goal of any growth strategy, and there can be no limit to such growth, unlike material growth which cannot continue indefinitely in the finite world.

Village Swaraj—Key to Sustainable Development

In most of the countries, environmental problems in urban areas have been aggravated by large-scale migration from rural areas. Gandhiji was aware of this and started what was know as the "Go Back to Village Movement." He believed in autonomous villages. His idea of village swaraj is that is a complete republic, independent of its neighbours for its vital wants, and yet interdependent for many others in which dependence is a necessity. Every village's first concern will be to grow its own food crops and cotton for its cloths. It should have a pasture for its cattle, playground and means of recreation for adults and children. Then, if there is more land available, it will grow useful cash crops, excluding ganja (marijuan), tobacco, opium and the like. The village will maintain a village theatre, school and public hall. It will have its own waterworks ensuring safe water supply. This can be done through controlled wells and tanks. Education should be compulsory. The Government of the village will be conducted by a panchayat of five persons, annually elected by the adult villagers. It should become absolutely clear that such a concept of village life takes into consideration the modern principles of ecology and resource management. It may not be exaggeration to say that Gandhiji outlined the ground plan for self-sustained or 'sustainable development' was conceived. Development of sustainable units in the form of "Solar Powered Village Ecosystems" will provide the most vital underpinning for the sustainable development of the country. It is important to educate the people in general and particularly the elected representatives of village panchayats, about the relevance of Gandhian approach for achieving real 'Village Swaraj'.

A brief discussion on the Gandhian philosophy given above strongly suggests that many of the environmental, economic and social ills can be effectively addressed by following the path of local self-sufficiency. The concept of "Village Swaraj" advocated by Mahatma Gandhi can serve as a blue print for a pragmatic approach for achieving sustainable development.

Making Khadi a Way of Life

Gandhiji's love for the hand-spinning of yarn and the hand weaving of Khadi cloth again indicates his grasp of the problems of industrialisation. He felt that all Indians, especially the peasants in the villages, should use their spare hours to weave Khadi cloth. The central fact of Khaddar is to made society self-supporting for its clothing. It is well-known that for the Indian climate the Khadi cloth is the best suited. It is non-polluting and much cheaper in terms of energy use and investment than the mill cloth. He pointed out that the destruction of hand-spinning has brought on slavery, pauperism and disappearance of fine artistic talents which were once well expressed in the wonderful fabric of India, which was the envy of the world. Gandhiji promoted Khadi to promote innovative talent, creativity employment and dignity of labour.

Gandhi and Food Security

Mahatma Gandhi, following Lord Buddha and other ancient Indian philosophers, practiced and preached vegetarianism with great belief and conviction. Modern ecologists, too, are advocating harvesting of food from primary production level, i.e., at the level of green plants, to get maximum food harvest, in preference to animal food products which on an average provide less than ten percent of the primary food energy.

The Gandhian philosophy of non-violence and vegetarianism is highly supportive of Nature conservation and ecological balance which have been jeopardised by the industrial culture.

Gandhi and Biodiversity Conservation

Gandhiji was a great lover of wild life and a champion of biodiversity conservation. He was of the view animals and other creatures have as much right to live as humans have. He observed, "I do believe that all God's creatures have the right to live as much as we have." He elaborated further, "It is an arrogant assumption to say that human beings are lords and masters of the lower creation. On the contrary, being endowed with greater things in life, they are trustees of lower animal kingdom." These observations amply demonstrate the Gandhian approach to biodiversity and beautifully summarise the main tenets of Biodiversity Convention. Gandhian concept of non-violence was not limited to human society only but it is holistic, including nature as a whole.

Concept of Freedom

In modern industrialised society, great emphasis is being placed on freedom. This is a fundamental right of every human being and provides the opportunity for individual growth and development. This basic concept, we are afraid, has often, not been properly understood. People take freedom to mean anything they please. Such an interpretation of freedom has lead to many complex social problems. This is not the true meaning of freedom. Freedom guarantees opportunity to individuals, but at the same time it also lays heavy responsibility on the individual to conduct himself rationally. Lord Buddha and Gandhiji have also laid emphasis on freedom, by which they mean freedom from wants, passion and greed to enjoy a fuller life.

In the name of freedom or modernisation, people in industrial societies are demanding more and more for less amount of work. Schumacher (1973) presents a very revealing analysis of the situation in the following way:

> "There is universal agreement that a fundamental source of wealth is human labour. How, the modern economist has been brought up to consider 'labour' or work as little more than a necessary evil. From the point of view of the workman, it is a 'dis-utility'; to work is to make a sacrifice of one's leisure and

* [At operational level, it is not difficult to visualize that self-sufficiency and innovative use of diverse local resources promote networking of entire community including creation of new jobs, social economic and communal well-being.]

comfort, it is earned wages are a kind of compensation for the sacrifice. Hence, the ideal from the point of view of the employer, is to have output without employees, and the ideal of view of the employer, is to have output without employees, and the ideal from the point of view of the employee is to have income without employment."

Gandhi and Human Labour

For Gandhiji human labour represented a great resource. He regarded it.

As a great potential capital, which must be utilised to its fullest (jobs for all people), if society wants to realise its greatest potential. Security against unemployment should be the first criteria of every healthy society. If this essential objective is sacrificed, then all other measures of economic development cannot bear fruit.

It is a "right" which people expect without pondering over the responsibilities which are inseparable from any form of right. The Gandhian philosophy does not approve the current values of our industrial civilisation. Gandhiji argues that "civilisation is a mode of conduct which points out to man the path of duty. Performance of duty and observance of morality are convertible terms. To observe morality is to attain mastery over out mind and our passion."

Promoter of Individuality

Let us now examine the relevance of Gandhiji's message in the context of individuals and institutions. His ideas may look ridiculous if we do not have in mind the fact that his approach to any problem presupposes that man is superior to the system that he has evolved and the institutions he has created. He asserts: "The individual is the one supreme consideration. I look upon an increase of the power of the state with the greatest fear, because, although while apparently doing good by minimising exploitation, it does the greatest harm to mankind by destroying individuality which lies at the root of all progress." "I have discovered that man is superior to the system he propounded." He believed in the innate goodness of man.

A Simple Philosophy

The concept of sustainable development, advocated by the world Commission of Development and Environment, has been interpreted variously by different people making it difficult to operationalise. Gandhiji believed in "Plain Living and High Thinking" and emphasised that man's happiness really lies in contentment. He who is discontented, however much he possess, becomes a slave to his desires." The Gandhian philosophy is simple, unambiguous and easy to understand by one and all. The relevance of his teachings is not restricted to Indian society but they have universal importance for fostering harmonious relationship between man and nature which is necessary to promote environment-friendly World Order.

7

Gandhi and Environmentalism

Ashok S. Chousalkar

Western World came to realize the importance of environmental issues after publication of the report of the Club of Rome in 1972. Before the West was enjoying its unique prosperity, which was achieved with the help of new developments in science and technology, theory of modernization, philosophy of rationalism and expanding world market. The welfare state policies in Western Europe greatly contributed to the growth and prosperity of the West. But the problem of protection of environment caused a deep concern as scholars like Andre Gory declared that both growth-oriented capitalism and socialism are dead thereby challenging the sustainability of Western model of social development.[1]

The model was based on the utilitarian philosophy of J. Bentham which believed in Maximization of pleasure and minimization of pain. It held that the individual should maximize his powers and capacities. The post-Second World War years saw prosperity and growth in the West. The experts from West argued that this model of development would ensure minimum level of living standards for the people, banish poverty and bring about economic development of the backward countries.

But by the beginning of 1970, it was realized by many perceptive observers that this type of development could not continue for a long time because it could bring about a total destruction of human civilization. Hence, it was said; "oceans are becoming sterile, soil infertile and air unbreathable. Capitalist growth is now encountering not only economic limits but physical ones."[2] Mahatma Gandhi was one of the first political thinkers who exposed the weaknesses of modern civilization and capitalist model of development. He warned the West that this type of development could not continue for a long time. He questioned the philosophical assumptions of modern development theory. In this article, Mahatma Gandhi's theory of environmentalism is critically analyzed.

I

Modern civilization gave birth to capitalist model of development. This model was based on a theory of man, which maintained that man was a rational being and, with the help of reason, he could decide what was in his interest. Every human being stove hard to maximize his interest. Hence, therefore was competition between different human beings. Independent, self-sufficing and rational individual sought to maximize his powers to live good and happy life. His concept of good life was essentially utilitarian, which posited that every one in this world tried to maximize his pleasures and minimize his pains. Pleasures could be maximized with the help of material goods, material goods could be secured from the markets which were free and competitive of each according to his abilities. Markets became the operative basis of development theory.

Capitalism expanded markets, which gave birth to colonialism and imperialism. The greed of capitalism could not be confined to national boundaries. Capitalists wanted profits. For that purpose, there was over production, and in order to sustain it, the cause of over consumption was promoted. The opulent lifestyle of the people in the rich countries was oblivious of its consequences. Capitalist model exploited natural resources of the world, caused environmental pollution of land, water and air.

Modern/Western civilization employed the institution of the state to facilitate the development of capitalist economy. The state took the help of science and technology to centralize all powers in its hands and hastened the process of political integration. The state channalised public resources to provide capital to the private industries. It encouraged private appropriation of social production. It successfully oppressed all the voices of dissent and legitimized its authority with the help of elected representative institutions. This state was called nation-state because all parochial ideas were invoked to bring about national integration of the people. Nationalism was not only an instrument of repression in the internal affairs of the state, but also an instrument for waging wars against neighbouring countries. Nationalism was responsible for the production of weapons of mass destruction, including the most dangerous of them—nuclear weapons. Thus, nationalism was the most destructive of passions.

II

Modernization theory was the most dominant paradigm of development during the first decade after Second World War. Belief in its efficacy was reinforced because of the relative prosperity the West had enjoyed during this period due to the success of welfare policies and Keynesian economics. But there emerged voices of dissent. There were three sources of criticism. First, modernization theory was criticized by the Frankfurt School and the New Left movement for its perverse positivism and regimenation of the people. Secondly, the theory was criticized by the scholars from Third World countries who argued that this policy was responsible for underdevelopment in the development countries. They blamed the First World countries for environmental degradation. They pointed out that the affluent sections of Western society were enjoying unprecedented living standards by exploiting natural resources of Third World counties. This policy destroyed their agriculture, denuded their jungles, polluted their oceans and rivers and depleted their natural resources. Thirdly, the environmentalists had begun to criticize the Western model after 1970's for giving birth to a deceased society. They argued that the economically advanced societies were undermining the infrastructure of the planet. Oceans were becoming sterile, soil infertile and air unbreathable. It is no longer enough to refrain from consuming more; it is time to being consuming less."[3] It was their argument that human activity found in natural world has reached its external limits and if this limit was disregarded, new forms of diseases would take birth and quality of life would decrease despite increasing levels of material consumtion.[4]

There are different versions of environmentalism such as the resource conservationists, environmental protectionists, green political theorists, eco-feminists and deep green theorists. Eco-centrism had acquired greater acceptability. It had, therefore, emotional 'romantic' appeal, an ethical aspect, and a rational scientific one.[5] environmentalism has completely changed the nature of debate in political theory and laid stress on totality and inter-relationship of different problems. Its viewpoint was global and communitarian.[6]

Adherents of environmentalism wanted to change the agenda of social development by inverting tools and technologies. They strengthened existing social relations hence, they pleaded that there was a need for development of technologies and methods of production which could be:

1. used and controlled at the level of neighborhood and community,
2. used to increase economic autonomy for local and regional collectivities,
3. not harmful to the environment, and
4. compatible with the exercise of joint control by producers and consumers over the products and production.

Finally, they stood for non-nuclearisation of polity.[7] it was the argument of environmentalists that total domination of nature resulted in domination of people by the few people who had control over techniques and technologies.[8]

Thus, in the West, the problem of protection of

environments has become an important problem as the environmentalists were trying to find out an alternative path of development which questioned the basis of the morally empty and hedonistic culture.[9] It is interesting to point out that the Mahatma Gandhi was one of the first thinkers who pointed out the dangers of capitalist model of growth and development.

III

Gandhi was critical of the West for ignoring vital aspects of human civilization. He had seen through the nature of English colonialism and evil effects of modernization. He blamed the West for ignoring the future. He wrote, "A wise man utilizes the present to undertake an act of production as it were. An ordinary man treats the present as an act of consumption. People of the West are new beginning to realize that they have sacrificed the future for the sake of present."[10] Hence, he asked Indians not to blindly imitate the West.

In his famous book *'Hind Swaraj'* Gandhi questioned the moral basis of Western civilization of argued that the problem of development should be seen through a total perspective. Gandhi wrote this book in 1907. *'Hind Swaraj'* or Indian Home Rule was Gandhi's political testament and throughout his life, he did not change his basic ideas and convictions. Gandhi's critique of Western civilization could be divided into the following 4 topics:

1. Gandhi's criticism of the ideology of modernization.
2. His criticism of modern civilization.
3. His criticism of railways, lawyers, etc.
4. His criticism of parliamentary democracy.

Gandhi's was critical of modern Western philosophy which was based on rationalism and utilitarianism. Gandhi was a believer in the spiritual values propounded by all major religions of the world in general and the religious values taught by the Geeta and Bhakti movement in particular. He was a 'Vedantin' who wanted to attain salvation or 'moksha.' He believed in the unity of man and held that all human beings were basically good, and because of that goodness only, man was ready for sacrifice and renunciation of wealth. He had the ability to bring about moral upliftment and enrichment by imbibing the spirit of non-violence and performance of duties as selfless action. Hence, he did not believe in the theory that self-interest was of prime consideration of man. Gandhi criticized rationalism and wrote, "Rationalism is hideous monster when it claims for itself omnipotence. Attribution of omnipotence to worship of stock and stone believing it to be God. I plead not for suppression of reason but an appreciation of its inherent limits.[11] He believed that faith transcended reason. He held that non-violence was the law of life and historically, man was nothing else but history of conquest of non-violence over violence. Human nature everywhere was working upward.[12] He did not subscribe to the theory of life struggle and held that service, sacrifice, caring for others and self less action were qualities of human beings. Relationship between man and man and man and nature was not competitive, but was essentially cooperative. He contended that the world would not survive for a day if it was believed that everybody was at war with each other and only the fittest survived. Gandhi did not take at nature as an adversary of man. He argued that nature was living and life giving source of water, food and air. Nature produced enough to meet the needs of all people, but not enough to satisfy the greed of everyone.[13] He wanted human beings to be compassionate with nature and not try to conquer it. Man was the maker of his destiny in the sense that he had the freedom of choice. His actions and results were governed by the law of causality. Hence, it was necessary to establish humane relations with nature.[14]

In his book *'Hind Swaraj'* Gandhi had criticized modern civilization and called it satanical. He held that India should not copy England because the condition of England was miserable. This was not due to the peculiar fault of Englan but she was reeling under modern civilization. It was civilization in name only. Under it the nations of Europe were getting degraded. They were promoting bodily welfare in the name of modernity. English people wore better clothes, they were better fed, they had better dwelling units, but were scarcely happy. Modern civilization had bred inequality, violence, divisiveness and laziness in society. Scientific innovations and inventions could not be considered true test of civilization when the condition of thousands of workers in England was worse than that of beasts. It was devoid of religion and morality. People lacked physical courage. Half a million women in England were slaving in factories or in similar institutions for a pittance.[15]

Gandhi said that the civilization was eating into the vitals of the English nation, but the English people did not want to abandon it because they wanted to expand commerce. Money was their god. They sought to convert whole world into a vast market for their goods.[16] It was his contention that India was not conquered by the English nation but she was conquered by modern civilization. It had introduced railways, lawyers, doctors and machines in India. Railways helped the English to spread and maintain their rule in India. Without the lawyers and judges, British rule in India could not survive for a day. They had enslaved India, accentuated Hindu-Muslim dissension and confirmed British authority. The different professions that arose taught immorality. He wrote, "Petty pleaders manufacture disputes. Their touts like so many leaches suck the blood of the poor people."[17] He held that the profession of doctors was equally parasitical as they were after money. They were scarcely interested in the welfare of the people. Gandhi criticized modern education for not developing the moral character of the students.

While criticizing modern civilization, Gandhi had criticized machinery. He pointed out that Indian handlooms were destroyed by machinery. It had given birth to modern capitalism and the factory system. Factory owners were amassing wealth by making people poor. He maintained that Indian mill owners would be as exploitative as the American or European owners.[18] He was of the opinion that machinery was useless because it impoverished a large number of people and made them dependent. It was against the spirit of 'Swadeshi.'

Gandhi held that industrialism was the result of modern civilization. Similarly, modern European state and parliamentary institutions were the instruments of modern civilization. He held that British parliament was not the mother of parliaments but a sterile woman and a prostitute. British parliament on its own accord had done not a single good thing, without outside pressure. It was like a prostitute because it worked under the control of ministers who changed from time to time. In the British parliament, honest people were not elected and elected members always thought about their own interest. It was either fear or self-interest that guided their actions. They always thought about their own re-election in the next round. It was a talking shop of the world. Members voted for their own party without a thought. A lot of money and time was spent in its functioning. It was a costly toy of the nation.[19] He thought that Prime. Minister and Minister were partisan and they imposed their will on the people. For English voters, newspapers were their Bible.! They were often dishonest.

After criticizing the Westminister model of democracy, Gandhi criticized modern state and argued that it was based on violence and repression. It was based on the principle of majority rule. But each and every time the decision of majority was not correct, and there was always a lurking danger of tyranny of majority. He did not approve of the fangled notion that the laws passed by the constituted authority should be blindly followed, even if they were against our conscience.[20] Gandhi argued that it was unmanly to obey unjust laws. Disobedience of unjust laws was the key to 'Swaraj'.

Gandhi contended that his 'Swaraj' would be different from English rule as he did not want India to copy the West. We should not aspire to establish English rule without Englishmen.[21] He gave the example of Italy to show that Mazzini's dream was not realized, though Italy became free of foreign domination. It became Italy of princes and nobles and the rich and not of the people. He pointed out that the rule by Indian princes was no better and just because they were born Indians their rule could not be considered 'Swadeshi.' He wrote, "My patriotism does not teach me that

I am to allow people to crushed under the heel of Indian princes if only the English retire. If I have the power, I should resist the tyranny of Indian princes just as much as that of the English."[22] He also criticized Japan for aping West and playing their game in the Second World War.[23]

IV

Gandhi's critique of moderm civilization was total in the sense that he saw different units of modern civilization inter-connected and inter-related. He said that blind pursuit of this would cause untold miseries. When Gandhi was writing this critique, the entire world was dazzled by new inventions of science and technology. He contended that the Indian civilization was a true civilization because it avoided mistakes of Greece and Rome, and survived due to its sound foundations. According to Gandhi, civilization was that mode of conduct which pointed out to man the path of duty. Performance of duty and observance of morality were convertible terms. To observe morality meant to observe control over mind and passions. Indian civilization believed in containing wants because "the more we indulge in our passions, the more unbridled they become. Our ancestors, therefore, set a limit to our indulgence. They saw that happiness was largely a mental condition. A man is not necessarily happy because he is rich."[24] Gandhi argued that India did not have life corroding competition as each individual followed his own profession. It was not that Indians could not have invented machinery, but they knew that, because of that, the people would become its slaves and would lose moral fiber. Hence, they laid stress on physical labor. They knew that large cities were dens of vice and the people would not enjoy happiness; hence, they lived in small villages. The cities were centers of exploitation of poor people. They did not respect kings and princes and gave more importance to 'Rishis and Fakirs'. The common people lived happily and followed their agricultural profession.[25]

Gandhi accepted that there were certain defects in Indian civilization and he contended that attempts were being made to remove these defects. He wrote, "In no part of the world, and under no civilization have all men attained perfection. The tendency of Indian civilization is to elevate the moral being."[26] Thus, Gandhi sought to face the challenge of modern civilization with the help of Indian civilization and questioned most of the assumptions of the former. It was his contention that despite our progress in the fields of science and technology, man had not become really happy in the West and it had caused untold miseries to the countries of the Third World because of its colonialism and exploitation of natural resources. This civilization was not good for the West and it was a curse for the people of poor countries. But Gandhi knew that the old Indian civilization could not be revived in toto, and a new political alternative would have to be put forward to replace the capitalist model of development.

V

Gandhi put forward his alternative path of development which was based on the following five principles:

1. New philosophy of man.
2. Decentralized economic development.
3. The concept of Gram Swaraj.
4. The concept of Satyagraha.
5. World peace and resolution of conflicts through peaceful means.

Gandhi was opposed to the modern Western philosophy that laid stress on rationalism and empiricism. He effused to accord the highest status to reason and science. He was essentially spiritual and the attainment of liberation was the goal of his life. He did not think that man should rob nature to achieve happiness. It was his contention that the essence of teaching of the 'Geeta' was non-violence and performance of one's own duty in the spirit of detachment and self-control. He did not favour indulgence in the pleasure of senses and wanted man to pursuer higher moral goals of life. While criticizing capitalist economy, he wrote,

"An economics that inculcates Mammon's worship, that enables strong to amass wealth at the expense of the weak is false and dismal science. It spells death. True economics stands for social justice and moral values. The people with full refrigerators, crowded clothes, closets, cars in every garage and radios in every room could still be psychologically insecure and unhappy. What shall it avail a man, if he gain human dignity to lose one's own individuality and become a mere cong in the machine. I want every individual to become full blooded member of the society."[27] Gandhi thus, put forward a new theory of man who preserved his autonomy and independence in relation to state, society, economy and nature.

Gandhi opposed modern capitalism and industrialism. He held that industrialism caused exploitation of Third World countries by the rich Western countries. It divided people into rich and poor and allowed concentration of power in the hands of a few rich people. Industrialism was nothing else but control of the majority by a small minority. This small minority exploited markets, destroyed competition in the market and reduced a large number of people to the status of unemployment.[28] He held that machinery was harmful. What machinery does could be done easily by millions of hands, otherwise unoccupied. Mechanization was good when the hands were too few for the work intended to be accomplished. Gandhi advocated spinning by Charkha and Khadi to give them independence and employment and to prevent exploitation of poor people by rich people and exploitation of poor countries by rich countries. He wrote, "(Khadi) touches life of every single individual, makes him feel a glow with the possession of power that had within himself and makes him proud of his identity with every drop of the ocean of Indian humanity."[29]

Along with Khadi, Gandhi supported the cause of nature cure and opposed modern medicines. He was of the view that all ailments were due to violation of laws of nature and conforming to those laws was the road to health. By shedding 'modern way of life' man could gain health of body and mind. Nature cure taught patients a right way of living which would not only cure them of their particular ailment, but save them from falling ill in future. The ordinary physician was interested in the study of diseases but nature curist was more interested in the study in the health. Eradication of patient's illness under nature cure marked only the beginning of the way of life in which there was no room for illness and disease. Nature cure was, thus, a way of life and not a course of treatment as it is aimed at purification of body, mind and soul.[30]

Gandhi was opposed to Western model of economic development because it gave birth to inequality. For him economic equality meant abolition of difference between capital and labour, bridging of gulf between rich and poor. This could be done by leveling down few rich and leveling up semi-starved naked millions of Indian.[31] Gandhi maintained that this change could only be brought about with non-violent methods which would make this change permanent. Thus, 'Swaraj' had to be built brick by brick with corporate self-help.[32]

In Gandhi's theory of environmentalism, an alternative model of economic development was enunciated on the basis of his concept of 'Swadeshi' as well as his concept of decentralization of economic power.

'Swadeshi' was India's answer to British colonialism and long before Gandhi entered Indian politics, it was preached by stalwarts like Dadabhai Naoroji, Sri Aurobindo and Tilak. Gandhi gave a new meaning to it and claimed that 'Swadeshi' meant self-dependent economy. Gandhi defined Swadeshi as "that spirit in us which restricts us to the use and service of our immediate surroundings to the exclusion of the more remote."[33] That meant a recognition of the special duty and obligation that one owed towards one's immediate environment. A supporter of 'Swadeshi' carefully study his environment and try to help his neighbour. He would not allow himself to be lured by the distant scene and run to the ends of the earth for service throwing out of gear his little world of neighbours and dependents. He hastened to add that 'Swadeshi' did not build a Chinese wall round itself. It only recognized and fact that all living beings were related to one another and everyone must serve according to his capacity.[34] It involved development of one's own surroundings, keeping in harmony with the concept of universal good. It did not believe in using mass produced cheap imported goods and letting millions of one's own countrymen get ruined. It was not a cult of exclusiveness or narrow parochialism. It believed in expanding the circles of friendship and mutual help.

Gandhi held that one could serve whole humanity through service of one's own neighbours; the only condition being that the service should be selfless and did not exploit other human beings. This duty of service would gather momentum, would snowball and encircle whole earth. Gandhi said, "A drop torn from ocean perishes without doing any good. As a part of ocean, it shares the glory of carrying on its bosom whole fleets of mighty ships."[35]

His concept of 'Swadeshi' was the basis of his passion for village and cottage industry. He was critical of destructive economic policies of the West because they laid stress on developing raw materials rather than utilizing manpower, which was abundant. If concentrated power in the hands of the few who rose to power and fortune at the expense of the many. Hence, Gandhi argued that so for as India was concerned, the real planning should consist in the full utilization of her manpower and distribution of her raw products to her numerous villages for being manufactured into goods instead of being sent out of villages or exported from the country to be repurchased as finished articles at a high premium.[36]

When Gandhi went to England in the early thirties, he was asked some pertinent questions about mass production. Gandhi pointed out that the mania of mass production was responsible for the world crisis. Gandhi's arguments against mass production were based on following points:

1. Mass production did not ensure proper distribution of production in the society.
2. Even if mass production was carried on in a decentralized manner, the real power would come from selected centers making the people dependent on their decisions.

3. The European powers used machinery to exploit so called weaker and unorganized races of the world, thus making contribution to global inequality.
4. One could control evil effects of mass production by following the policy of producing that much of goods which were needed by the people. But it should not be continued for securing more gold and wealth for the country.
5. Distribution could be equalized only when production was localized. But this could not be done so long as capitalists wanted to tap markets of the world for the sale of the goods they had produced.
6. He was not opposed to mass production as such. Mass production was desirable at peoples' own houses using simple machinery. Thus, even mass production could be localized.

Thus, equality was a major concern of Gandhi and he opposed modern civilization for its partiality towards the privileged few. Hence, he wrote, "I hate privileges and monopoly. Whatever can not be shared with the masses is taboo to me."[37]

Gahdni laid stress on the growth of agriculture and handicraft industries. He did not think that cities represented true India. He was of the opinion that cities exploited hinterland for the benefit of the rich few living in the urban areas.

Gandhi drew a picture of his concept of ideal 'Gram Swaraj' and pointed out that it would be a casteless and classless society where everybody would get according to his need and capacity. There would be no high or law and all services had equal status and carried equal wages instead of personal advancement, self-expression and self-realization through service of society was the goal of the people. Everybody was a toiler with ample leisure, opportunities and facilities for education and culture. It was a world of cottage crafts and intense small scale forming co-operatives where there was no room for caste and communalism. He wrote, "It is the world of 'Swadeshi' in which the economic frontiers are drawn closer but the bounds of individual freedom are enlarged to the maximum limit. There is no conflict between part and the whole; no danger of nationalism becoming narrow selfish or aggressive."[38]

Decentralization of power was a necessary condition for Gandhi to reduce the power of state. He held that due to centralization of power and force, which was based on violence, the modern state had become enemy of the rights of the people. In the *'Hind Swaraj'*, Gandhi raised his voice against the Western model of state building and asked Indians not to imitate it. He wrote, "the state represents violence in a concentrated and organized form. The individual has a soul, but as the state is a soulless machine, it can never be weaned from violence to which it owes its very existence."[39] He wanted to reduce the power of the state and put it on sufferance.

In order to reduce the power and help of the state, Gandhi devised the method of Panchayat democracy, which gave decision-making powers to people at the grassroots level. He thought that it was superior to parliamentary form of government. His Panchayat democracy was based on the following principles:

1. Village republic will be self-reliant and it will produce food, milk, cotton and cloth.
2. Everybody will be literate and village will maintain school, theatre, public hall, playgrounds, etc.
3. Every activity will be carried out on a co-operative basis. Village will supply clean water and maintain water works, public wells, etc.
4. There will be no castes and untouchability.
5. Non-violence with its technique of non-cooperation will have the sanction of the village community.
6. There will be compulsory service of village guards selected by rotation.
7. Panchayat of five work as executive, legislature and judiciary of the village republic.
8. All the decisions will be taken unanimously.[40]

The major cause of inequality in the society was the existence of three-fold differences in it. The three are: (1) division between physical and mental labour, (2) division between rural and urban areas, and (3) division between agriculture and industry. Gandhi sought to bridge the gap in his 'Gram Swaraj.' He saw no difference between physical and mental labour and held that everybody should earn his bread through the sweat of his brow. The difference between urban and rural areas could be bridged by preventing excessive mass production, by preventing establishment of big industrial units and by decentralizing economic activities. His concept of cottage and village industries was specifically designed to reduce the gap between industry and agriculture as he sought to have a fine interweaving between them.

In Gandhi's ideal state of 'Swaraj,' people would enjoy all rights and the weakest would have the same authority as the strongest. He wrote, "the real 'Swaraj' would come not by the acquisition of authority by a few but by the acquisition of capacity by all the in resisting authority when abused. The capacity to resist will depend on the independence of spirit which such a disciplined corporate life would generate."[41]

Gandhi's village republics will be the unit of public life. "In this structure composed of innumerable villages, there will be ever widening and never ascending circles. Life will not be a pyramid with the apex sustained by the bottom but it will be an oceanic circle whose centre will be individual always ready to perish for the village. The whole becomes one composed of individuals, never aggressive in their arrogance but ever humble, sharing the majesty of oceanic circle of which they are integral unit. The outermost circumference will not yield power to crush the inner circle but will give strength to all within and will derive its strength from within."[42]

Gandhi wanted individual to enjoy full rights and authority and sought to limit the power of state. He held that with the help of civil disobedience or 'Satyagraha' the people would be in a position to challenge the might of the state. The purpose of 'Satyagraha' was to non-violently oppose wrong policies of the state, purge social and political institutions of its evils and ailments, and assist the wrong doer in realizing his mistakes and to encourage his to affect a change of heart. Gandhi always held that 'Satyagraha' was the weapon of the strong and fearless.

Gandhi was opposed to violence and war, he criticized modern nationalism for spreading the poison of hatred. Science of war led to dictatorship pure and simple.[43] Gandhi argued that those who stood for peace should not succumb to the pressure of the tyrant and always offer their services for peaceful resolution of disputes because war and conflict ultimately did not solve the problem. But peace could not be bought under duress. The peace Europe gained at Munich was a triumph of violence.[44]

In the preceding pages, we have briefly discussed the political theory of environmentalism as propounded by Gandhi. It is to the credit of Gandhi that he visualized most of the arguments of environmentalists and presented a blue print of his alternative model of development which took care of most of the concerns of modern environmentalism.

VI

Modern environmentalists propounded important principles which included localized production, limited use of machines, economic autonomy for regional and local collectivities, exercise of joint control by producers and consumers over the products and production process and opposition to war and nuclear weapons. If we carefully go through Gandhi's ideas on economy, polity, war and peace, we would realize the Gandhi sought to implement many of these ideas in his social and political life. It was his contention that environment could not be protected in isolation or by taking some remedial measures, but ignoring the basic problems of development. Unless, the existing capitalist system, based on exploitation of the markets and excess mass production was challenged and its policies reversed, it would not be possible for us to prevent degradation of nature and the ruin of ecology. Centralization of power, repressive state machine, instrumental use of science and technology and perverse interpretation of rationalism provided the base to modern civilization which Gandhi considered a curse. He was right in saying that the use of huge and complicated machines caused inequality in the society because modern methods of production helped the rich. It was his argument that nature should be treated properly. He put forward alternative methods such as nature cure, village sanitation, Panchayat democracy, Gram Swaraj, Khadi and cottage industries, co-operation farming and decentralization of political power and the method of Satyagraha based on the principle of democracy.

It was to the benefit of Gandhi that he belonged to the country where different forms of production existed and there was ample scope for making experiments. The West had destroyed its plural cultural forms; hence, it did not enjoy this advantage. Gandhi made a creative use of different forms of economics, politics and culture in Indian civilization so as to put forward and alternative. Gandhi praised Indian civilization, but he did not want to resuscitate the old civilization in toto as he knew its weaknesses. He wanted to change it from within by introducing the spirit of freedom and autonomy in it. Thus, village republic of his dreams was very clean, with well laid out roads and all important facilities for education and recreation. It consisted of well-built but simple houses, supply of clean water and facilities of sanitation for all.

Environmentalism has raised certain important question about sustainable development and the limits of growth because we have to husband our natural resources carefully. But both the things are not possible unless we decide to contain our wants and revise our concept of progress and material pleasure. Gandhi agreed that minimum basic needs and decent living standards had to be given to the people. He was opposed to excessive indulgence in the material pleasures because its costs were exorbitant. Gandhi's political theory was essentially green political theory as it laid stress on sustainable development, containment of wants and peace. Gandhi's contribution to green theory was his concept of Satyagraha or civil disobedience which could be used to firth against injustice. Peace movements world over should take note of this fact and use this weapon against unjust regimes.

Politics of ecology is still in the stage of infancy. The discipline of Political Science is dominated by the supporters of modernization. The supporters of environmentalism do not have the advantage of Gandhi who had waged an ideological war against British imperialism. Hence, we can say that their politics is yet to be tested against the most entrenched opponents. Therefore, when their struggle for establishment of a just and sustainable society and world order begins in right earnest, they will have no body else but Gandhi to fall back upon.

Notes and References

1. A. Gory, "Ecology and Freedom in S.E. Browned ed., Twentieth Century Political Theory: A Reader, (New York: Routledge, 1977), p. 345.
2. *Ibid.*, p. 343.
3. *Ibid.*
4. *Ibid.*, p. 346.
5. M. Clark, "Environmentalism" in R. Bellamy ed., Theories and Concepts of Politics: An Introduction (Manchester and New York: Manchester University Press, 1993), 247.
6. *Ibid.*, pp. 256-7.
7. Gory, *op. cit.*, p. 350.
8. *Ibid.*, p. 351.
9. S.S. Pandharipande, Anvaya (Pune: Partima Prakashan, 1995), pp. 47-75.
10. P.N. Seth, Theory and Practice of Environmentalism: Green Plus Gandhi (Ahmedabad: Gujarat Vidyapeeth, 1999), p. 60.
11. R.J. Terchek, Gandhi: Struggling for Autonomy, (New Delhi: Vistaar, 2001), pp. 79-80.
12. Pyarelal, Mahatma Gandhi: The Last Phase, Vol. 1, Book 1, (Ahmedabad: Navajivan, 1966), p. 114.
13. Seth, *op. cit.*, p. 66.
14. Pyarelal, *op. cit.*, Vol. 2, pp. 67-68.
15. M.K. Gandhi, *Hind Swaraj* or Indian Home Rule (Ahmedabad: Navajivan, 2003), pp. 31-33.
16. *Ibid.*, p. 36.
17. *Ibid.*, pp. 48-49.
18. *Ibid.*, p. 84.
19. *Ibid.*, p. 28.
20. *Ibid.*, p. 92.
21. *Ibid.*, p. 26.

22. *Ibid.*, pp. 58-59.
23. Pyarelal, *op. cit.*, Vol. 1, p. 114.
24. Gandhi, *op. cit.*, p. 53.
25. *Ibid.*, p. 54.
26. *Ibid.*, p. 55.
27. Louis Fisher, The Life of Mahatma Gandhi, 8th End (Mumbai: Bharatiya Vidhya Bhavan, 2003), p. 422.
28. M.K. Gandhi, Khadi: Why and How? (Ahmedabad: Navajivan, 2003), pp. 18-21.
29. D.G. Tendulkar, Mahatma: Left of Mohandas Karamchand Ghandi, Vol. 6, (New Delhi: Publications Division, Government of India, 1969), p. 20.
30. Pyarelal, *op. cit.*, Vol. 1, pp. 139-40.
31. Tendulkar, *op. cit.*, p. 26.
32. *Ibid.*, p. 27.
33. Pyarelal, *op. cit.*, Vol. 1, Part 2, p. 187.
34. *Ibid.*
35. *Ibid.*, p. 189.
36. *Ibid.*, p. 187.
37. Tendulkar, *op. cit.*, Vol. 3, p. 136.
38. Pyarelal, *op. cit.*, p. 181.
39. N.K Bose, Selections from Gandhi (Ahmedabad: Navajivan, 1957), p. 42
40. D. Joshi, Gandhi on Villages (Bombay: Manibhavan Sangrahalaya, 2002), p. 3.
41. Tendulkar, *op. cit.*, Vol. 2, pp. 168-69.
42. *Ibid.*, Vol. 7, p. 168.
43. R. Duncan ed., The Writings of Gandhi (New Delhi: Rupa and Co., 1993), pp. 79-80.
44. *Ibid.*, p. 79.

8

Indian Environmentalism and Gandhian Values: The Relevance of Satyagraha in Contemporary Environmental Movements in India

Sarmistha Pattanaik

INTRODUCTION

Environmentalism in India, like in most parts of South Asia, began mainly as an integral part of local level activism for broad social justice. The spontaneous resistance and protests by the affected parties, when and where the lives or livelihoods of a number of people or communities were threatened by the environmental impacts of activities initiated by others, came to be identified as 'enviromentalism'.[1] The beginnings of the environmental movement in India are conventionally dated to the early 1970s. Beginning with the Chipko movement in the Garhwal Himalayas in the 1970s and reaching global prominence with the movement against the Narmada dams in the next two decades, India has witnessed a series of popular movements in defense of community rights to natural resources. In many of these movements of the present time, environmental activists have relied heavily on Gandhian techniques of non-violent protest or satyagraha, and have drawn abundantly on Gandhian polemic against heavy industrialization. Gandhi has been the commonly acknowledged patron saint of the Indian environmental movement. He was the principle architect of India's independence and nationalism and set his head and heart to stop the blatant exploitation of India's people and its natural resources.

Gandhi and Ecology

Ideas of environmental consciousness, ecological understanding, environmental conservation, sustainability and survival are very much found in Gandhi's philosophy, teachings and ideology. Much before the environmental consciousness began to expand in modern times, Gandhi and brought out a manifesto of counter culture in his *'Hind Swaraj'* or 'Indian Home Rule' in 1909.[2] His *'Hind Swaraj'* is a manifesto warning against the mad race after civilization of modernization characterized by materialism and a distorted model of development. Today, environmental hazards pose a greater danger to our survival than even the nuclear stockpile. The Stockholm conference in 1972 had proclaimed that "the protection of the environment is a major issued which affects the well-being of people and economic development throughout the World." It is, therefore, here that the teachings of the Mahatma become increasingly meaningful and relevant. The present paper tries to explore the Gandhian values and principles of non-violence or 'Satyagraha' in relation to nature. "Nature is to be approached with a sense of reverence" according to Gandhi. In fact, Gandhi has not said anything specific on environmental degradation and alternative solutions although it had become a problem even during his period. For instance, he himself was never associated with forest satyagrahas, but his name was frequently invoked by peasants and rebels. We can find the ways and solutions in his writings, his speeches and his life. Once, when asked for a message to humanity, Gandhi said, "My life is my message."

Gandhi was a practicing yogi, although he never claimed to be so. The various formal disciplines like yamas and niyamas pertain to environment and ethics or resource use. In fact, these were actually first practiced and then preached by the Mahatma. The yamas are ethical commandments relating to human behaviors in relation to other humans and living creatures and non-living resources. Essentially, these are a set of don'ts; the five yamas are: no-violence (ahimsa) towards all animate and in-animate creation, truth (satya), shunning the use of materials obtained by illegitimate means and avoiding destruction vandalism (asteya), celibacy (brahmacharya) because humans need to keep their numbers in check, otherwise demand on resources will increase, and lastly, not coveting or amassing materials and wealth beyond one's requirement (aparigraha). Gandhi practiced all the yamas, encouraged indigenous capability and local self-reliance (swadeshi), self-rule and local self-governance (swaraj) at the level of village and welfare of the weakest (antyodaya) leading to welfare of all (sarvodaya).. It is said that 'if environment is to be saved from degradation we have to avoid or limit the use of machinery.' That is why Gandhi's promotion of Khadi and Village Industries has become more relevant today than during the freedom struggle.

A Gandhian ecology, therefore, begins with individual and collective self-rule (swaraj), premised upon truth, non-violence and self-sacrificial actions or (tapas). It insists upon respect and compassion for all creatures and for nature itself. If encourages economic self-reliance and self-sufficiency at the local (village, town, or neighborhood) level. Gandhian ecology addresses the practical environmental and economic issues of our present day grounded in ultimate values and truth seeking.[3]

The Organizing Legacy of Mahatma Gandhi—Satyagraha

After Gautam Buddha, Gandhi has been the prophet of non-violence and truth-sticking to the truth (satyagraha) even under greatest and provocation. He has been acknowledged as an unquestioned apostle of applied human ecology. Gandhi argued that no one could know with certainty the absolute truth, and that without such certainty, we could not presume to punish our opponent by using violence. Self-suffering, another important element of Satyagraha, guarantees the sincerity of the satyagrahi's own opinions, and restraints the person from asserting ambiguous truths.[4]

Gandhi believed that there is divinity in all life, and a fundamental unity in divinity. His faith in non-violence and vegetarianism made him a votary of conservation of all diversity including all forms of life, societies, cultures and religions. His argument for conservation of biodiversity was indeed simple. Since a "human being has no power to create life, he has, therefore no right to destroy life" further, he felt that there cannot be any ecological movement designed to prevent violence against nature unless the principle of non-violence becomes central to the ethos of human nature. Hence, the centrality of Gandhi in non-violent activism is widely acknowledged and has been important source of inspiration for contemporary environmental movements in India. In other words, the environmentalism in India in the form of Satyagraha very closely mirrors elements of Gandhi's philosophy. His entire life and work is an environmental legacy for all humanity. Gandhi's environmentalism amounts to being pro-nature, pro-poor, pro-women and pro-job generation. He combined social, economic, environmental, equity and ethical imperatives for obtaining political independence and economic salvation through rural development for the teeming millions of India. In 1920, in *Young India*, he wrote: "We want to organize our national power not by adopting the best methods of production only, but the best method of both the production and distribution."[5]

Hence, the important elements of Gandhian environmentalism are:

- Human being should act in a manner so as to reinforce its identity as a part of nature rather than severing connections with nature;
- Materials available on the earth should not be used with greed;

- Human beings practice non-violence not only towards fellow humans but also towards other living organisms and inanimate materials because over-use of such materials also amounts to violence;
- Bottom up shared value is preferred to the top-down totalitarian overview;
- Conservationist and sustainable life-saving approach prevails over the unsustainable self-destructive approach;
- The human race thinks about how much is enough for a simple need-based, austere and comfortable lifestyle;
- Human care for and share with the poor and the destitute in the society is a moral obligation towards them;
- All development as far as possible should lead to local self-reliance and equity with social justice; and
- Ethics and self-discipline in resource use is and overriding criterion of development.[6]

This article analyses the teachings and ideals of Mahatma which have a tremendous impact upon various environmental movements of contemporary India, its present relevance and significance in the twentieth and twenty-first century and argues that those who want to make an informed study of 'social movements' or 'environmental movements' with livelihood issues, protecting our biodiversity and people's rights to natural resources and particularly those who are interested in the philosophy of non-violence and satyagraha for the success of the movement, should, therefore, go back to Gandhi for a fuller picture. Drawing insights from three contemporary popular environmental movements in India—Chipko, NBA (Narmada Bachao Andolan), and CBA (Chilika Bachao Andolan) of the present time, this essay tries to explore the influences of Gandhian values and principles upon the movements' better known figures popularly known as Gandhian activists and who have underlined their own debt to Gandhi in these movements. The paper seeks answer to various questions: Does the life and practice of Gandhi have been the single most important influence on the Indian environmental movements?

Can his teachings, his work give us an 'alternative perspective' on development while explaining how 'the current mode of development is exploitative of man by man and of nature by man?' In fact, what is the relevance of Gandhi today in the present day environmental crisis? To find answer to these questions we need to revisit the environmental movements in India and locate the role of satyagraha in it.

Environmentalism in India and Philosophy of Satyagraha

There are critics about whether Gandhi could be considered an 'early environmentalist'.[7] Ramachandra Guha, one of the foremost scholars of environmentalism in India and abroad, argued that although Gandhi anticipated our environmental concerns, but did not demonstrate practically where and in what ways he did so.[8] He also showed his disagreement on Gandhi's *Hind Swaraj* (published in 1909) by critically arguing that "although the book gives an 'alternative perspective' on development while explaining how the current mode of development is exploitative of man by man and of nature by man, the book does not say anything about man's relationship with nature and hence, offers less to an alternative perspective in development."[9] However, in spite of noting down certain limitations in viewing Gandhi as an 'early environmentalist' for his purportedly poor recognition of the distinctive social and environmental problems of urban areas, Guha readily acknowledges that the value and philosophy of Gandhian thinking is to be felt in the life and works of many of India's most well-known environmental activists in various environmental movements.

Madhva Gadgil, the pioneering environmental writher in India, says that "the origins of India environmentalism lie in the early 1970s, when a number of movements and events heralded a new awareness." The philosophical moorings of early Indian environmentalism were largely Gandhian. But, prior to 1970s, there were also few thinkers who worked with the tradition of Gandhi for a "village-centered economic order", of which resource conservation was an integral part. It was J.C. Kumarappa, who studied the agrarian economy with a view to rehabilitating it on sound social and 'ecological principles'. The environmental implications of his work could be better highlighted through his writings where his observation about profound ecological consequences could be sought. He asserted, "if we produce everything we want from within a limited area, we are in a position to supervise the methods of production; while if we draw our requirements from the ends of the earth it becomes impossible for us to guarantee the conditions of production in such places."[10] As a follower of Gandhi he went on to challenge the modern civilization for disembedding the economy from its ethical and cultural moorings.

Kumarappa could be said to be the first Gandhian who began task of building an ecological programme on Gandhian lines much before the initiation and popularization of environmentalism in India. After Kumarappa's work the Gandhian values and principles of ecology are more visible and observed in various environmental movements in the 1970s starting with the Chipko movement in the Garhwal Himalayas.

Another Gandhian with environmental ideas was Mira Behan (originally known as Madeline Slade), the daughter of an English admiral who joined Mahatma's Sabarmati Ashram in 1925. During her stay in rural north India, she made some perceptive comments on the environmental problems of Indian agriculture, i.e., the large scale water logging the appears to be an almost inescapable feature of canal irrigation, the ploughing up of lands more suitable for growing pasture for cattle and rampant soil erosion. Like Kumarappa her primary concern was with the rehabilitation of the village economy of India, but her interest in the natural environment was not merely instrumental; at times, she expressed a spiritual affinity with nature of a Wordsworthian kind, similar to the European romantic tradition. Herself a 'devotee of the great primeval Mother Earth', she wrote in April 1949 that,

> the tragedy today is that educated and moneyed classes are altogether out of touch with the vital fundamentals of existence—our Mother Earth, and the animal and vegetable population which she sustains.... we have got to study Nature's balance, and develop our lives within her laws, if we are to survive as a physically healthy and morally decent species.[11]

Revisiting Chipko, NBA and CBA: Experiments with Satyagraha

The Chipko Movement

The Chipko movement is historically, philosophically and organizationally an extension of the traditional Gandhian Satyagraha. It is India's first celebrated environmental struggle. Started in the early 1970s, its roots lie more strongly in a century old tradition of present resistance in defence of forest rights. The movement was the result to hundreds of decentralized and locally autonomous initiatives. It pitted hill villagers against state forestry policies that gave priority to commercial exploitation over subsistence use. The Forest Department's replacement of the mixed deciduous forests with pine plantations in the Garhwal region undermined an economy where forests provided fuel, fodder, timber and many other basic requirements. Protest in the hills was marked by large-scale involvement of women and peasants. The campaign to manage forests for guaranteeing subsistence usufruct acquired an explicitly ecological dimension after the devastation floods of 1970, which brought into public consciousness the links between deforestation, social erosion, floods and landslides. A key element in Chipko ideology since then was opposition to commercial tree felling on both ecological and social grounds.[12] The movement's better known figures were Sri Dev Suman, Mira Behan and Sarala Behn—regarded as true Gandhians. The influence of these two European disciples of Gandhi-Mira Behn and Sarla Behn, on the heritage of Chipko struggle for social justice and ecological stability in the hills of Uttar Pradesh has been immense and they generated a new brand of Gandhian activists who provided the foundation for the Chipko movement—Sunderlal Bahuguna and Chandi Prasad Bhatt.

These two Gandhians have been regarded as the extraordinary Gandhian environmentalists of the present day.[13]

Bhatt and his organization the 'Dashauli Gram Swarajya Mandal' (DGSM), became the main organizing base of the Chipko movement. The tree-hugging technique of protest was itself suggested by Bhatt to the peasants of the Upper Alkananda valley. In referring to the Chipki's crusade to protect the region of Uttarkhand from ecological abuse, Chandi Prasad said;

> Our movement goes beyond the erosion of land, to the erosion of human values.... the centre of all of this is humankind. If we are not in a good relationship with the environment, the environment will be destroyed, and we will lose our ground. But, if you halt the erosion of humankind, humankind will halt the erosion of the soil.[14]

Such was the philosophy of Chandi Prasad's Chipko movement, which draws its inspiration from Gandhian Sarvodaya (good or welfare of all) teachings and practices.

In a similar manner, where Chandi Prasad Bhatt has been reckoned as the pioneer of Chipki, another movement's ideological and charismatic saintly figure has been Sunderlal Bahuguna, who has spread the Chipko message in India and abroad through his tireless padayatras (long marches) across the Himalayas, fasts, lectures and writings. His indefinite fast in 1981 demanding a total ban on commercial felling above an altitude of 1,000 meters was a major success for the movement based on the Gandhian principle of satyagraha. It was in response to this event that the government imposed a fifteen-year moratorium on commercial forestry in the region. Thus, the Chipko movement was an example of how non-violent resistance and struggle by thousands of people at the grassroots can succeed under certain circumstances. It is, in fact, a voice from the margins of Indian civil society that managed to demonstrate that crucial environmental conflicts are not just city-based (such as pollution) or related to the depletion of non-renewable resources useful for industry, but arise directly from the philosophical premises embedded in the modern, western and capitalist vision.[15]

Gandhian values and principles of ecology animate the lives of both the leaders of the Chipko movement who are also the greatest living Indians in Guha's terminology. Bahuguna is a prophet and moralist who appeals to the conscience of individuals, urging them to abjure consumerism and return to a simpler way of life. In contrast, Bhatt and his groups are more in line with Gandhi who emphasized constructive work by training activists in his Sabarmati and Wardha Asharmas since he believes in a 'sustainalable economic alternative' to centralized development. His work has helped to infuse a new ecological meaning to the Mahatma's ideal of 'Gram Swaraj' or village self-reliance.

The Narmada Bachao Andolan (NBA)

A second successful example of environmental campaign which has succeeded Chipko as the most significant environmental initiative in India today is the 'Narmada Bachao Andolan', the campaign for the stopping of the Narmada Vally Project (NVP), a hug hydro-electric dam and irrigation project. The movement has tried to pressure the Indian government and foreign investors to stop construction dams that submerge huge sections of the valley and displace hundreds of thousands of people. It has won some victories too, most notably in 1993 when the World Bank expressed concern about human rights problems and withdrew its funding. But the Indian Supreme Court, which at one point, had stayed construction of the Sadar Sarovar Dam, ruled in October 2000 that the project could go forward. Beyond several specifics of these projects, the NBA has challenged the reigning 'development paradigm', the very idea that these large-scale projects are always beneficial to ordinary people. Observes Amita Baviskar, "the very attempts of the administrative mechanism through the elites to exploit the resources have been challenged and collectively resisted by the very people whom India had 'sought' to maraginalize."[16]

The movement's charismatic figures—Medha Patkar and Baba Amte—regarded as eminent Gandhian activists, have been fighting in a non-violent manner over the past two decades. Medha Patkar, a social scientist, environmentalist and human valley rights activist, who has lived among the tribals of the Narmada valley since the mid-1980s, played a crucial role in starting the Gandhian satyagraha which, for the past two decades, has resisted the destruction of rural villages and the displacement of traditionally poor and underprivileged tribals by the state and its allies such as the global financial institutions and accompanying corporate interests. During an interview with Robert Jensen, she argued that "while such projects generate large profits for a small number of people, they also bring social and environmental devastation to threat to "the very life-supported resources of the world" posed by corporations and the so-called 'free market' of the new-liberal economic programme, which bring "displacement, destruction and disparity." She linked the goals of the movement to challenge corporate globalization to the longstanding struggles of the adivasi (indigenous or tribal) people and dalits in India to control their own lives by saying "without community rights, no human rights can be sustained in the face of corporatization, communalism and corruption."

The movement's another saintly figure, a veteran social activist, Baba Amte is a living legend and a shining example of the Gandhian spirit and approach to current and compelling social problems of Narmada struggle. Amte is regarded as the first man in post-independence India who has so passionately carried forward the Gandhian movement for swaraj in the country. During July 2001, he had launched a mass Narmada satyagraha or non-violent resistance against the Sardar Sarover Project, against inhuman displacement and unjust development. His message was "satyagrahis should stake their lives and assert people's right to life and resources."[17]

As a tireless social activist, he has been propagating his ideas among the common people, especially among the youth of the country. He described the 'Narmada Satyagraha' as a new battle front for youth action in independent India, and therefore, said, "it was an outburst of Gandhian courage and concern for antyodaya." Further, Amte said poignantly, "now that the sun of life is about to set I have set out to catch the rising sun of environmental consciousness."[18]

Thus, in our present developmental efforts, India and the world have to willingly come to terms with the ideas of Baba Amte as a true satyagrahi fighting for the cause of the common people.

Finally, I round off my discussion on the 'Gandhian satyagraha' by citing recent environmental movements in eastern India, popularly known as 'Chilika Bachao Andolan' (CBA) or 'Save Chilika Movement'. Chiplo and Narmada movements are outstanding examples of Gandhian satyagraha, but they are by no means isolated examples of Gandhian satyagraha, but they are by no means isolated examples of the living heritage of Gandhi. The CBA also represents Gandhi-like spirit and ideology and is a most significant icon of contemporary environmental struggles of in India.

Chilika Bachao Andolan (CBA)

The ongoing struggle of the fisher-folk of Chilika lake in recent years in Orissa is an example of environmental protest by the local, traditional, cultural fishing communities against the development policy of the state and also one of the successful movements based on the line of Gandhian principle of satyagraha. The initiative in the movement was carried out by the local traditional fishermen communities in the early part of nineties against the commercial shrimp aquaculture projects promoted by the state and outside capitalist interests. The movement was successful in campaigning against the state government's lease of large parts of Chilika lake to the Tatas, one of India's biggest industrial conglomerates.

Chilika lake, a lake of about five thousand years old situated in the east coast of penisular India, in the Bay of Bengal, is one of the popular Ramsar sites in Asia. It is the biggest brackish water lake. Fishery resources of Chilika lake are one of the most potential sources of income for the local people and for the government of Orissa through export and inland supplies. The lake and its ecosystem have a cultural location and cultural significance in the life of the fishermen community.

When the Tata group started intensive shrimp culture inside the lake, along with a tie-up programme with the Government of Orissa, it ignored the interest and requirement of the marginalized class, i.e., the traditional fishermen community of Chilika. When their livelihood became threatened by the move of the agencies by taking lease over the surrounding areas of the natural resources, the outcome was obviously violent protest and resistance. In the wake of all these development, a powerful people's movement emerged in Chilika in the name of Chilika Bachao Andolan (CBA) or 'Save Chilika Movement' to protect the lake economy as well as its people from the commercial exploitation by big businessmen and to restore people's right to manage the lake.[19]

There are mainly three strata of social forces operating in Chilika contributing to the emergence of this protest movement. They are the traditional fishermen, farmers and students. Among them the fishermen and the farmers are directly affected either by the Tatas or the mafia's invasion on Chilika. Students group are in extraneous force, but deeply involved in the Chilika's struggle. The traditional fishing communities, however, were the people who are deeply concerned with the destruction of both their livelihood and also that of Chilika which are in a way complementary to each other. The traditional fishing communities and farmers were mobilized through the support of the 'Orissa Krushak Mahasangha' (Orissa Farmers' Federation) or O.K.M. a farmers' organization under the leadership of late. Shri Banka Das, a veteran of Quit India movement and president of the then federation. In fact, of the diverse ideological streams comprising the Chilika people's movement, the most well known name is that of B.B. Das, a leading Gandhian activist of the movement whose leadership and mobilization was singularly important. He had spread the movement's message all over India and abroad.

The O.K.M. under the leadership of B.B. Das gave a new dimension to Chilika's struggle in 1992 by raising the question of ecological health of the Lake along with the impairment of livelihoods. Mr Das led the case of Chilika to the Supreme Court by invoking the C.R.Z. Notification (under CRZ notification, prawn culture ponds are either in the prohibited zone between High Tide line and Low Tide line or within 500 metres of the High Tide line for which prior permission is needed. The Central Government had no policy about coastal prawn culture 'till recently and the State Government of Orissa did not enforce the existing laws till the early part of 1995.[20] While opposing the aquacultural bill he emphasized that, "the real roots of the popular participation, necessitate the preservation of environment and people's livelihood."[21]

By invoking the CRZ notification and raising the question of environment Das broadened the compaign base of CBA in Orissa and elsewhere in the country the O.K.M. with the help of 'Chilika Matshyajivi Mahasangha' (Chilika Fishermen's Association) mobilized the fisher-flok and organized big rallies and Dharnas at Chhatrapur, the district headquarters of Ganjam.[22] By this, all the villages surrounding Chilika were involved and it also attracted people outside the lake area. The result was that the movement became broad-based and powerful. With the help of O.K.M., the movement continued the environmental awareness programmes, meetings and conventions. Emphasis was being given on cultural programmes including 'street drama' and 'folk drama' to arouse awareness among fisher-flok. The movement in its second phase of its struggle had given a call for 'Rasta Roko' and 'Rail Roko' on December 14th 1994 in order to force the government to evict the encroachers. Dharnas, padayatras and demonstrations were the means through which it used to create awareness among the people and attract the attention of the government to understand their plight. This was the beauty of the peaceful movement run on Gandhian principles as expressed by late B.B. Das.[23]

Lessons from Satyagraha in Environmentalism: Organizing for Activism

In analyzing Indian environmentalism through satyagraha, my analysis suggests that Gandhism, the dominant strand in Indian environmentalism of today, is grounded in a moral imperative. In other words, many of the methods by which communities have resisted environmental degradation and external control of natural resources fall under the rubric of satyagraha (truth force or non-violent resistence).[24] The ways in which satyagrahis deal with different forms or means of protest are strongly integrated into a broader, more holistic approach, which helps the groups to build and create broader environmental or social movements.

Among the various methods used by activists and groups resisting environmental degradation (as witnessed in our earlier discussion), six are easily discernible. First comes the pradarshan, a collective show of strength by communities at the receiving end of environmental degradation, be they peasants of Chipko or fisher-flok of Chilika protesting against the pawn aquaculture project. The pradarshan shades imperatively into a more militant form of protest called as dharna or sit-in which aims specifically at stopping economic activities that threaten the survival options of resource dependent communities. Further, a more sharply focused variant of the dharna is gherao, where a senior bureaucrat or politician perhaps is surrounded by protestors and locked till he accedes to their demands or is rescued by the police. More militant still is the *rasta roko* which was born out of a more general disgust with state policy as could be found in the case of NBA and CBA. Fifth, we have the resurrection of a classic technique of Gandhian satyagraha used and applied by our activists in environmental movements—the *jail bharo andolan* (literally means the movement to fill the jails). Here, protestors deliberately court arrest by violating a law, most frequently section 144 of the Criminal Procedure Code (CPC), used to prohibit large gatherings. At the same time, the inadequacy of Indian jails to handle large number of prisoners assures them a relatively swift release. And, finally, the sixth technique of Gandhian satyagraha is the *bhook hartal* or hunger strike. In fact, the *bhook hartal* is most frequently carried out in the presence of a charismatic figure such as Baba Amte, Medha Patker and Sunderlal Bahuguna. In fact, the fast unto death by a widely respect popular leader is coercive technique to compel the state to yield in fear of the consequences of the leader succumbing to the fast. Above all, the Narmada movement has already witnessed a major Sangharse Yatra (struggle march), while its participants have frequently threatened a spectacular Jal Samadhi (literally, water burial through immersion in the rising waters).

The various environmental movements drawn on the above mentioned means of satyagraha provide, perhaps, the best insight into the structural dimension of Gandhian ecology: its steadfast adherence to a non-violent and self-reliant ecological philosophy. The Chipko movement, NBA and CBA—all stress a harmonious and sustainable relation between humans and nature. Second, the Chipko movement encourages local control of basic modes of economic production and recommends village-base industries, since Gandhi identified India's villages as the locus for political, economic and personal swaraj or self-rule. Here, the inner logic of Gandhian ecology emerges since swaraj is understood in the context of satya, ahimsa and tapas the inner logic of non-violent respect and compassionate concern for those persons and institutions that threaten local self-rule, self-sufficiency (swadeshi) and control of natural resources.

The non-violent, self-sufficient village life is an antidote to the 'brutal force' of capitalism and is a precondition for any form of national, political or economic self-rule as propagated by Gandhi. However, in spite of all these ideals, philosophy, teachings and morals, Gandhian non-violent views are also not free of critics. Some criticize his views as too idealistic. Critics raise the question as to whether Gandhi or his philosophy of satyagraha provide all the answers to those working for environmental and social renewal today? These eternal values ran like a fine chain through all his (Gandhi's) ideas, actions experiments and ideals. Although there are certain limitations to the Gandhian approach such as inadequate understanding of the urban context and its distinctive social and environmental problems and the wilderness.[25] Still, for many, he is a great contributor to the environmental resistance movements aimed at the restoration of the relationship between the agrarian economy and its natural environment. Therefore, the environmental movements must perennially return to Mahatma Gandhi. It is important today for Gandhian activists, people and decision-makers to take a serious stock of the situation and reallocate their priorities for a better and healthy environment. As Gandhi says, "the earth provides enough for every man's need, but not for every man's greed", has proved to be true in today's fast growing culture throughout the World. The land of the Mahatma has also got trapped in the same trend. Therefore, if India is to be saved from the unabated environmental pollution, the process of consumerism should be reversed before it is too late. Above all, the sarvodaya-based values of truth, non-violence and goals of Gandhian model of development offer a grand non-violent revolutionary strategy for the reconstruction of humanity.

To conclude, my analysis suggests that rather than critically examining Gandhi's ideology and philosophy, it is the hour of need to emphasize the importance and significance of his principle of satyagraha which offers a grand non-violent revolutionary strategy for the reconstruction humanity. In order to protect our environment and to obtain sustainable development, the Gandhian satyagraha is the only means. In other words, a wider Gandhian satyagraha for our environment and its conservation is a viable force for resisting globalization and consumerism in India and for promoting social and ecological justice worldwide. Gandhian ecology is one that engages environmental issues on a practical level through non-violent means as a way to find ultimately peaceful and sustainable solutions. The eco-system of a Gandhian model is based on the ecological values of harmony between its four major components, namely, population, organization, energy and technology. Hence, the harmony will be established through decentralized handicraft-based, community-oriented production system which promotes the values of dignity of labour and bread labour thus giving an opportunity for individuals to be direct with nature and environment.

Notes and References

1. Jayanta Bandyopadhyay, "Between Local and Global Responsibilities", Seminar, 516 (2002), p. 21.
2. Mahatma Gandhi, *Hind Swaraj* (Ahmedabad: Navajivan Publishing House, 1909, New edn. 1938; 1982, p. 44.

3. R.C. Sharma, ed., Gandhian Enviromentalism (Delhi: Global Vision, 2003), p. 108.
4. Kavita Mediratta, and Clay Smith, "Advancing Community Organizing Practice: Lessons from Grassroots Organizations in India"—research paper developed in New York city (2001):http://comm.-org.wisc.edu/papers2001/mediratta/mediratta.htm. Downloaded on 05th November 2007.
5. Mahatma Gandhi, *Young India* (Ahmedabad: Navajivan Publishing House, 1924), p. 318.
6. T.N. Khoshoo, "Gandhian Environmentalism: An Unfinished Task", *IASSI Quarterly*, 16, 1 (July-september 1997), p. 10.
7. See Sharma 2003, p. 4.
8. Ramachandra Guha, "Mahatma Gandhi and the Environmental Movements in India", in Kalland Arne and Gerard Persoon, eds., Environmental Movements in Asia (Surrey: Curzon, 1999), p. 67. See also Ramachandra Guha, and J. Martinez-Alier, Varieties of Environmentalism: Essays North and Sough (Delhi: Oxford University Press, 1997), p. 155.
9. *Ibid.*, p. 155.
10. J.C. Kumarappa, The Gandhian Economy and Other Essays (Wardha: All India Village Industries Association, 1948), p. 10.
11. Krisna Murti Gupta, ed., Article in Khadi Gramodyogas (New Delhi: Himalaya Seva Sangh, 1992.), p. 141.
12. Amita Baviskar, "Red in Tooth and Claw? Looking for class in struggles over nature", in Raka Ray and M.E. Katzenstein., ed., Social Movements in India: Poverty, and Politics (New Delhi, Oxford, 2005), p. 165.
13. See Guha and Martinez Alier, *op. cit.*
14. Quoted in Sharma, *op. cit.*, p. 108.
15. Harsh Sethi, "Survival and Democracy: Ecological Struggle in India", in Wignaraja Ponna, ed., New Social Movements in the South: Empowering the People (New Delhi: Vistaar Publications, 1993), p. 127.
16. Amita Baviskar, In the Belly of the River: Tribal Conflicts over Development in the Narmada Valley (Delhi: Oxford University Press, 1995), p. 38.
17. Robert Jensen, School of Journalism, University of Texas, Interview with Medha Patkar, 2004, http:/uts.cc.utexas.edu/~rjensen/freelance/patkar.htm. Downloaded on 05th November 2007.
18. Baba Amte, "Speech by Shri K.R. Narayanan, President of India while conferring the Gandhi Peace Prize for 1999 on Baba Amte" (14th Jan 2000), http://pib.myiris.com/speech/article.php3?f1=010526181810, Downloaded on 5th November 2007.
19. Sarmistha Pattanaik:
    (a) "Globalization and a Grassroots Environmental Movement: The case of Chilika Bachao Andolan (CBA)", *Journal of the Indian Anthropological Society*, 38, 1 (2003), pp. 36-39.

(b) "Tradition Development and Environmental Movement of the Marginalized: A Study of Fishing Community's Resistance in Orissa, Indian Anthropologist, 33, 1 (2003), pp. 57-60.

"Conservation of Environment and Protection of Marginalized Fishing Communities of Lake Chilika in Orissa, India", *Journal of Human Ecolgoy*, 22, 4 (December 2007), p. 299.

20. B.B. Das, Chilika: The Nature's Treasure: Will it be Allowed to Die? (Bhubaneswar: Orissa Krushak Mahasangha, 1996), pp. 3-5.
21. *Ibid.*, p. 5.
22. Debendranath Jena, "Chilika Bachao Andolan: Reflection on Sociological Issues", *Social Change*, 28, 4 (1998), 9, 54.
23. See B.B. Das, 1996, p. 33.
24. Madhav Gadgil, and Ramachandra, Guha, "Ecological Conflicts and the Environmental Movement in India", in Mahesh, Rangarajan, ed., Environmental Issues in India: A Reader (Delhi: Pearson Education, 2007); p. 409.
25. See Ramchandra Guha, 1997, p. 167.

9

War with Nature—At What Cost?

SUNDERLAL BAHUGUNA

The author and the Chipko Movement are synonymous. In a society where destruction of Nature has become an accepted part of life, respect for life manifested in the form of worship of Nature must look an outdated doctrine. But somebody has to wake up to the dangers of Man's look like an outdated doctrine. But somebody has to wake up to the dangers of Man's war with Nature. The present article is an attempt in that direction.

A few years ago, just after the United Nations' Conference on Environment at Stockholm, the UNESCO Courier published a cartoon. A pygmy was running with a big tree under his arms. Somebody asked him, "Where are you going?" Without stopping he replied, "To find some safe place for this tree." He was looking behind, as if he was afraid of something. The next question was, "What are you afraid of?" And the reply came, "the cement road is chasing me."

Living with Pollution

The cement road is the symbol of our civilization. But, wherever the cement road goes, Nature has to disappear. We try to create a world of our own, but every few people know that this whole creation is just like a mechanical man, with no heart and feelings. Nature is living, creative and she has a system of her own in which all life is interdependent. All living beings need oxygen to breathe. We can not live more than five minutes without oxygen, but as far as oxygen, but is concerned, we are heading towards bankruptcy. It is not only the shortage of oxygen is concerned, we are heading towards bankruptcy. It is not only the shortage of oxygen, but the increase of carbondioxide and other pollutants in the atmosphere, which has made life miserable. This is more so in big cities and specially in the industrial centres. In October 1984, I was in Berlin Cold winds were blowing very fast. I asked my German friends, "Do you always have such winds?" They replied, "Not in winter, when there is snow, but life in winter is very miserable." Why? There is concentration of pollution at certain places. Dhildren cannot bear this and there is a children's disease 'Pseudo crupp', which takes many lives.

The evil effects of air-population are not confined to human beings but in Europe and in all the industrialized countries of the world, forests are in danger due to acid rains. And when plans disappear, there is a real crisis of survival. Forests are not only the oxygen Banks of humankind, but are also the Sinks of carbondioxide, which is increasing at an alarming rate on our planet.

Water Scarcity

What about water? We, in the cities of North India cannot imagine that there was water-rationing in a number of South Indian cities including Hyderabad for a long time. The condition in villages was all the more critical. Water was transported from far away. Imagine the villagers waiting for a tanker or a train coming with water. It is not only scarcity of water, but in many places human beings and animals are forced to drink polluted water. From where does this pollution come? From our cities and industries. The recent tragedy in Gomati in Lucknow, where the dying fish cautioned people of water pollution, is not an isolated problem. We have polluted rivers everywhere. In Bailadilla a river has been flowing for years with iron ore. We take notice of these things when there is some big tragedy, but all our underground water wells, specially in areas of the Green Revolution, are polluted with residues of chemical fertilizers and pesticides.

The third essential things for the survival of life is soil. The increasing rate of soil erosion, 6,000 million tons a year and salinity, is causing grave concern.

Ecological Disasters

The can be a long list of ecological disasters. Are these nature or man-made? Or, are these peculiar to undeveloped regions of the world or due to ignorance and poverty, because these are the causes often attributed to it? No, these are unfortunately the gifts of our materialistic civilization. The materialistic civilization, which developed after the Industrial Revolution, changed the whole attitude of man towards life. There were, of course, some very good developments, Human beings developed a scientific outlook and superstitions and dogmas disappeared; but it laid stress on only one aspect of human life and that was material prosperity. Affluence became synonymous with development. In order to achieve more and more things, man became the butcher of Nature. Nature became a commodity to be exploited for the fulfilment of the never ending desires of human beings. With the help of science and technology, he acquired unlimited powers to exploit the treasures of Nature. Not only the non-renewable resources like minerals and metals are fast disappearing, but the four renewable source like grasslands, forests, crop lands and oceans have become non-renewable due to over-exploitation. Thousands of plant and animal species have become extinct. Our planet is poorer with respect to genetic resources as compared to a century ago.

The Cultural Way

The progress we are trying to achieve can not be continued, because we cannot have unlimited growth with limited resources. In many cases, we are producing more either at the cost of non-renewable resources as in the case of the Green Revolution or at the cost of our two basic capitals—the soil and water. Moreover, the poor regions of the world have to suffer to maintain the standard of the rich regions and even in the same country it happens. In order to keep this intact, they have to create a war psychosis and encourage the sale of arms. War and poverty are the outcome of this system.

Humankind, today, needs Peace not war; clear environment, not pollution and prosperity for all, not poverty. Fortunately in India, the path to achieve this was searched long long ago. Here, a culture was born in the midst of forests, like many ancient cultures and has survived the onslaughts of material civilization. Gurudev Rabinarnath Thakur named it Aranya (forests) culture. The sages who lived in the forests developed a philosophy of life in which besides science, which is the systematic study of the laws governing the process of the physical world, they developed a new science of the inner-self, atma jnana. Insight into the inner self was regarded as the highest objective of life. They reached the following conclusions:

1. There is life in all creation—human beings, birds and beasts, plants and trees, rivers and mountains.
2. All life is one and life is sacred.

Gandhi, Vinoba and Buddha

Respect for life manifested in the form of worship of Nature—rivers, trees and even animals. This in recent times when we came in close contact with materialistic civilization and when the world became smaller, has been named as Vedanta. The experience of unity of life is termed Vedanta. Nature is the supreme power according to Vedantic saints. To keep check on the greed of man and to maintain the harmonious relationship between 'Man and Nature', they preached 'Ahimsa' (non-violence). 'Ahimsa', as Vinoba Bhava—the spiritual heir of Gandhi and the walking saint of India said, "is the way of living and Vedanta is a way of thinking."

Buddha was the first to make this a way of life for the common people. He was in search of the causes of miseries and a way to end these. After hard penances it occurred to him that the root cause of all distress (dukh) was insatiable desire (trishna). In order to achieve permanent peace, happiness and ultimately fulfilment, he preached the ending of desires. There is a basic difference between needs and desires. Our needs should be fulfiled, but we should not run after desires, which make man greedy and ultimately the butcher of Nature.

This message in our times has become more relevant for human survival, when human kind is faced with triple problems of war, pollution and poverty, which are interrelated. The root cause of these is human greed and the answer is in man's relationship with Nature, Gandhi has in very simple words put this, 'Nature has enough to sustain all, but nothing to satisfy the greed of a few'.

What is Progress?

Materialistic civilization in a vain attempt to achieve prosperity has exhausted non-renewable resources and made renewable resources as non-renewable due to over-exploitation. The prosperity thus achieved is short-lived, and that too at the cost of peace and happiness. It keeps individuals in a state of permanent discount, which is the result of insatiable desires. The individual discontent is finally seen in the form of 'war psychosis', since war is the collective manifestation of individual dissatisfaction. Man is at war with Nature or his fellow beings. The end of this war is in adopting a way of life in which austerity is practised. Austerity, on the other hand will bring inner satisfaction. This will help man and society at large to get rid of tensions, which have become an integral part of our lives.

It is often asked, "What is progress?" Progress can never be a lifestyle which is based upon the butchery of Nature and creates a number of problems—like pollution and extinction of species. Real progress is in a lifestyle, where quality of life improves and the individual adds to the betterment fo the whole universe. This is "Sanskriti" or culture, which is achieved as a result of the sublimation of

Nature for the welfare of all living beings. It is only in such an atmosphere that art, literature and peace flourish. Antithesis to this is perversion (vikriti), the challenge before us to come back vikriti to Nature and proceed towards culture. Science will give speed to it and spirituality the right direction.

It is hoped that if many international organizations take up this cause, we will certainly bring 'Hope' to our dying planet and a smile to the millions, because they can bring together the message of the spirituality of the East and the benefits of the science of the West together for this cause.

10

Environmental Sabbath and Gandhi

RAMJEE SINGH

Much before the environmental consciousness began to expand in modern times, time from the Stockhlom Conference to the RIO consensus (5-7 June, 1992), including the Report of the World Commission on Environment[1] and Development[2] and the *United Nations Environmental Perspective to the year 2000 and Beyond*[3] and the Declaration on the Right to Development[4] in many U.N. General Assembly Resolutions,[5] Gandhi had recognized the imminent danger threatening the existence of the Earth as a result of violence and environmental destruction in his revolutionary small hand-book called *Hind Swaraj* or the Indian Home Rule. Written in 1908/1909. This was soon prescribed in 1910 by the then British Government declaring it to be seditious. This hastened its translation into English in 1910. To some, it was anti-science, anti-civilization and anti-machinery while others dubbed it as ecological dystopian vision created as a reaction against dehumanization and alienation of man in modern technological culture. John Middleton Murray, however, acclaimed the book as "the spiritual classics of the world" and "the greatest that has been in modern times"[6] which pleaded for a society capable of using machine without incurring material and spiritual devastation. According to G.D.H. Cole, "Gandhi's case against the West Looks infinitely stronger than it looked to us Westerners thirty years ago."[7] This is why Gerald Herard described *Hind Swaraj* as superior to Rosseau's Social Contract and Karl Marx's *Das Kapital*[8] Gandhi's *Hind Swaraj* is a warning against growing consumerism, materialism and wrong model of development. Both capitalism and Marxism adopt the same western model of development and industrialization to meet the ever-growing material standard of life, leading to ruthless exploitation of natural resources. This leads to unrestrained urbanization with all its attendant evils of crime, prostitution and corner societies. In the famous publication *Only One Earth*, Dr. Noel J. Brown, Director of U.N. Environment Programme (1987)[9] explains in the same voice as Gandhi did: "The need for establishing a new spiritual and ethical base for human activities on Earth has never been greater as the deterioration of our Planetary Home makes the protection of the human environment a new global imperative." In his address to the world's scientists, politicians and spiritual leaders at the Global Forum (Jan. 1990), the Secretary General of the U.N. dramatizing the urgency of the situation called for fundamental changes in societal attitudes. But "for that change, we need to draw, not only upon the intellectual, but also the spiritual resources of the world." No doubt, this is a vital and auspicious moment for Humanity, to reassert our compassion, care and respect for our Earth. All human societies are built on fragile ecological foundations. Without clean air, fresh water, productive soil and a sustaining web of life, Home sapiens can neither survive no prosper. In a few short decades we are eroding these foundations beyond repair. By the year 2000, if present trend continues, one-third of the world's productive land will be driven to extinction, the sharpest setback to life on earth since our remotest ancestors first appeared on the planet: And the world climate will almost certainly change, with enormous, but incalculable consequences. In each case, human activities will be to blame."[10] Union of Concerned Scientists, in a comprehensive statement said: "Human beings and the natural world are on a collision course.

Human activities inflict harsh and often irreversible damage on the environment and on critical resources and warned.[11] A great change in our stewardship of the earth and the life on it is required if vast human misery is to be avoided and our global home on this planet is not to be irretrievably mutilated. It further declared that the developed nations are the largest polluters in the world today. "They must reduce their over consumption, if we are to reduce pressures on resources and global environment." This is exactly what Gandhi had said while bitterly criticising modern civilization whose emblem is consumerism and bodily welfare. Even Pitrim Sorokin described the modern western civilization as "sensate" and came to the conclusion that man would have to future and would be completely lost if he does not abandon his man must become more altruistic, other regarding, ecologically conscious and adopt early enough a new stance based on them.

Rifken, the author of *Entropy*, pleaded for simpler lifestyle in the name of second law of Thermodynamics. Today, U.S.A. consumes 30 to 50 of world amul production.[12] The former Soviet Union had to move into Hungary, Poland, Czechoslovakia and many developing countries. It was in this context that Gandhi had exclaimed: "God forbid that India should ever take to industrialism after the manner of the West. The economic imperialism of a tiny island (U.K.) is today keeping the whole world in chains. If the entire nation of 300 (new 890) millions took to similar economic exploitation, it would strip the world bare like locusts."[13]

The publication of the club of Rome thesis on the limits to Growth point out two major criticisms of this wrong model of development: (a) depletion of non-renewable resources, and (b) the environmental pollution threatening human life with extinction. Like Gandhi, Fritij of Capra thinks that industrial technology is the root cause. All this means that "whatever befalls the earth befalls the sons of the earth. Man did not weave the web of life, he is merely a strand in it. Whatever he does to the web, he does to himself."[14] Industrialization everywhere has brought dirtier air. The story of airborne lead illustrates the connection between industrialization and air pollution.[15] When fossils fuels are burnt, sulphur dioxide and oxides of nitrogen released into air. This acid rain is most dangerous for human lfie.[16]

Ozone depletion[17] and "greenhouse effect" are signals of Doomsday. According to Environmental Protection Agency, water supplies of 80 American cities contained chemicals that may cause cancer.[18] The U.S. Global 2000 Report say that the demands for fresh water in the world will increase by 2000-3000% from 1975 to 2000 A.D. Lone canal disaster is only the tip of the iceberg.[19] The U.S. Congressional Office of Technological Assessment has estimated that it will require about 50 years and 100 billion to clean up toxic wastes.[20] The World Health Organisation estimates that half a million species are poisoned yearly by pesticides and the most of those people live in the Third World Countries.[21] It has taken 42 billion years for life to reach its present state of development on this planet but one million species out of 5-10 millions could be extinct[22] because of atmospheric poisoning and a full-scale nuclear holocaust could lead to Sussane, Gowan, *Moving Towards a New Society*, Philadelphia, 1976, pp. 64-65.

> total extinction[23] accidents like the one at Cherneby raises the basic question—whether governments that claim to function in the name of the people have the right to tamper with the right of man to survive, and to preserve the environment on which it depends.[24] Deforestation is also a serious problem, because it can lead to significant changes in the climate which usually mean less rainfall.

During the past several years the international coordinating Committee on Religion and the Earth (ICCRE) has cooperated with the world council of churches, the world conference on Religion and Peace, the World Wide Fund for Nature, the South American Conference on Religion and Ecology and other international and interfaith organizations in formulating the *Earth Charter*. In October 1985, when U.N. was celebrating the 40th anniversary, a core group of religious and political leaders met for the first time in a village north or New York city. The politicians were members of the Global Committee of Parliamentarians on Population and Development. The spiritual leaders were invited by the Temple of Understanding. The dialogue proved so fruitful that they decided to continue and expand it scope. The First Global Survival Conference in April, 1988 drew nearly 200 spiritual and legislative leaders. The second meeting of the Global Forum was hosted in former Soviet Union in January 1990 in which more than 1000 spiritual and other leaders attended. President Gorbachev hailed it as "a major step toward the ecological consciousness "of humanity." Co-sponsored by the National Congress of Brazil and the Global Forum, the Parliamentary Earth Summit gathered in Rio during the first weekend of the U.N. Conference on Environment and Development. (June 1992), in which delegates from 178 Governments and 300 parliamentarians and spiritual leaders, attended. Another general assembly was held in Kyoto (Japan) from April 17-23, 1993.

Rio vision is essentially factual when it says that "the planet earth is in peril as never before. With arrogance and presumption, humankind has disobeyed the laws of the creator which are manifest in the divine natural order. The crisis is global. Nature does not depend on human beings and their technology. It is human beings who depend on Nature for survival." Hence we mush evolve "Earth Ethics." Ecological disruption is violent intervention into the web of life. Hence Mr. Mauria Strong, the Secretary-General of UNCED in his opening remarks at the Earth Summit (3.6.1992) opines that "the changes in behaviour and direction called for here must be rooted in our deepest spiritual, moral and ethical values. We must reinstate in our lives the ethic of love and respect for the earth, which traditional peoples have retained as central to their value systems." The National Religious Partnership for the Environment representing too million people wrote "Problems of such magnified and solutions demanding so broad a perspective must be recognized from the outset as having a religious as well as a scientific dimension. Effort to safeguard and cherist the environment need to be infused with a vision of the sacred." In January 1990, an open letter to the Religious community from the scientific community was addressed including 50 religious leaders and 50 Nobel laureates in which "a much wider and deeper understanding of science and technology" was emphasized.

After two years of preparations, 178 governments at the Earth Summit (UNCED) reached agreement on three texts: (1) Agenda 21, a comprehensive strategy for Global Action on Sustainable Development; (2) The Rio-Declaration or Environment and Development, outlining the rights and responsibilities of governments in this area; and (3) a statement of principles to guide the sustainable management of forests world-wide.[25] However, three of the biggest causes of environmental destruction were:

Overlooked at the Earth Summit presumably because of the vested interests: (a) multi-national corporations, the military, and inappropriate development models.[26] A myriad of other problems were not dealt with because they are too controversial including the unsustainable consumption patterns of the riches peoples of the planet, and the fact that one billion people have no access to fresh water supplies. Instead of discussing policies that lead to pollution, the government signed tailpiece solutions such as checking carbon-dioxide emissions and cataloging rare species in the world's remaking forests. Gandhi had neither any vested interest nor he proposed any ideology with reservations or inhibitions. Hence Mr. Hugh was right when he said "the whole purpose of the book (*Hind Swaraj*) is to save India, not from Englishmen, but from the modern civilization which is eating into the vitals of the west."[27] The Price of Progress[28] is too great for its results in a neurotic society. Modern technicality and centralism appear to be the inherent tendencies of industrial growth involving a great sacrifice of human values, and excessive capital costs. Schumacher re-echoes Justice Brandic's lamentation on the qualities of contemporary life and the curse of bigness.[29] Mechanics and technics have become a source of idolatry. Machine qua machine is madness. Apart from the loss of meditative, creative and spiritual enrichment, the industrial culture has also resulted in "forced labour" society, totalitarian monopoly of mass media and mass indoctrination, enabling rulers perfect and project their controls over the whole range of social life, decline in skilled labour, lack of community satisfactions,

> rise of a commercial system and conflicts between capitalists and the labourers. We have seen the industrial hazards like industrial disease, poison, accidents, loss of life, etc. But it is impossible to sum up the emotional loss tension. The cause of all contradiction is centralism in production and in power leading to exploitation and oppression.[30]

Gandhi attacked both the ideology ad technology as both go together. Technology has influenced social consciousness as well as economic and social structure of society. We find the Frankenstein of modern technology with the horrors of war and technological unemployment. But the ideology behind modern civilization is much more dangerous.[31] Whether it is "Rape of the Earth" or use of super-advanced technology for the accepted notions of economic growth, they all are rooted to meet and suit the needs and interests of the greedy and acquisitive person resulting in the imbalance in society leading to violence and war. "Nature has given enough to satisfy our needs but not our greed"—said Gandhi. Gandhi went further to assert that single person.[32] Our desires are infinite and unlimited. Hence we need a new design of living. Arnold Toynbee[33] has been shown that ease and luxury had been the most fatal foes of the twenty-seven civilizations which have passed into oblivion of antiquity. John Galabraith laments that "we have becomes slaves of machine, we have created to serve us and the servitude is felt comfortable as a result of mass suggestion to which consumers are subjected."[34]

Mareuse's observations are more biting.[35] Gandhi therefore, pleaded for limiting our wants or indulgences. He is true when he says that "the mind is a restless bird, the more it gets, the more it wants, and still remain unsatisfied." The more we induge our passions the more unbridled they became.[36] It is a unique coincidence that in the land of affluence and veritable plenty, i.e. U.S.A., millions of people have been pursuing lifestyles of a more home spun but richer quality of life.[37] Gandhi knows that "a man is not necessarily happy because he is rich, or unhappy because he is poor." The measuring rod of a good civilization is morality or to raise man to a higher moral level, or unhappy because he is poor. The measuring rod of a good civilization is morality or to raise man to a higher moral level, whereas the hallmark of modern civilization is materialism and selfishness. Hence prophet Muhamad calls such a civilization as satanic or the Hindu scripture calls it the Black Age (Kaliyug). Gandhi disliked that man should be taken as a limited, material, mechanistic being functioning under the force of wants. The satisfaction of wants through the consumption of goods gives 'pleasure', which he seeks to maximize. Hence, he is reduced to be a consumer having unlimited wants. This craving for unlimited pleasures has accelerated blind industrialization leading to rapid depletion of the non-renewable world resources and to the problems of pollution. Hence, Gandhi pleaded for a technology and economics within the framework of ecological balance of a holistic paradigm. He tried to foster a new lifestyle based on simple living and high thinking. There is thus bound to be "a shift from the mechanistic to the holistic conception of reality"—says Fritz of Capra. So Alvin Toffler thinks that there will be "a shift back from mass production to home production." Gandhian model of technology and development is based more on renewable resources like animal, water, oil and solar energies, etc. and less on non-renewable ones. It does not lead to environmental pollution or disturbs the ecological balance. But this is impossible without a decisive and clear moral and spiritual lead; that will be full of idealism, even with a touch of romanticism. We can not have an extravagant and ever-growing comfortable or luxurious lifestyle without a mega-technology and consequent environmental hazard and pollution. We cannot have a strong military-structure without large-scale super technology. Hence Gandhi said an emphatic "no" to organization of bruti force or army, multi-national centralized large-scale industrial base and materialistic consumerist development model. Let not environmentalists beat the bush only. Let then be sincere and courageous. The real enemy of environment is within our own selves our unlimited desires and wants. We cannot have both 5-star air condition culture as well safety of our mother earth. Some body had asked Socrates: "what is the secret of happiness?" the reply was "How many things we can do without." I think that is also the reply to our environmental challenge.

Notes and References

1. Report of the U.N. Conference on the Human Environment, 16.8.72.
2. U.N. General Assembly Resolution 42/187 of 11.12.1987.
3. *Ibid.*, 42/186 of 11.12.1987.
4. *Ibid.*, 41/128 of December 1986.
5. *Ibid.*, 39/11 of 12.11.1984 (Declaration of the Right of Peoples to Peace).
6. *Ibid.*, 33/73 of 15.11.1978 (Declaration on the Preparation of Societies for Life in Peace).
   Ibid., 37/199 of 18.12.1982.
   Ibid., 37/7 of 28.10.1982; 38/124 of 16.12.1983.
   Ibid., 37/7 of 28.10.1982; 42/186 of 11.12.1987; 42/187 of 11.12.87.
   Ibid., 42/186 of 11.12.1987 and 42/187 of 11.12.1987.
   The Aryan Path (Special Number of *Hind Swaraj*, Vol. 67, Sept., 1978 pp. 200-438.
7. *The Aryan Path* (Special Number on *Hind Swaraj*), p. 429.
8. *Ibid.*, p 436.
9. U.N.E.P. DC. 2-803, U.N., Newyork, NY-10017, USA.
10. Excerpted and adopted from the UNEP Profile in Only One Earth.
11. Endorsed by 1680 members or fellow 104 Nobel laureats, senior officers from organizations such as the Third World Academy of Sciences, the Brazilian Academy of Sciences, the Royal Society of London, the Chinease Academy of Sciences, the Pontifical Academy of Sciences coming from 71 countries including all of the 19 largest economic powers.
12. Sussane, Gowan, *Moving Towards a New Society*, Philadelphia, 1976, pp. 64-65.
13. *Collected Works of Mahatma Gandhi*, Vol. 38, p. 243.
14. Steve van Matra and Bill Weiler, (eds.), *The Earth Speaks*, Warren Ville III, Institute of Earth Education, 1983, p. 122.
15. Studies show that today's Americans contain 500 times more lead than those of pre-historic humans. *New York Times*, 13.5.1980, p. 82.
16. Law-Barry Commoner, *The Closing Circle*, New York: Alfred Knopf, 1971, p. 39.
17. *Collected Works of Mahatma Gandhi*, Vol. 38, p. 243.
18. Steve van Matra and Bill Weiler, (eds), *The Earth Speaks*, Warren Ville III, Institute of Earth Education, 1983, p. 122.

19. Studies show that today's Americans contain 500 times more lead than those of pre-historic humans. *New York Times*, 13.5.1980, p. 82.
20. Law-Barry Commoner, *The Closing Circle*, New York: Alfred Knopf, 1971, p. 39.
21. Eckholm, E., Down to Earth, New York, W.W. Norton, 1992, p. 93.
22. *The Global 2000 Report to the President*, New York: Penguin, 1982, p. 26.
23. A decline Levine, *Lone Canal: Science, Politics and People*, Levington: 1982, and Michael Brown, *Laying Waste: The Poisoning of America by Toxic Wastes*, New York: Pantheon Books, 1980.
24. *The New York Times*, 11.03.1985, p. 12.
25. Martin Wolterding, *The Poisoning of Central America*, Sierra, Sept-Oct. 1981, p. 63.
26. Norman Myors, "The Fate of the Earth", *Foreign Policy*, 42, Spring, 1981, p. 141.
27. J. Schell, "The Fate of the Earth", New York: Avon Book, 1992, p. 93.
28. Ravindra Varma, "Warning from Chernobyl", *Gandhi Marg*, New Delhi, May 1986, p. 69.
29. From the Press Summary of Agenda 21 and Earth Summit Press Release.
30. Madanlal Handa, "The Existing World Order: A Gandhian Interpretation", *Gandhi Marg*, Nov. 1980, pp. 427-30
31. B. Ginsberg, "Science", *Ency. of Social Sciences*, Vol. XIII, p. 602.
32. Archbishop Angelo Fernandes, "God's Rule and Man's Role, *Gandhi Marg*, March 1982, p. 699.
33. S. Pandey, The Ultra-Modern Gandhi," *Gandhi Marg*, April 1976, p. 23.
34. J.K Galbraith, *The New Industrial State*, Calcutta, 1993, p. 19.
35. "The slaves of developed industrial civilization are sublimated slaves, but they are slaves, for slavery is determined." One Dimensional Man, Boston, 1986, p. 32.
36. M.K. Gandhi: *Hind Swaraj*, p. 61.
37. C. Hunderson, "Learning to Live Frugally", Span, New York, Vol. XX, No. 7, July 1979, p. 14. About 60 million people will begin to live full voluntary simplicity of life by 2000 according to studies of Standard Institute of California.

Ecology and Gandhism

Bindeshwar Pathak

The term 'ecology which has its root in the Greek word 'oikos' (household or living place), came into use in the latter part of the nineteenth century in the works of zoologist and botanists to describe the study of the ways in which organisms live in their environments. Soon two branches of ecology were distinguished: autecology, the study of the individual organism's interaction with environment, and synecology, the study of the correlations between the organisms within a given unit of environment. The latter study has prevailed, however, and has become the principal connotation of ecology, since it became evident in numerous field studies that organisms, whether plant or animal, establish viable relationships with environment, not independently but collectively, through the mechanism of a system of relationships. Bioecologists were thus led to employ a set of concepts and techniques of investigation that imparted a markedly sociological coloration to their work.

The ecological approach was introduced as human ecology into the field of sociology at a critical period in the development of the latter discipline. In the 1920s the reformistic phase of sociology was drawing to a close, and the subject was gaining acceptance as a respected discipline in the curricula of American universities. That the transition would be effected so quickly without the aid of a theoretical framework lending itself to empirical research seemed doubtful. Ecology opportunely provided the necessary theory. A period of vigorous research followed that was to prove instrumental in launching sociology on its career as a social science.

Sociologists made free use of analogy as they borrowed heavily from the concepts of plant and animal ecology. The Darwinian nation of animate nature as web of life became at once a general orienting concept and a basic postulate; it directed attention to the necessary interdependence among men as well as among lower forms of life. A second concept, the balance of nature, denoting a tendency toward stabilization of the relative number of diverse organisms within the web of life and of their several claims on the environment, provided human ecology with its characteristic equilibrium position. The more or less balanced web of relationships, when viewed in a specific local area, presented an aspect of community, a concept with obvious appeal for students of human social life.

The term Cultural Ecology is also used to study the processes by which a society adapts to its environment. Its principal problem is to determine whether these adaptations initiate internal social transformations or evolutionary changes. It analyzes these adaptations, however, in conjunction with other processes of change. Its method requires examination of the interaction of societies and social institutions with one another and with the natural environment.

Cultural ecology is distinguishable from but does not necessarily exclude other approaches to the ecological study of social phenomena. These approaches have viewed their special problems—for example, settlement patterns, the development of agriculture, and land-use—Hindi Swarajin the broad context of the complexly interacting phenomena within a defined geographical area. Explanatory formulations have even included the incidence of disease, which is related to social phenomena and in turn affects societies in their adaptations. This modern concept of ecology has largely superseded other concepts, such as 'urban', 'social' and human ecology, which employed the biological analogy of viewing social institutions in terms of competition, climax areas, and zones.

Although the culture of any society constitutes a holistic system in which technology, economics, social and political structure, religion, language, values, and other features are closely interrelated, the different components of a culture are not similarly affected by ecological adaptations. Technology, which exemplifies progress in man's control of nature, tends to be cumulative. A language, unless replaced by another one, slowly but continuously evolves into divergent groups of languages. Humanistic and stylistic cultural manifestations may retain their formal aspects during social transformations but acquire new functions. Societies change through a series of structural and functional transformations.

Social structures respond most clearly to environmental requirements. This basic structuring is related most immediately to cooperative productive activity, and it is manifest in community and band organization and in essential kinship systems. Among simple societies, any interpersonal or interfamilial arrangements necessary for survival in particular areas are virtually synonymous with social organization. Because food collecting, such as in the case of seed gathering, is competitive, societies in unproductive environments tend to become fragmented into nuclear family units. Societies of hunters are more productive under cooperative arrangements and attain various patterns of cohesion. Societies that depend primarily upon farming tend to have permanent community organization, whether in dispersed or nucleated settlements, because cooperation in such activities as clearing plots and irrigation projects facilitates production. Increase in productivity is delimited by the environmental potentials, crops, and farm methods, but it may lead to larger communities and to internal specialization of role and status.

The industrial revolution enormously expanded the areas of exploitation through its improved transportation, mass manufacturing, communications, and economic and political controls. Its technology also gave importance to many latent resources. Modern nations and empires embrace highly diversified environments and draw upon areas beyond their political boundaries. Their technology may modify environments to meet their cultural needs, and, above all, any localized sub-society reacts to a complex set of state institutions, to a diversified social environment, and to a large number of goals other than survival. Although people necessarily live in particular places, members of highly industrialized nations must be viewed as increasingly non-localized to the extent that their behaviour is determined by a great overlay or elaboration of cultural patterns that are only remotely connected with particular environments and are even minimizing some of the child rearing and economically complementary functions of members of the nuclear family. It can be imagined that nuclear power, hydroponic and synthetic food production, and other technological developments might create wholly artificial environments, as in a permanent space station.

Sacred groves are small patches of native vegetation type, traditionally protected by the local communities. Reverence for nature and nature resources in this country is part of our cultural heritage. Stretching into pre-historic times, the concept of "sacred grove" in India has its roots in antiquity (Ramakrishnan, 1996) even before the Vedic age, the Vedas representing the only recorded remains of the thought of the ancient Aryans. Vedic people of pre-historic times assimilated new environmental values; they also incorporated into their values system the concept of the "scared grove" from the inhabitants of the Indian sub-continent. Though many traditional societies value a large number of plant species from the wild for a variety of reasons. Thus the already existing landscape/ecosystem level sacred grove concept of the pre-Vedic habitants of India was extended by the vedic migrants down to the species level.

It is reasonable to assume that the traditional Hindu society recognized individual species as objects of worship, based on accumulated empirical knowledge and their identified value for one reason or the other (Ramakrishnan,

1996). Thus "Peepal tree" and other species of the same genus from components of a variety of ecosystem types and support a variety of plants and animal bio-diversity. Tulsi (Ocimum samtum) is worshipped in all traditional homes as a Goddess, and indeed is a multipurpose medicinal plant, according to the traditional Indian pharmacopia. Other like Quercus (oaks) may not be worshipped in a religious sense, but one part of the socio-cultural traditions in Kumaon and Garhwal region. They are considered to serve a variety of functions: help in improving soil fertility and conserve soil moisture. Consequently, they support a rich biodiversity in the ecosystem. The ecological value of the species within them and the ecosystem function of most of these are yet to be fully evaluated. Modern science is rediscovering the ecological principles roots in over ancient wisdom. Mahatma Gandhi's words 'Path is the Goal' is most appropriate at this juncture of human evolution.

Before we embark on an exploration and analysis of Gandhism and ecology it will be useful to take into account the time in which Gandhi lived, the social milieu in which he was brought up and the political matrix in which he worked.

Gandhi born in a princely state of Gujarat, a state of India, in a traditional Hindu religious social milieu. Reverence for nature and nature resources in such a social milieu was a part of cultural heritage. Attaching sacredness to trees and greenery was a part of thinking, thought process and a way of life. From times immemorial people of pre-historic times believed in environmental benefits and related value system. Thus, the concept of sacred grove, worshipping trees and vegetation symbolizing Gods and Goddesses became a part of their thought process. This worship was rooted in realization of usefulness of plants, trees and vegetation. Gandhi imbibed this attitude and was deeply influenced by it.

Gandhi was born in 1869 when Industrial Revolution had started in England, the imperial power which ruled over India. Early in his life he saw the developing conflict between the ruthless march of industrialization, mass production, urbanization on the one had and need for protection of environment on the other. As early as in 1927, he had warned the world that the large scale industrialization would create problems of the type we are confronting today. He said, "the world influenced by the Western culture was going in the wrong direction, and like the proverbial moth would burn itself eventually in the flame around which it was dancing carelessly." He foresaw the exhaustion of scarce nature resources which are essential for survival of mankind on earth; poisoning of the life sustaining air, water and soil by toxic pollutants from industries, automobiles and modern agricultural practices; the threat of submergence of land mass under sea due to "greenhouse effect" resulting from carbon dioxide build up in the atmosphere; the fear of ghastly disease like cancer, blindness, etc. due to radiation hazards resulting from depletion of ozone in the stratosphere: and large scale deforestation, soil erosion and desertification all being the results of ill conceived development strategies perpetuated by the Western technology and which has brought the whole human civilization closer to the path of ecological disaster about which Gandhi had predicted very early. The concept of environmental conservation, sustainability and survival are inherent in the philosophy of Mahatma Gahdhi. A man far ahead of his time in comparison to modern environmentalists. Ecologists all over the world today seem to share Gandhi's view that the industrial society is no longer sustainable.

He was, however, not against industrialization but against industrialism and dehumanized machine culture. Gandhi was concerned trying to find a way out of the inexorable march of industrialization, mass production, fulfiling the needs of rising populace. The way out according to him was to lay emphasis upon small-scale enterprises for "production by the masses and not mass production by any individual." He emphasized upon small scale enterprises for "production by the masses and not mass production by any individual." The latter would mean prosperity for a few and poverty for the rest and that is what exactly has happened in India. Small-scale enterprises are also free from any developmental conflicts between man and nature and economic conflicts between management and labour. They are less energy-intensive and therefore less polluting.

Small scale enterprises result in greater dispersed employment and can have the effect of dispersing urban settlements. After all when he consider the development of communication technology we find emphasis being placed on home installed computers, mobile, lap tops, telephone systems. We have been witness to the phenomenon where small scale enterprises, cottage industries with simple technologies giving way to mass production, integrated factory establishments. But they in turn gave way to development of auxiliaries and ancillaries, interdependent industrial units and now even interdependent international trade. It there is today need for political pluralism, there is even greater demand for pluralism in production activities, communication net work, etc. I am laying emphasis on all this with a view to stressing the importance of dispersal of production activates and human habitations which promote protection of environment and ecology.

Gandhiji always stressed human factor in technological and economic development. For this he emphasized the village and cottage industries with "simple" indigenous appropriate technology. Scale of economic activity is the key to permanence of human values and living in harmony with nature and its environment maintaining ecological balance. Gandhiji's great insistence on village as the unit of production and minimisation of wants as the centre of economic, cultural and spiritual life echoed in Schumacher's, "Small is Beautiful" and Gunnar Myradals' "Asian Drama" makes Gandhi relevant to the present day world.

Gandhi's personal philosophy influenced his political goals. Gandhi's philosophy of "non-violence" is of great ecological significance. His concept of non-violence not only meant absence of injury to the living world but also to the nature and its non-living entities such as air, water and soil. The ecological movement of the world today is essentially to preserve nature from the onslaught of industrialization, unplanned growth of human habitation. But it will be meaningless unless it is simultaneously directed against piling up of deadly weapons. Potential threat to environment and ecology due to arms development is enormous, besides polluting the biosphere and indiscriminate use of the fossil fuel on defence preparation.

In modern societies, nature is becoming a victim of "human greed", indiscriminate misuse of nature resources in the name of economic development disregarding its ecological implications has landed mankind in the present impasse. Gandhi said, "the Earth provides enough to satisfy every man's need but not every man's greed." He was of the view that as long as the greed prevailed and the fruits of economic development were not shared equitably among the masses, poverty and hunger would exist and till the evils of hunger, malnutrition and exploitation of the poor continued in any part of the world, there could be no economic stability and ecological sustainability of the human society. Poor people and poor nations tend to over-exploit the resources in order to survive.

Gandhi's simple lifestyle also had a great ecological bearing. Conspicuous consumption, "over-consumerism" and "throw away" attitudes is ecologically destructive and cannot be sustained for long in a world suffering from dwindling resources. In this age of technology, it is necessary that a spring of compassion should gush forth and non-violence should be enthroned as the queen.

Against the background of the ecological crisis of today, a new set of norms are required for Mankind. Acceptance of a completely different world view is essential. The basic requirement is to realize that modern man cannot subdue or exploit nature as he likes, and if he does, it is at his own peril. There is no and should not be any more dispute between developmentalists and environmentalists.

Gandhiji, as we have seen, had questioned the very foundations of Western civilization, of the modern scientific, industrial growth centred, materialistic self-centred world view and way of life. He emphasized the spiritual and ethical aspects, not only at the individual level, but at the national and global level as well. The twenty-first century, if it is to survive, will have to change its world view, its paradigm of domination and perpetual growth and focus more on Gandhiji's holistic truth.

REFERENCES

Gandhi, M.K., *Hind Swaraj* or Indian Self-Rule, Navajivan Trust, 1939.

Sachs, Wolfgang. (ed), The Development Dictionary, Zed Books Ltd., London, 1992.

Goldsmith, E., and Hildyard, N., Green Britain or Industrial Wasteland, Polity Press, London, 1986.

Lester Brown, Interview on CBC Survival, Worldwatch Institute, Washington.

Saral Sarkar, *Lokayan Bulletin*, 5:3, 1987, New Delhi.

"Cities, Gasping from Life", *India Today*, December 1996.

Gordon Amta and Suzuki, David: It is a Matter of Survival. Harvard University Press, Cambridge, Mass, 1991.

Fromm, Erich, To Have or to Be? Jonathan Cape, London, 1978.

Sachs, Aaron, Humboldts Legacy, Worldwatch, March-April, 1995.

Merchant, Carolyn, The Death of Nature, Harper, San Francisco, 1883.

Chaturvedi, Badrinath, "The Roots of Violence", *Times of India*, October 21, 1996.

Nehru, Jawaharlal, Speech delivered at Nagpur airport, July 12, 1958.

Dogra, Bharat, *The Hindustan Times*, June 8-10, 1996.

Chakravarthy, S., Redeeming the Pledge, *Mainstream Annual*, 1994, New Delhi.

Farzand, Ahmed, Endless Hunger, *India Today*, December 1996.

Kishwar, Madhu, *Manushi*, January-April 1996.

12

Impact on Ecology of the Two Views of Life

SACHCHIDANAND SINHA

"End justifies the means", the idea attributed to the Jesuits has been quite pervasive, and a substantial segment of the left movement also came to accept this view. But a close examination would reveal that after the end flows out of the means and is shaped by it. It has been observed that the French Revolution inspired by Rousseau's "Age of Reason", ended up in the "Reign of Terror", and ultimately in the empire of Napolean Bonaparte. Perhaps it was inevitable in the violent nature of the revolution. And yet the idea of the inevitability of violent revolution has kept shaping powerful social and political movements ever since. Marx, perhaps did not accept that precept, but in a different way became a victim of that fallacy.

No one has exposed more thoroughly and clearly than Marx the mendacity and cruelty through which capitalism has grown and maintained its grip on the economic and political life of society. But in his apocalyptic view of a proletarian revolution, capitalism had to acquire maturity by expanding its industrial base, destroying all pre-industrial societies, to ensure the brans formation from capitalism to communism. So capitalism had to became the means (the via media), the essential launching pad to catapult society into an era of equality and amity. Marx had failed to see, that (1) the expansion of capitalist industry was closely linked with the acquisition of vast markets and sources of raw materials outside its European base; and (2) the new industrial society had to be inspired by an acquisitive ethos. In short, as a great economist Menand Keynes put it, "Greed and Jealousy" had to persist to ensure economic growth. Both these factors posed previous problems for society and the biosphere.

During the time of Marx, to the Europeans, the world was still a boundless area in which to expand. What happened to India, Australia or the vast expanses of the American had little impact at home. The greed paid as acquisitions from distant lands still legendry to most European gave them grains and gold.

But with the expansion of trade and transport and the native peoples of other hands slowly evening from the shadowy world of legends began making their real presence felt as human being with their own demands of life and dignity—that world has begun to shrink. So the greed had to be limited. How could that be when greed is the chief ingredient of the capitalist ethos and the motive power of the industrial society? So we face the frenzied activities of the supra-national organizations, the trade and tariff negotiations, the great wars and the little wars—little nations and big powers measuring their wit against each other, each trying to have its greed the upper hand. But owing to the frenzied activities of industrialisation, more and more forests are axed, more land is dug and denuded for their minerals, farmlands and plantations are stripped to make way for express ways and factories. Millions of factories belching for their noxious effluents, and millions of ears with then exhaust fumes, pollute the earth to such an extent that we are confronted with global warning an euphemism for impending heat death.

What we have been said is not a story of distant lands. All this is happening even in our own dear motherland.

Commercial forestry is destroying the traditional forests which sustained the life of the tribals and other forest people. Their villages are devastated to provide iron ore, bauxite, coal and other minerals to national or multinational corporations. Forest people are driven from traditional habitat to make way for wild life sanctuaries so as to attract tourists. These people, driven from their traditional land and life support systems crowd the city slums or take up arms and become rebels, variously named as Maoists or recessionists.

All this is inevitable result of the type of industrialization and the style of life that sustains it. Little wonder that the two major revolutions the one of Russia in 1917 and the other in China under the leadership of Mao-tse-Tung in the end made way for the most aggressive capitalist system. Besides, they created huge bureaucratic structures with their own massive usurpation.

This is not surprising. Heavy industrialization needed rapid capital for nation, and that could take place only if the common people were to create the surplus to ensure fast accumulation of capital. Capitalism had already shown the way for if in what Marx had described as primitive accumulation. Besides, the colonisation, preceding and following the Industrial Revolution, had shown the glorious path of industrialisation. Greed in its starkest form had been distilled to accomplish this feat. So the so-called communist revolutionaries of Russia and China had only to follow the trodden path in order to industrialise and we are face to face with the consequences.

Gandhi had a different perception of human nature and path of development. His famous saying; "there is enough in the world for every one's need but not enough for one man's greed", summaries his whole attitude. Once you discard greed, the craving for acquisition which powers modern industrialisation vanishes. A person's endeavour one under this system would be to take minimum from nature, just enough to sustain his life. This could be had with whatever is offered by nature in his neighbourhood. He could farm and spin and weave with the simplest tools which he or his neighbours could make. He lives in harmony with his fellowmen and the plants and animals around him.

Freed from the acquisitive drives, he has enough time to help or play with his neighbours or to nurse the plants and animals, which render from the minimal goods and services. In this system there are no polluting gases, nor the incessant war that is going on against the forces of nature either to tame them or to destroy them. Ecology is not alone. Man does not aspire to godly powers, nor does he need to stop to bestiality to sustain his own ego. One may argue that it is not practical. But with the industrial civilization moving towards doom, this alternative on the contrary appears the only practical way of survival.

13

Gandhian Environmentalism

MANOJ SINHA

Albert Einstein paid Gandhiji rich tribute: "Generations to come, it may be will scarce believe that such one even in flesh and blood walked upon this earth."[1] This expression of Einstein reflects the importance of Gandhiji as a visionary par excellence. The catastrophe that is looming large over our planet Earth has forced us to rediscover him and wonder how we managed to miss his message to which he devoted his life.

Mohan Das Karamchand Gandhi, as perhaps the tallest leader of our time in Indian history, not only resisted the external influence in shaping his ideas, he also retained his indigenous identity. He strengthened his convictions on the basis of traditional and scriptural native resources. His development a unique conversion-mechanism to turn a foreign concept into his own idiom. He was thus able to transform the tradition-modernity syndrome to suit his paradigmatic needs.

While we are progressing day-by-day, there is a simultaneous need for the re-examination of our development. Like any great leader, Mahatma Gandhi, the greatest among Indian leaders, mobilized millions of Indians and launched a protracted mass struggle against the mighty British empire. He also cherished a dream. In his dream, the villagers in independent India would have initiative not live in dirt and darkness as animals. Both men and women would be free and able to hold their own against any one. There would be no plague, cholera, small pox; no one would be idle, nor wallow in luxury. "The contemplated form of the Government in independent India, consistent with the realization of the dream, is one which is completely decentralized and fully democratic."[2] What did Gandhiji perceive for India, and where are we now? The fact is that we are approaching the end of 54 years since our independence, but we have gained no ground in the eradication of poverty, unemployment, etc. We are at a stage where the unequal distribution of the fruits of development has left society at crossroads. In view of all these facts, a scholar of Gandhian economics concludes, "it becomes imperative under such circumstances to insist that neither modernization, nor the extension of capitalist relations of production, is contributing in any way to the welfare of the people. Before any improvement in condition of living of the masses can be looked for, growing structural unemployment can be halted only by revitalizing the labour-intensive occupations of the traditional sector. This is the kernel of Gandhian economic thought, the fundamental analytical insight from which the rest of Gandhian thought can be derived as a series of elaborations."[3] Four days before his death, Gandhiji wrote, "What are we celebrating for"? It was 26th January 1948, and 54 years on, we're still asking the same question.

Apart from these contentions, there is a global crisis facing mankind. It is here in the midst of all the problems, that we need introspection and a serious pursuit of the problems, that we need introspection and a serious pursuit of the philosophy of Gandhiji. "Conserve the world for tomorrow" has become the slogan of humankind around the world. So it is our duty to protect it at any cost. To many, the ultimate solution to the threat of ecological disaster in a world of escalating human wants and population explosion, is to be found in Gandhian philosophy.

The Need for a New Perspective

At the time when Adam Smith was writing, life was short and harsh for most people. There was a constant struggle to satisfy even basic economic needs. Mankind was at Nature's mercy. Today the position seems broadly to the opposite. At the time it seemed appropriate to emphasize the importance of increasing the material economic welfare of all by increasing their consumption of desired commodities. But per capita consumption levels in development countries today greatly exceed that of those earlier times. Consumption levels are much greater than is needed to satisfy basis needs, and for most, permit a measure of luxury. Indeed, the health and welfare of some individuals in advanced countries, suffers as a result of their 'excessive' consumption of commodities, and as result of their restless and never-ending desire for greater income and levels of material consumption. Therefore, it is legitimate to question in the case of the more developed countries whether an even higher level of material consumption per head is an appropriate goal.[4]

There are also other reasons why we need a new perspective. Today we face prospects on a global scale of irreversible environmental damage from economic activities, of which the greenhouse phenomenon is just one example. Not only this, but we are uncertain about the occurrence of such impacts, their rate of onset, and their likely consequences. We face the possibility of sudden and irreversible leaps and bounds in environmental conditions. Past trends, and signs may provide little forewarning of approaching economic and environmental collapse due to resource depletion and environmental degradation. By the time signs of future collapse become apparent, it may already be too late to reverse the deteriorating situation and avoid catastrophe.

The great English economist Alfred Marshall was able to declare in the last century that Nature does not proceed by leaps and bounds. In his framework of thought, marginal certain change is almost assured. But now we fear that nature may sometimes proceeds by leaps and bounds and can do so in irreversible and unpredictable ways.[5]

Since the effects of environmental changes can be

widespread, even global, we can all be affected. Thus, everyone has a stake in what is happening to the environment. Our global environment is a shared resource. However, resolving our conflicts about the use of our shared environment is no easy task as many of us have varying attitudes to risk-taking and uncertainty, and there are differences in the relative gains and losses for each individual. This must be recognized and taken into account in forming our decisions about resource use.

Humans have come to dominate nature but are still subject to its laws. There is no guarantee that mankind will be able to continue to sustain and expand economic activity in the same way as in the past, despite all technological changes and optimism. There is a possibility of unwanted ecological impacts or disasters from economic growth. In such circumstances, it is essential to bring flexibility into resource and response systems.

Gandhian Perspective

Awareness about the importance of the environment is not recent or Western in origin. The great political theorist and economist of ancient India, Chanakya, also known as Kautilya, said as far back as the 4th century BC, that the "stability of an empire depends on the stability of its environment."[6] Gandhi did anticipate the current catastrophe an warned us, that the alternative to urban industrial civilization was villagization, a society based on harmony between humankind and nature.[7]

The unit of society should be a village, or a small manageable group of people who would ideally be self-sufficient (in the matter of their vital requirements) as a unit and bound together in bonds of mutual co-operation and interdependence.[8]

The ideas and thoughts of Gandhi could have many benefits, not only for India but for the Gandhi could have many benefits, not only for India but for the whole universe, as it aims to create an environment of great peace and harmony with nature. But some criticisms are also leveled against this philosophy, such as: (a) Gandhi conceived the village as an insulated system; and (b) He opted for rural primitivism disregarding the tremendous advantages that accrue humanity through advances in technology.

But we can say that both of these accusations emanate from a widely prevaility ignorance about his position in this regard. He persistently advocated independence along with interdependence. "Let us not forget that is man's social nature which distinguishes him from the brute creation. It is his privilege to be independent, it is equally his duty to be interdependent... it will be possible to reconstruct our villages so that villages collectively, not villagers individually, will become self-contained."[9] Further, he says that to be self-sufficient is not to be altogether self-contained. In no circumstances would we be able to produce all the things we need. So, though our aim is complete self-sufficiency, we shall have to get from outside the village what we cannot produce in the village. We shall have to produce more of what we can in order to exchange what we are unable to produce. Thus when Gandhi speaks of villages collectively striving for a self-contained system, he is advocating integrated area development. Similarly, having ruled out the possibility of attaining complete self-sufficiency, he recognized the need for regional specialisation and exchange of goods between regions, a nation ask into balanced regional development.

Gandhi did not mean by village primitivism, a village society not having and using modern machines and tools. He was in favour of technology and machines which were within the affordable limits of the villagers, as only a technologically well development village can make modern machines, and only economically advanced villages can afford them. So it is clear that Gandhi was not in opposition to the villages being technologically or economically advanced, but objected to villages being exploited by cities. He did not wish for villages to get infected by the germs of industrialism. The coexistence between city and village is possible only if balance between them is pursued, and the Gandhian perspective provides for it. He says: "Under my scheme, nothing will be allowed to be produced by the cities which can equally well be produced by villages. The proper function of cities is to serve as clearing house for village products."[10]

It is often alleged that under the Gandhian scheme, villages will not be able to produce sophisticated, high quality goods. But he writes, "When our villages are fully developed, there will be no dearth of men with high degrees of skill and artistic talent. There will be village poets, village artists, village architects, linguists and research workers. In short, there will be nothing in life worth having which will not be had in villages."[11] It is indeed dishonest to dismiss such high quality village life as 'primitive'.

Why did Gandhi opt for villagization? The Gandhian rationale in this context has two dimensions: negatively viewed, it was an onslaught against the exploitative tendency of industrialism and the domination by urbanism; and positively considered, it was an attempt to establish a non-violent social order, free from explotation.[12]

Gandhi was a strong follower of the principle of non-violence, and domination of one life by another was considered a violence of certain degree in the eyes of Gandhi. He writes: "Today the cities dominate and drain the villages so that they are crumbling to ruin ... exploiting the villages is itself organized violence."[13] Further, "You cannot build non-violence on a factory civilisation, but it can be built on self-contained villages... rural economy as I have conceived it, eschews exploitation altogether and exploitation is the essence of violence."[14]

In a rural situation there are several factors which facilitate building non-violent social order. Firstly, it is possible to evolve a non-violent occupational structure. "A non-violent occupation is ... that occupation which is fundamentally free from violence and which involves no exploitation or envy of others. When a man is content to own only so much land as he can till with his own labour, he cannot exploit others. Handicrafts exclude exploitation and savery."[15] That is, a peasant way of life is conducive to a non-violent society. Secondly, village life promotes the Swadeshi spirit. Swadeshi is that spirit in us which restricts us to use and service our immediate surroundings to the exclusion of the more remote. This necessarily insulates a spirit of independence and self-reliance. Thirdly, the rural set-up provides a reason for everyone to perform physical labour, which is a great social leveler return to village life means a definite, voluntary recognition of the duty of bread labour and all it connotes. Viewed against the background of India's caste-liked occupational structure and the abhorrence with which the twice-born varna groups viewed manual labour, the notion of compulsory bread labour prescribed by Gandhi was a measure potent with revolutionary vitality for social transformation. Fourthly, the land-based economy of villages is more amenable to institutionalizing the principles of trusteeship, invoking the traditional maxim, that all land belongs to God, that is the community, Gandhi argued that land should be collectively owned and operated. He wanted the landowners to be the trustees and trusted friends of the entire village community, a factor which would facilitate the emergence of non-violent society. Here, it should be clear that Gandhi's conception of the village was not anchored in the modern (urban-industrial) notion of development.

Human Ecology and Mahatma Gandhi

Although during the life time of Mahatma Gandhi there was no wide ranging debates on environment and development *per se*, he was nevertheless ahead of his times, on account of his being deeply conscious of the very environmental concerns we perceive today. This shows Gandhi's forethought and vision. This is abundantly clear from his statements and writings. Above all it is most obvious through the simple and sustainable personal lifestyle that this great socio-economic and political reformer followed in his life. He renounced luxury, and willingly experienced the pangs of deprivation, despite being from a willingly experienced the pangs of deprivation, despite being from a wealthy family. As a barrister at-law, he could have led a very comfortable life. He identified himself with the poorest of the poor (daridranaraian) in the country. Indeed, he had a very holistic approach towards all such problems. His strongest point was that he preached what he practiced. His strongest (ashrams) stood as testimony to this. These were located in an open and rustic rural setting and were based on self-help, local self-reliance, participatory management and gender equality, the importance of which has now only been realised. According to N. Radhakrishnan: "The ashrams or the communities Gandhi founded, both in South Africa and India, were meaningful centres where Gandhi demonstrated with convincing success how each member of community could live in harmony with nature. The community life Gandhiji developing consisted of manual labour, tree planting, agriculture, simple life, and carfts."[16] This precept of Gandhiji is also reflected in the writings of the Nobel Prize winning physicist Gritj of Capra. Capra says that many modern scientists support a society which is currently based on a mechanistic and fragmented world view, without appreciating that science points beyond such a view. It towards oneness of the universe, which includes, besides our natural environment, our fellow human beings. He believes that the world-view implied by modern physics seems inconsistent without present society, which does not reflect the harmonious inter-relatedness one observes in nature.[17] Thus Gandhi did not merely speak about harmony with nature, but realised it in a living sense through his ashrams a live demonstration of his theories and beliefs.

Gandhi's underlying philosophy was need, not greed, and some comfort, but no luxury. In the final analysis, these are also the basics of sustainable development. Environmentalism was a part of his daily routine. In every sense he had foreseen the environmental crises that were on the horizon.

Gandhi's view of he relationship between human kind and Nature was influenced by the Vedic perceptions about Earth being a home of very large family of living organisms (Vasudhaiva Kutumbakam). Atharv Veda presents the concept that the earth is our mother (Dharti Mata) or the universal Mother. Furthermore, the earth, as a whole, is considered a gigantic super-organism which is living, dynamic, evolving, and continuing. Earth is the only planet in our solar system that harbours life as we know. Today, due to unsustainable industrial development, the earth system is not only under considerable stress and strain, it is in jeopardy. Many physical and chemical changes have taken place in the system which are cause for serious concern. Changes in life-support systems ultimately affect the survival potential of different organisms, including the quality of life of human beings.

One of the important foundations of Gandhi's environmentalism has been the age-old ethical doctrine that India has given to the world: non-violence is the highest dharma (ahimsa parmo dharma).[18]

Gandhi and Green Thought

Cultivation of an eco-centric culture is crucial to achieving a lasting solution to the ecological crisis. Such a culture was embedded in Gandhi ideas and behaviour.[19] Only in a political community where consensus is for ecology preservation, can substantive reforms that protect biodiversity and life support systems be achieved.[20]

Such a comprehensive ecocentric perspective:

- (i) accepts the needs for the protection of large tracts of representative eco-systems;
- (ii) the development of a humane population policy that respects the carrying capacity of eco-systems;
- (iii) ensures the "rights" of other species to share the Earth's life support system;
- (iv) promotes a fundamental re-evaluation of human needs, technologies and life-system a way as;
  - (a) to minimise energy and resource consumption; and
  - (b) to minimise or eliminate pollution;
- (v) the provision of adequate compensation whenever ecological reforms are likely to produce inequitable consequences for certain social groups, classes, or nations; and
- (vi) believes in non-violence.[21]

Though many environmentalists do not share this opinion, it is the blueprint of post-environmentalism in which discerning theorists will find the fabric of Green political thought inter-woven with fine threads of Gandhian thought. Seven Social Sins and find ways of avoiding them."[22]

Harmony with Nature and Gandhi

Mahatma Gandhi realised that not only man must desist from exploiting man, but he must also desist from violence in any form, and therefore from the exploitation of nature and natural resources. The resources of the earth should be used as God's gifts to the whole human race and used with due consideration for the needs of present and future generations. As long as the rhythmic cycle of life is not destroyed that soil renews its fertility and provides health, sustenance and peace to those who depend on it. But when greed prevails, nature's balance is upset and there is all round biological deterioration. Nature's balance is very delicate, a slight disturbance is enough to upset the ecological system.

His ideas were based on the Indian Philosophy of Vedanta, which is a combination of spiritual faith and scientific thought.[23] The activities of modern industrial hi-tech 'civilisation' has to be held responsible for the present situation. In 1927 he had warned the world that the large scale industrialism would create problems of the type we are confronting today. He said, "The world influenced by the western culture was going in the wrong direction and like the proverbial moth world burn itself eventually in the flame around which it was dancing carelessly."[24] Ironically, that same year, Jawaharlal Nehru returned from the Soviet Union, greatly impressed with the success of Soviet industrialization. Gandhi described modern civilization—its unabated exploitation of resources, multiplication of wants, production for the market and consumerism-as satanic.

Ecologists all over the world today subscribed to Gandhi's view that industrial society in its present form is no longer sustainable. He was not against industrialization but against industrialism and the dehumanised machine culture. He stressed, "Machinery merely helps a few to ride upon the backs of millions."[25] He emphasized upon small-scale enterprises for production by the masses and not mass production by any individual. The larger the unit of production, whether in field or factory, the more detrimental it is to individual development. In a decentralized society, way of life is more important than means of production.

Gandhi stressed the importance of the individual. For him, supreme consideration is to be given to human.

We derive no benefit from a high standard of living which is linked with a deprived way of life. The price of mechanical, comfort amenities and a high standard of living will be paid from through violence and war. Modern man thinks that on many fronts he has achieved victory over nature, but as a matter of fact man and human freedom are continually being vanquished.

The simple lifestyle of Gandhi and his frugal living habits had a great ecological bearing. He put greater stress on moral than on material values. The accepted values of life should be truth and non-violence. Science has given us unlimited mastery over nature, but it has not been able to teach us self-control. Today man is swayed by jealousy, hate, fear, desire, greed, acquisitiveness, anger and egoism.

Petra K. Kelly writes: "Recently I came across an article by Frienda Berrigan, the daughter of Philip Berrigan on 'Becoming an Audit.' She mentioned the "Seven Social Sins" listed by Gandhi on her wall—

- Politics without principle.
- Pleasure without conscience.
- Wealth without work.
- Knowledge without character.
- Commerce without morality.
- Science without humanity.
- Worship without sacrifice.

> "I think it is most important that we being to understand these seven social sins and find ways of avoiding them."[22]

In the life-cycle of plants, animals and men, the principle of balance must replace that of competition. We shall have to develop both humility in our dealings with nature, and respect for all forms of life. For the protection of our race, people should be motivated by moral laws in their daily life. It will be possible to achieve this spiritual power if we consciously establish unity with man and nature, and collectively work to ensure its realization. The whole of humanity is benefited by one man's spiritual development, the whole of humanity is harmed by one man's spiritual downfall. Through achieving unity with all living creatures, we can approach non-violence.

Ecologist Edward Goldsmith seeks guidance from the vernacular man who was once committed to maintaining the critical order so necessary to preserve the planet in a habitable state. He points out that, "the present world view, I am afraid serves to rationalize and legitimize today's policies. It's most basic tenet is of progress and the idea that science, technology and industry are going to create a paradise."[26] This Modernisation does not consider the natural climate and environmental conditions. Our so-called sophisticated and life-improving technological developments simply fail to do any good.

Gandhian Society: A Revolution

Mahatma Gandhi pronounced his views on various issues, and also formulated a comprehensive programmes for implementation of his ideas. Included in his thinking was the notion that unless every village turned itself into a village republic with the provision of elementary civic amenities, guaranteed employment and a living wage to everyone for securing the basic necessities of human existence, one word could claim that the country was really free. In order to secure this result, individuals, both in the villages and in the urban areas, must follow the principles of truth and non-violence. In order to effect this, Panchayati Raj should be established and the members charged with the responsibility of keeping the village clean, and of finding a source of employment for every family in the village. To quote him: "We have to tackle the triple malady which holds our villages fast in its grip and severely retards the healthy, progressive growth of the village community. The village movement is an attempt to establish healthy contract with villagers by inducting those who are fired with the spirit of service, and encourage them to find self-expression in the service of the villagers."[27]

While we should welcome the creation of large-scale

industries that could be capital-intensive, we have to lay equal stress on cotton and small scale industries. This would help reorientate our rural economy and bring about an economic transformation in our villages which are the backbone of the body politic. Pointing out the merit of this approach, Mohit Chakraborti pointed our that, To Gandhi, as to Swami Vivekananda, Sri Aurobindo and so many others, science and technology were always means are never ends. Again, they were never considered to be the most important or the only means for the progress. Gandhi favoured small scale industry. He wanted to build his ideal society on a rural basis. In his ideals, not science but religion, not technology but ethics, had the highest place. Gandhi could easily foresee the doom or mankind, due to unbridled faith in science and technology. Today we have arrived at a point, where the evils of science and technology are as clear as their advantages. The realization has dawned that if man has to survive on this planet, or rather if earth has to survive, there should be a planned and controlled development of science and technology. Science and technology are not the ends, the end is Ram Rajya or Sarvodaya. The world has become small today. No single country may go on accumulating atomic weapons without any danger to others. A nuclear explosion anywhere is a risk everywhere. Futurologists have clearly pointed out the ruinous results of unbridled industrial pollution.

It is here that Gandhi's views have become so relevant today. These should be planned and moulded in the service of Sarvodaya. The ecology of a country is the most precious thing to be saved, at all cost.

A Philosophical Relevance

The international community seems to be involved at the moment in a candid reappraisal of the efficacy of Gandhian philosophy, particularly the Gandhian model of development. It may be noted that there is a global non-violent awakening, and many of the alternatives Gandhi suggested to humanity, are being examined and put into practice vigorously. For years his non-violent alternatives were not treated with the kind of conviction that befit great ideas. Such was humanity's pre-occupation with "wonderful things", of science and technology which subsequently have altered the basic human approach to man and matters. Everybody seems to have forgotten the simple truth as to where these developments will take humanity. The tremendous strides of innovation that have brought astonishing new things through the communication explosion, has also added to as insatiable appetite for more and more. A side effect of the new culture which came with this development was rising consumerism at a micro-level, and materialism at a macro-level little. No one seems to have noticed that these two tendencies have reached such saturation point, that materialism and consumerism have started to consume us.

Gandhi warned humanity against the rising tide of materialism and consumerism when he advocated the necessity to limit one's wants, rather than hoarding consumer and luxury items. The manner in which nature is being exploited under the mistaken notion that it has inexhaustible resources also attracted the attention of Gandhi and he advocated discipline in the use of resources, pointing out that nature provides enough to satisfy every man's needs, but not for anybody's greed. The alternative sources of energy and his insistence on the use of these alternatives were initially scoffed at or just ignored. It appears that humanity has now woken up and is looking around desperately for alternatives. Here stands Gandhi, whose holistic vision of life is offering them the much needed break through.

Ecological Balance and Harmony

Gandhi was against blind urbanization and industrialization in India. He visualized that this would create ecological imbalance, both at village and city levels. He cautioned against the ruthless exploitation of nature for the progress of industry. In the tradition of ancient Indian thoughts, he insisted upon harmony of man and nature, individual and society, citizen and the state, the Hindu and the Muslim, man and woman and the human beings and the animals, even the trees and plants, rivers and oceans, mountains and plains, whenever there is a question of interrelationship between two or more elements, the Indian formula harmony. So was the solution offered by Gandhi in all fields of life.

Harmony with nature is basic to Gandhian thought. Thankfully, most countries have realised the danger of disturbing the ecological balance Greater attention is now being paid to forestation, social forestry; protection of top soil from erosion, prevention of damage resulting from the use of chemical fertilizers, urbanization, use of synthetics, fast foods, excessive use of petroleum products, and social problems of alienation. Now there is greater appreciation of the value of the holistic approach, integrated development, and of psychological problems? Gandhi believed that prevention is better than cure; that a long-term view is more rewarding than a short-term view. Unnecessary movement of raw materials and men is at the root of many ills.

Even in 1910, Mahatma Gandhi had predicted crises after crises on our environment as result of modern technology, "Nature works unceasingly according to her laws, but man violates them constantly"[28] in a variety of ways and in different Periods thoughout the ages; nature has signelled to humanity that there is nothing in the world which is not subject to change.

The 'Need' for Rethinking

There is now a desperate need for major rethinking on social, economic, environmental, and cultural fronts, so as to translate sustainable development into reality. Transformation of individuals is very necessary as Gandhi envisaged. This means ushering in a programmed for environmental education with regard to long-range ecological security. Natural ecosystems, agro ecosystems and industrial economic systems have to be both conserved and used in a sustainable manner. In other words, there has to be a healthy blend of environmental, social development, and economic imperatives. A sustainable society has faith in science and technology as an instrument of environmentally friendly social and economic change. Furthermore, economic growth is not at the expense of ecological assets. The sustainable society has to aim at working in partnership with nature and conserve non-renewable resources. It must produce goods that are easy to recycle, reuse, and repair after use. Such a society must also recycle and reuse discarded matter. The sustainable economy aims at maintenance at a constant and manageable level, of both the number of people and livestock, and quantity of goods. These should be within the carrying capacity of the concerned systems: natural-ecosystems, agro-ecosystems or industrial-economic systems. The methods of growing food and raising livestock must be based on soil and water conservation, bio-fertilzers, biological control of pests and minimal use of non-renewable energy. There has to be extensive use of bio-technology in a sustainable society. Basic needs of the people should be met without any serious determent to environment.

Following this path of development, people must believe that resources of the earth have to be protected and sustained not only for human kind, but also for other species; and not only for this generation, but also for generations to follow. To manage and sustain resources of the earth, the approach must not be centered around any one species, i.e. the human being, it should encompass the entire life support system. People should work with nature and not waste resources unnecessarily, nor interfere with other species.

A sustainable society and economy is based on the firm belief that belief that earth has a finite area, both for purposes of colonization of species and utilization of resources. Furthermore, increasing population growth, production and consumption, stress and strain place on the natural processes. These processes, renew and maintain the life support system (air, water, soil, forests, and biodiversity). It is essential not to over load the system with environmental degradation and depletion of resources. We must work in harmony with nature, reducing unnecessary use and wastage of resources, preserving other species. Therefore, for short-term gains, long term environmental and economic cost must be avoided.

To recollect Gandhi's prophetic statement, "The earth provides enough to satisfy every man's needs, but not every man's greed." This statement of his has absorbed into the folklore of world environmental literature. Some points that emerge from such thinking are given below:

- The physical, chemical, and biological assets of the earth constitute the capital. The capital should not be in deficit on account of the conventional economic activities of humanity. It has to be conserved.
- A sick earth system will lead to a sick environment and a sick economy, degraded; polluted, and unsustainable environment with a ravaged and plundered resource-base.
- The human race must willingly practice population control and ensure its stabilization at the level of the carrying capacity.
- The human race must owe responsibility for whatever damage occurs during development, and restore degraded eco-systems and protect those that are endangered on other counts. This is because the earth system is the only habitat for living species (including the human race). Protection of all life our primary duty.
- Since resources of the earth are finite, humankind must willingly set a limit to its requirements for sustenance, need, and comfort rather than for greed and luxury.
- There is an urgent need for change in present day lifestyles of affluent countries, as these lead to over-extraction and over-consumption of resources. The result is pollution and eco-degradation of a very serious kind with equally serious environmental impacts. Their management will take time because it is not easy. Equally important is the improvement of the lifestyle of the poor, because subsistence lifestyles also lead to pollution and eco-degradation of different, albeit mostly manageable kind.
- Short and long-term external environmental costs must be internalized. In other words, market economy must include both the present and

future costs of pollution and eco-degradation so that these are not passed on the society at large and to the environment as a whole. Using the polluter pays principle, these costs must be met by the manufacture and/or country concerned for not using environmentally friendly technology.

- Progressive replacement of environmentally harmful goods by environmentally friendly ones must take place.
- Serious attempts have to be made to evolve and encourage the use of technologies that lead to more output from minimum amount of resource inputs, i.e., that produce more goods and services from less and less resources. Such technologies should produce a minimal amount of pollution and use a minimal amount of energy.
- Both cost and time-wise, anticipatory or preventive action is need for cheaper than restorative action.
- There is need for taking a hard look at all tax rebates and subsidies; because in their present form, these lead to resource waste. These may enhance production in the short range, but are disastrous to the environment in the long-run. There is need to replace the present day technologies with those technologies and production systems of goods such system should as far as possible, encourage efficient resource use and avoid resource waste, eco-degradation and pollution. Such technologies need to be rewarded and awarded.

From the preceding account, it is clear that in order to improve suitability, we need appropriate environmental policies, and a whole range of environment-friendly technologies.[29]

Gandhi and Sustainable Development

"Gandhi worked and wrote in a time which the parlance of development was not yet current, and so his writings may not be recongised automatically as literature on development. In the mainstream of international development literature, his insights have not been ignored completely, but interest in them has been clearly much less than his influence on post-Independence India. While millions of people outside India have heard and taken to heart his message of non-violence (Ahimsa), even though sometimes missing its deeper spiritual and social active connotations. It is more difficult to pin point his influence on development policies and action outside India."[30] This contention of J. George Waardenburg may not be correct, but it is very much true that during contemporary period of Gandhi, such diverse problems on all fronts as humanity faces today, did not exist. But we can trace the influence and relevance of Gandhi in today's context. Today Gandhi has become an alternative not only for India but for the whole world. Because his solution-oriented discourses keep simplicity at its core. What Gandhi has written himself about his philosophy, in his own What Gandhi has written himself about his philosophy, in his own words, "I do not claim to have originated any new principle. I have simply tried in my own way to apply the eternal truths to our own daily life and problems. Well, all my philosophy, if it may be called by that pretentious name, is contained in what I have said, you will not call it 'Gandhism': there is no 'ism' about it. And no elaborate literature or propaganda is needed about it."[31]

The philosophical core of 'Gandhism' can be applied in any field today for a solution. Adi H. Doctor writes, "It is not my contention that Gandhi had consciously developed a well reasoned thesis on suitability. Gandhi had neither the time nor the patience or inclination to formulate theories. He wrote voluminously. He arrived at several concepts almost intuitively. He would make extreme statements and often then proceed to qualify them in many ways. Nevertheless, his political and economic ideas or his political and economic perspectives, provide us with the raw materials for subsequent theorising."[32] So, the philosophical depth of Gandhi's writing has become more realistic today. Through Gandhi we have the philosophical foundation and practical tools needed for sustainable development, cultural and biological diversity through Swadeshi, a thirst for justice, a capacity for compassion, and Yoga to feed the transpersonal self. Gandhi believed that man was single integral personality whose life could not be compartmentalized into different lives like the religious and the secular, the political and the economic. Man lived life as a whole and hence he urged, that we adopt a holistic view of life. Gandhi found modern man dehumanized and suffering from a pervasive feeling of loneliness and helplessness in a hostile world, and he attributed this to the prevailing social, political and economic structures we had adopted.

Gandhi saw his countrymen crippled by colonialism and incessant caste hostilities. He found that the contemporary West minister Parliamentary model of government and the capitalist economy based on large scale production, stifling and constraining to individuals liberty and his capacity to realize his potential or best self. Worse, he considered present days civilization too pre-occupied with ever-rising standards of living, potentially destroying the well being of future generations. After Gandhi, it was Jaiprakash Narayan who was to warn fellow socialists along similar lines. He cautioned them against making the mistake of allowing the capitalist mode of production to re-entrench itself under the garb of democracy and constitutionalism.[33]

With rare insight, Gandhi saw both the contemporary systems, socialism and capitalism, carrying the elements of exploitation. Exploitation stemmed from the method of large scale production that was a common feature of both the economic systems. The only difference between the two systems lay in the fact that large scale production gave rise to private enterprises capitalism in one system, while it paved the way for state capitalism in the other. Gandhi foresaw that exploitation was bound to be present in any system exhibiting centralization of power.

According to Gandhi, the capitalist mode of production exploited man and constrained his freedom in numerous ways. Based on the principle of economics of scale, the capitalist mode naturally resulted in larger and larger units of production. Such centralized production concentrated power in the hands of the few who owned or managed the large enterprises. That is why he claimed that it was machines that divided society into two classes of those who have and those who do not have, of owners, managers, and of industry and it's workers.

The capitalist mode of production not only exploits man for profit, but also exploits nature. It is indeed to Gandhi's credit that he foresaw, why before the new-classical economists and the advocates of sustainable growth, the truth that humanity cannot survive if it does not learn to live in harmony with nature. A moral order as Gandhi saw it, was one which neither exploited man nor nature. Just as a father ought to consider not only providing for the present needs of his wife and children but also with providing for their future needs, in like manner must the community think not only of the present generation but also of future generations. But the community can provide for future generations only if it follows what Gandhi called the Law of Return, that is, return to the soil in organic from what is taken from the soil. What Gandhi was saying was that if a community or economy wanted to ensure the welfare or future generations it must restrict consumption as for as possible to renewable resources. Gandhi's lament was that the capitalist mode of production, with eyes for productivity only, measured in terms of output and profit, was indulging in and indiscriminate exploitation of non-renewable resources. Thus, he lamented the fact that in industry we were increasingly relying on non-replenish able resources like oil and coal; while in agriculture we were indulging in an improvident denudation of forests for greedy exploitation of their timber wealth. In like manner, he issued warnings against overgrazing, use of fertilizers, and mechanization in agriculture which exposed the soil to the elements.

In a materialistic civilization, Gandhi argued, man has no rational incentive to be truly human. He squarely blamed the West and its materialist, acquisitive philosophy, for the invention of labour saving technologies and the preference for the mode of large scale production based on economics of scale. In Gandhian thought, any economy worth its name must aim at promoting the happiness of both present and future generations. But happiness and welfare for all is not synonymous with more and more material prosperity. "The man", said Gandhi in *Hind Swaraj,* "is a restless bird, the more it gets, the more it wants and still remains unsatisfied. The more we indulge in our passions, the more unbridled they become." Peace and happiness are mental states or conditions which are better realised when we set limits to our indulgence. Peace emanates from contentment and hence like the Vedic Rishis (Sages), Gandhi preached that man should learn to live content with his real needs. He should not crave for more than what is necessary in order to live a life of reasonable comfort. What Gandhi objected to was unlimited wants which establish an imbalance in human life. He claimed that an economy based on unlimited wants was bound to prove a disaster. It would give rise to new and more exploitative technologies. It would lead to indiscriminate exploitation of non-renewable nature resources. In Yervada Mandir, Gandhi observed, "Civilisation in the real sense of the term, consists not in the multiplication but in the deliberate and voluntary reduction of wants. This alone promotes real happiness and contentment and increases capacity of services."[34] This alone can be said as a guarantee for a safe future.

Mahatma Gandhi gave us the example that thought out our lives we can be dissenters, even rebels but never through violence, and this is what we must try to teach our children, by our example; to teach the example of freedom. Of freedom of expression as the first Article of the Declaration of Human Right, "All human beings are born free and equal in dignity and rights."[35]

While taking a note of the importance of Gandhi, Kaka Kalelkar has written, "More than a personality, he is an institution and the harbinger of a new culture that knew no limitations of geographical or racial barriers. Some of the seeds scattered will no doubt will take time to germinate, but he has already changed the face of India, and promises now a hundred years after his birth to change the face of the world."[36]

As we enter the last century, human beings are compelled to sit up and reassess their own environments, nature, culture and future. "Has man a future?" asked the great mathematician and philosopher, Bertrand Russell, in the mid-sixties when the world was experiencing a possible nuclear tragedy under the pressure of cold was situation. Now that worry is over temporarily, other worries are creating nightmares in the minds of millions around the world, and one of the serious concerns is environmental. It has been the job of reckless industrialization that the world has followed during the last hundred years. It is in this context that Gandhi will be well remembered by posterity, apart from other significant areas in which his thoughts and contributions have unparalleled value and acceptance.

Traditional Knowledge

The concerns for the natural environment have been married to the idea that human respect for nature is lost in the pursuit of material gains. Materialism, the production of goods from nature, represent an abdication of human responsibility for the natural world. It is possible to recognize the strength of ethical commitments in the environmental perspective. And these ethical concerns are not as recent as one may imagine. In a country like India, people have been conscious of environmental problems ever since the vedic times. One finds mention in almost all ancient Hindu scriptures, including. those of Jainsim and Buddhism, that nature and mankind form an integral part of the life support system. The Earth as the source of all life—non-human as well as human—has been considered to be an object of awe, love, reverence and worship as the mother goddess. The Sufi and the Bhakti saint poets like Kabir, Chishti, Nanak and Tukaram, all sang of the unity and oneness of all, that a wound inflicted on any element hunts the total system. That all things are useful to human beings and therefore should learn to live in harmony with non-human nature, is very well established by the story of Jivaka, who was not able to find even a single plant which was of no use to humans.[37]

The ancient Hindu scriptures show that it has always been considered as a dharma or divine duty of individuals to protect the environment not only for their self-interest, but for the sake of protecting the environment itself. It also finds wide mention of specific duties of human beings towards humanity and God's Creations, that are called, Manav

Dharma. This concept of Manav Dharma, applies to every individual on the planet, and demands that all individuals must pay due respects to all other creation. It can be derived therefore, that a country like India, is deeply rooted in the concept of respect for nature in its culture and this respect forms a part of its social life.

The significance of nature is not merely due to the resources that it gives us in order to meet humanities daily requirements. Nature is not just a conglomeration of resources, it is a complete system, which we are a part of. We cannot afford to nature the idea conquering nature, as it will turn on us. Hitherto, it seems as if we have proven that we do not comprehend the all pervasive character of nature, as we have not been prepared to see it as a holistic system, and have failed to see our role in it.

The mysteries of nature revealed to man so far by science are only a negligible fraction of the processes of nature. Despite the various revealations science has made about nature, it shall remain true that a great deal more remains concealed from us. The knowledge derived from sense organs, or instruments, or by inference is always one-dimensional. Understanding nature is a multidimensional activity which can be experienced through intuition and not through sensory perception. A point which was continually emphasized by Mahatma Gandhi. Therefore, to fully grasp the meaning of scientific knowledge, we have to depend on our intuition. Our ancestors, who had experienced the truth internally, always held that metaphysically all existence is one and that it is not divisible. The divisions are only illusory. Our external experience of the world reveal its plurality but through our internal experiences it is possible to see the world as one. This ultimate reality experienced internally has been traditionally termed God, and this is the way Mahatma Gandhi tried to link God and Nature.

This kind of knowledge had helped Indians to maintain a constant link with nature, because nature in its infinite forms and countless modes was believed to be the manifestation of God Himself. This is why all beings in the universe were said to be interrelated. To maintain this relation, there was a need to strike a harmonious balance with each other. As soon as this harmony is destroyed, the internal organization of nature will break down and there will be none who would be able to escape its effects.[38]

This knowledge from which constitutes how to live in harmony with nature without upsetting its balance, is termed as traditional knowledge. Loss of such valuable knowledge due to blind pursuit of materialism may be one of the reasons why mankind has scored such spectacular success in destroying harmony. All over the world the bio-centric tendency to traditional native thinking is now in the process of the being redefined, as exemplified above in the case of India. Traditional native world views seem to have stressed several themes at odds with industrial capitalism: The unity and inter-relatedness of life; the belief that the world unfolds in a cyclic, not uni-linear way; a communal system of property, as against private ownership; detailed knowledge of nature; living in place (bio-regionalism); population self-regulation; respect for all life—forms and their sacredness; a sustainable harvest of wild-life over thousands of years; and rituals that severely limit the destruction by humans of flora and fauna and the land itself. Obviously, such traditional native perspectives have a great deal of compatibility with ecology.[39]

The knowledge base built up by tribal societies that evolved over a period of time, rationalises their particular way of life which is formulated in a different language, the language of mythology. It rationalizes something which lasts, is fulfilling, and is sustaining. The people who have lived in India for centuries are likely to know how to farm the land. They obtain excellent yield methods, E.F. Schumacher points out, "bear the mark of non-violence and humility towards the infinitely subtle system of the modern world. If we now realize that the modern lifestyle is putting us into mortal danger, we may find it in our hearts to support and even join these pioneers rather than to ignore or ridicule them.[39]

The Past as Future: The Prithvi Sukta

O.P. Dwivedi and Neelam Trivedi, in their treatise Prithvi Sukta and Environmental Stewardship describe in detail The Prithvi Sukta meaning An Ode to the Earth, from the ancient Indian book, The Atharva Veda. The prithvi Sukta describes ways to live in Harmony with Nature. The most important ones being welfare of all and giving up. Of hatred, and the concept of trusteeship. The Suktas also describe how the villages and cities are to be planned so that environment is not endangered. It stresses on the unity of all living beings and their co-existence. Maintenance of purity of air, water and soil should be integrated into living. Based on the above Sukta, the authors prescribe a code, named as the environmental code. This code is reproduced below:[40]

- Human beings have the obligation for the stewardship of the Earth and the planetary system.
- Nations should aim for sustainable development that is ecologically sound.
- Recognition of the fact that there is an interdependence among all species on earth and obliteration of any one particular specie shall have disastrous consequences on all others.
- Acceptance of responsibility by all individuals, and state holders, that we are the trustee and the guardians of the environment for present and future generations; and that we ought to be environmentally accountable.
- Acknowledgment of responsibility, individually and collectively, for sensitizing our fellow humans, concerning environmental protection and conservation.
- Many local and indigenous people have a unique knowledge of their regional ecosystems, a knowledge and culture which should be respected and sustained.
- Pursuance and adoption of values that address current consumptive patterns and the growth of human population.

It is not very difficult to see the similarities of the Gandhian approach with the environmental code proposed by Dwivedi and Trivedi. Indeed, Gandhi may himself have derived his principles from the same source, The Prithvi Sukta. This environmental code addresses the roots of environmental degradation, and looks to the entire problem in its totality. Therefore it is bound to succeed, if adopted. However, minds steeped deeply in Western materialistic culture and consumptive patterns may take a while longer to appreciate the divine knowledge presented to them in simple code. What has not been discussed here from the Prithvi Sukta, is the ways it prescribes to deal with violators of this environmental code. Governments and societies might have to consider those too in the future.

What is to be Done?

There is a need for massive, environmental reclamation. This includes preservation and regeneration of existing forest areas, deforestation of denuded lands, soil conservation measures, cleaning up drives and anti-pollution measures, energy conservation and use of renewable energy sources to name a few. To quote J. Krishnamurthy; "Now, when we are in a state of conflict, of suffering, there is no comprehension: in that state, however cunningly and carefully thought out our action may be, it can only lead to further confusion and sorrow."[41]

But these are all only fragments of a solution, fragments which would be rendered meaningless, or ineffective and inadequate, if not placed within the framework of a very different socio-political and economic structure, from the one we have today. Some major elements of changes required stem from an understanding of the social causes of environmental problems. Most important is a much more equitable control over natural resources so that their use is no longer in the interests of only a minority. Drastic land reforms are an example of such a change. Much greater public control over the use of forest resources is another example. We desperately need a system in which industrial workers can effectively demand cleaner work environments, slum-dwellers can orient urban planning towards their needs, women can articulate and get action taken on environment-related problems which affect them, tribals can live in peace in their forest dwellings if they desire, and so on. We need, in other words people's control over their own lives and environment.

Gandhian Model and Alternative

Gandhian model as an 'alternative' is village-oriented, decentralized and labour-intensive, and has agriculture at complete harmony with nature, to satisfy of the natural and basic needs of society, and not the 'induced' demands of the elite consumer.

Alternative technology which aims at meeting the needs of everyone in rural as well as urban sectors, would reduce movement towards urbanization. With decentralization of production based on the use of local material, agricultural products with low energy consuming process, urbanization pressures would be reduced. Further, communities would develop in a manner in which they would be able to occupy themselves usefully, meet a set of their requirements, development facilities for their work and thus would be able to contribute creatively to society as a whole.

There should be complete co-ordination between policy-markers, planners and environmentalists in protecting and conserving the environments. The development process has to be modified in such a way that there is complete harmony with the needs of the people and with the need to maintain ecological balance. A slight distortion in this pattern will bring catastrophe. Until and unless, we don't change our luxurious lifestyles and start living in harmony with self, society and nature, no numbers of 'conferences' or 'agendas' can save mother earth from disaster.

In India, where there is no greater source of moral authority, Gandhi has emerged as the patron saint of the environmental movement. In providing an environmental gloss to Gandhi's ideas, leading activists have invoked his ethics of self-restraint, his attacks on consumerism, and his celebration of village society as providing building-blocks for the construction of a environment friendly and harmonious alternative to modern industrial development. "By comparison, the cultural icons of the Western environmental movement are more often individual, such as John Muir, who have tended to downplay human concerns in their defense of the unspoilt wilderness."[42]

Gandhi's environmentalism had its roots in a deep antipathy to urban civilization and a belief in self-sufficiency, in self-negation and denial rather than wasteful consumption. Gandhi was not going back to nature but to the village and to peasantry as the heart and soul of India, to rural asceticism and harmony as against urban bustle and industrial strife. It is in this context that the Gandhian view of a sound and sustainable economy becomes a matter of interest to people of the non-Western world. Gandhi looked beyond the market and into the consequences of industrialism for humans.

In a lecture delivered at Allahabad on 22 December 1961, Gandhi dealt with this basic issue. "Does economic progress clash with real progress. By economic progress, take it, we mean material advancement without limit, and by real progress we mean material advancement without limit, and by real progress we mean moral progress which again is the same thing, as progress of the permanent element in us.... in a well-ordered society, the security of one's livelihood should be and is bound to be the easiest thing in the world. Indeed, the test of orderliness in a country is not the number of millionaires it owns, but the absence of starvation among the masses."[43]

The Gandhian approach provides on alternative to both individualism and socialism. This view gets confirmation and reinforcement from the stand point of Rajani Kothari; "Thus the attitudes engendered by our given perspective are somewhat different from those that move either to the establishment intellectuals . committed to modernizing the world in the image of the Western Technological Civilisation, or the anti-establishment intellectuals from the same centres who are roaming the world after the fashion of new missionaries and preaching revolution."[44]

The modern industrial urban civilization makes it difficult to cultivate the values and virtues of civility personal initiative and responsibility concern for neighbourhood and community, and accountability for public conduct. High technology makes for large scale operations, automation, anonymity and alienation, migration and rootlessness, and fluid neighbourhood relations in urban settings. In addition it propogates centralization of power in decision-making and large organizations that breed oligarchy, and mass media that create not only homogenization of mass society but also destroy local culture and traditions. The risk is greater for those people and societies that are backward in technology and know-how. Such people are unable to note the power and influence of alien governments and cultures. The acquisition of modern gadgets and frills is hardly a healthy substitute for the loss of cultural identity, personal virtues and contentment. Gandhi set before himself the tasks of achieving through Satyagraha, political liberation from the alien rule, moral regeneration of the people through constructive programme, and economic self-reliance with eradication of unemployment and poverty. Gandhi perceived the challenges and problems the world is facing today. Although Gandhi laid the foundation, the edifice has yet to be built. His was a heroic effort, but all the sings indicate that the world has yet to live up to his message.

Gandhian Solution

Gandhi's approach to economic development was an attempt to preserve the traditional socio-economic structure to fight poverty and idleness of the masses, to ensure independence and self-respect the Indian people in the face of British imports and economic exploitation, exploitation, and to rescue labour-intensive means of production from the onslaught of capital-intensive, technologically advanced, machine-based industry. The merit of this approach lay not only in the solution to the problems of mass unemployment and poverty, but also in finding both the alienation and harmlessness of the individual in the liberal capitalist economy on one hand, and the oligarchy of large organizations inherent in the highly bureaucratic, centrally planned and regimented economy on the other. Gandhi rejected both liberal individualism and social collectivism, which were abstractions and concerns, and their symbiotic relationship with nature, and the changing seasons. The traditional way of life was deeply, almost religiously, related to nature through festivals, weddings, farming and other socio-cultural practices. The economy was woven into the fabric of social and cultural life which stood threatened with disruption by urban industrialism. Gandhi was very much serious about the consequences of the undue muddling with nature. His concern is evident from his techniques. The Swadeshi principle placed emphasis on utilizing local materials and renewable raw materials, eco-friendly to the highest degree adopting such techniques. Encouraging village industries and rural life, is accepted as a principle of progress today. The Gandhian approach also helps us in understanding the value of our environment and maintaining the safety of the environment, as well as a lifestyle away from urban complexity to rural simplicity, but not necessarily backwardness.

Frit of Capra has noted that the patterns scientists observe in nature are intimately connected with the pattern of their minds; with their concepts, thoughts, and values. How facts are investigated, selected, and interpreted depends on one's values, which are influenced by how one sees the world. The following comparison clearly shows out the various dimensions of the holistic Gandhian clearly shows out the various dimensions of the holistic Gandhian approach to the building of an alternative model of development with an eye on Harmony with Nature:

Mechanistic *versus* Ecological World Views[45]

Mechanistic/Cartesian	Ecological/holistic
Descriptors	
Mechanistic, reductionist, Objectivist, technocentric	Organic, holistic, Participative, ecocentric
Primary Characteristic	
Fact and value unrelated	Fact and value closely related
Ethics and ordinary life separated	Ethics and ordinary life integrated

Subject and object separate	Subject and object interactive
People and nature separate relation is one of domination	People and nature inseparable relation is one of systemic synergy
Linear concepts of time and causation	Cyclical concepts of time and causation
Knowledge divisible, value free, value-empirical, controlling	Knowledge indivisible, hidden, both empirical and intuitive, empathetic
Nature understood as being made up of discreete parts; the whole is no more than the sum of its parts	Nature understood as being made up of interrelated wholes which are greater than the sum of their parts
The power of a unit equated with well-being (money, influence, resources)	The quality of interrelationship between systems equated with well-being
Emphasis on the quantitative	Emphasis on material reality
Concern with the qualitative	Concern with physical and metaphysical reality
Analysis key to understanding	Synthesis given greater emphasis
Instrumental values	Instrumental and intrinsic values integrated through systemic values
Few or no technical or ecological limits	Ecological limits determine technical limits

Secondary Characteristics	
Centralization of power	Decentralization of power
Specialisation	Multidimensional approach
Emphasis on the competitive	Emphasis on the co-operative
Increasing homogeneity and disintegration	Increasing diversity and integration
Undifferentiated economic growth	Steady-state economy or qualitative growth

The thoughts of Gandhi were not only relevant for his own time but they are even more relevant and necessary for the present as well as future. His approach will ensure national development without the deterioration of the environment. We do not need a materialistic culture, but we need the collective life of villages simplicity. Our desires are infinite and unlimited. We need a new design of living. Arnold Toynbee writes that ease and luxury had been the most fatal of the twenty-seven civilizations which have passed into oblivion of antiquity.[46] John Galbraith laments that: "We have become slaves of machines we have created to serve us and the servitude is felt comfortable as a result of mass suggestion to which consumers are subjected."[47] It is here at this crucial juncture we feel the need of Gandhi who gave the simplistic vision of human society based on rural economics at this crucial juncture we feel the need of Gandhi who gave the simplistic vision of human society based on rural economics.

Gandhi pleaded for limiting our wants or indulgences. He is right when he says that, "the mind is a restless bird, the more it gets, the more it wants, and still remains unsatisfied."[48] The more we indulge our passions, the more unbridled they become. It is a unique coincidence that in the land of affluence and veritable plenty, that is the United States, millions of people have been pursuing lifestyles of a more home-spun but richer variety in terms of quality. Gandhi knew that a man is not necessarily happy because he is rich, or unhappy because he is poor. The measuring rod of a good civilization is to raise man to a higher moral level, whereas that hallmark of modern civilisation is materialism and selfishness. Gandhi disliked that man should be taken as a limited materialistic, mechanistic being, functioning under the force of wants. The satisfaction of wants through the consumption of goods gives pleasure, which man seeks to maximise. Hence, he is reduced to a consumer having unlimited wants. This craving for unlimited pleasure has accelerated blind industrialization leading to rapid depletion of non-renewable world resources and to the problems of pollution. Hence, Gandhi pleaded for technology and economics within the framework of ecological balance of a holistic paradigm.

Gandhi's views about a sound economic policy were faithfully articulated and elaborated by J.C. Kumarappa. He maintained that the highest form of economy was the economy of service and this was best seen in the relation between parent and child. And he explained that "In animate life, the secret of nature's permanency lies in the cycle of life by which the various factors function in close co-operation to maintain the continuity of life."[49] About the approach and aims of economic policy to be followed for India, he said, "Our objective is to organize the villages for a happier, more prosperous and fuller life in which the individual villager will have the opportunity to develop both as an individual and as a unit of a well integrated society. This has to be done by using local initiative and local resources to the utmost extent possible in the economic, political and social fields, building these on co-operative lines. Self-reliant and properly organized life in the village will thus be the aim of our planning."[50]

Looking for the important elements of Gandhian environmentalism, one has to base the search on his utterances and writings, and above all on the very lifestyle he adopted, and then try to echo some of his ideas and ideas. It is possible to derive that he would have wanted us to follow the path of social democraticism where empowerment of women and weaker sections of our society was guaranteed. Secondly, he would have liked us to link environmentalism with some basic social, economic and ethical tenets. He would have also liked the society at large to take the full responsibility of carving its own future, where:

- human kind would act in a manner that it is a part of Nature rather than apart from Nature;
- materials available on the earth (possible humankind's only home), are not used with an element of greed;
- human beings practice non-violence, not only towards fellow humans, but also towards other living organisms and inanimate materials because over-use of such materials also amounts to violence;

- women are respected, and are made partners in and given their rightful place in all spheres of human endeavour;
- bottom-up shared view is preferred over the top-down totalitarian over view;
- conservationist and sustainable life-saving approach prevails over the unsustainable consumerist self-destructive approach;
- humans care for and share with the poor and the destitute in society as a moral obligation towards them;
- the human race thinks about how much is enough for a simple need-based, austere and comfortable lifestyle;
- all development as far is possible leads to local self-reliance and equity with social justice; and
- ethics and self-discipline in resource-use is an over riding criterion of development.[51]

Such a code of human ecology would help humankind to enter into a dharmic or a yogic phase of environmentalism where the human being is not only totally self-controlled, but in the thought process; becomes an honest human being practitioner.

Gandhi's entire life and work is an environmental legacy for all humanity. This was not because he wrote a treatise on the environment, or led a movement to stall a dam, or clean a river. This was because he was a practitioner of sustainable development in the real sense of the word. Here there was a man who was in harmony and peace with the environment and with himself, although for his whole life he was licked in an unequal battle with the British. His strength came to him on account of his spirituality and practice of non-violence and truth. Taken in a wider sense, these are the very critical elements for the success of sustainable development. In brief, it may be said that, his whole life was his message and lesson on environment and development for Indians and the world at large to follow.

Notes and References

1. Das, Amritnanda, Foundation of Gandhian Economics, (Madras; Allied Publishers, 1979), p. 59.
2. Prasad, Pradhan H., Gandhi, Marx and India; An Alternative Path of Progress, (New Delhi; Manak Publications, 1994).
3. Tisdell, Clem Environmental Economics: policies for (Environmental Management and Sustainable Development (Kent: Edward Elgar Publishing Ltd., 1993), p. 193.
4. Das, Amritnanda, Foundation of Gandhian Economics, (Madras; Allied Publishers, 1979), p. 190.
5. *Ibid.*, p. 194.
6. Oommen, T.K., State and Society in India: Studies in Nation Building (New Delhi: Sage Publications, 1990).
7. Gandhi, M.K., in *Harijan*, October 6, 1945.
8. *Ibid.*
9. *Young India*, June 10th, 1926.
10. *Harijan*, January 28th, 1939.
11. *Harijan*, November 10th, 1946.
12. Oommen, T.K., State and Society in India: Studies in Nation Building (New Delhi: Sage Publications, 1990), p. 31.
13. *Harijan*, January 20th, 1940.
14. *Harijan*, November 4th, 1939.
15. *Harijan*, September 1st, 1940.
16. Khoshoo, T.N., Mahatma Gandhi: An Apostle of Applied Human Ecology, (New Delhi: Tata Energy Research Institute, 1995), p. 47.
17. Fritof Capra, The Tao of Physics (London: Flamingo, 1991).
18. Khoshoo, T.N., Mahatma Gandhi: An Apostle of Applied Human Ecology, (New Delhi: Tata Energy Research Institute, 1995), p. 56.
19. Gandhi, M.K., *Hind Swaraj* or *Indian Home Rule*, (Ahmedabad: Navjivan Publishing House, 1959), p. 12.
20. Verma, Vinod Kumar, "Harmony with Nature: A Gandhian Vision", in A.D.Mishra (ed). Gandhian Approach to Contemporary Problems (New Delhi: Mittal Publications, 1996).
21. *Ibid.*, p. 7.
22. Kelly, Peter K., "Gandhi and the Green Party", in *Gandhi Marg*, Vol. 11, No. 2, July-September 1989.
23. An Appeal by Saria Devi, Catherine Mary Heilenann to "Revive our Dying Planet": An Ecological, Socio-Economic and Cultural Appeal.
24. Pyarelal, Towards New Horizons (Ahmedabad: Navjivan Publishing House, 1959).
25. *Ibid.*
26. Goldsmith, Edward, The Way: An Ecological World, (Buston: Shambhala, 1993).
27. Ahluwalia, B.K., Facets of Gandhi, (New Delhi: Lakshmi Book Store, 1968), p. 35.

28. *Gandhi Marg*, "Gandhi's Predictions on Environment Coming True: Events and Comments", Vol. 10, No. 7, UCT, 1988.
29. Khoshoo, T.N., Mahatma Gandhi: An Apostle of Applied Human Ecology, (New Delhi: Tata Energy Research Institute, 1995), pp. 47-48.
30. Nanda, B.R. (ed.), Mahatma Gandhi, 125 Years: Remembering Gandhi, Understanding Gandhi, Relevance of Gandhi, (NewDelhi. Indian Council for Cultural Relations and New Age International Publishers Limited, Wiley Eastern Limited, 1995), p. 357.
31. Datta, Dhirendra Mohan, The Philosophy of Mahatma Gandhi (Madison, The University of Wisconsin, 1953), p. 21.
32. Doctor, Adi H. "Gandhi and the Discourse on Sustanability", in Ramjee Singh and S. Sundaram (eds., Gandhi and the World Order (New Delhi: APH Publishing Corporation, 1996), p. 151.
33. *Ibid*.
34. *Ibid*.
35. Radhakrishnan, N., Gandhi, The Quest for Tolerance and Survival, (New Delhi: Gandhi Smriti and Darshan Smriti, 1995).
36. Kalelkar, Kaka, Foreword in B.K. Ahluwalia, Facets of Gandhi (New Delhi: Lakshmi Book Store 1968), p. X.
37. Jain, R.B. and Kanchan Sharma, "Environmental Stewardship and Sustainable Developments: The Emerging Conceptual Issues, in R.B. Jain (ed.) Environmental Stewardship and Sustainable Development (New Delhi: Freidrich Ebert Stiftung, 1997).
38. Banwari, Panchvati, Indian Approach to Environment, (New Delhi: Shri Vinayaka, 1992).
39. Schumacher, E.F., Small is Beautiful: A Study in Economics As If People Mattered (London: Macdonald & Co., 1973).
40. Krishnmurthy, J., Education and the Significance of Life, (New Delhi: B.I. Publication Pvt. Ltd. 1987), p. 63.
41. Krishnmurthy, J., Ramchandra Dutta (eds.), Introduction—Nature, Culture, Imperialism: Essays on Environmental History of South Asia (Oxford: Oxford University Press, 1995), p. 90.
42. Arnold, David and Ramachandra Dutta (eds.), Introduction-Nature, Culture, Imperialism: Essays on Environmental History of South Asia (Oxford: Oxford University Press, 1995), p. 90.
43. The Collect Works of Mahatma Gandhi, Vol. XIII, pp. 311-12, (The speech at Muri College Economic Society, Allahabad, December 22nd, 1916) (New Delhi: Government of India, 1990), pp. 311-12.
44. Kothari, Ranjani, "World Politics and World Order: The Issue of Autonomy", in Lovit, Mend (ed.) On the Creation of a just world Order (New York: Free Press, 1975).
45. Sterling, Stephen R., "Towards an Ecological World View" in J. Ronald Engel and Joan Gibb Engel (eds.), Ethics of Environment and Development (London: Pinter Publishers, 1990), p. 82.
46. Panday, S., "The Ultra Modern Gandhi", in *Gandhi Marg*, April, 1976.

47. Galbraith, J.K.., The New Industrial State (London: Hamish Hamilton, 1993).
48. Gandhi, M.K., *Hind Swaraj* or *Indian Home Rule*, (Ahmedabad: Navjivan Publishing House, 1959).
49. Kumarappa, J.C.., Economy of Permanence (Kashi: Akhil Bharat Sarva Seva Sangh Publications, 1958).
50. *Ibid.*
51. Khoshoo, T.N., Mahatma Gandhi: An Apostle of Applied Human Ecology, (New Delhi: Tata Energy Research Institute, 1995), p. 8.

Index